The Sociologically Examined Life

....

Pieces of the Conversation

FIFTH EDITION

MICHAEL SCHWALBE
NORTH CAROLINA STATE UNIVERSITY

New York   Oxford
OXFORD UNIVERSITY PRESS

Oxford University Press is a department of the University of Oxford.
It furthers the University's objective of excellence in research,
scholarship, and education by publishing worldwide. Oxford is a
registered trade mark of Oxford University Press in the UK and
certain other countries.

Published in the United States of America by Oxford University Press
198 Madison Avenue, New York, NY 10016, United States of America.

For titles covered by Section 112 of the US Higher Education
Opportunity Act, please visit www.oup.com/us/he for the
latest information about pricing and alternate formats.

Library of Congress Cataloging-in-Publication Data

Names: Schwalbe, Michael, 1956- author.
Title: The sociologically examined life : pieces of the conversation /
   Michael Schwalbe, North Carolina State University.
Description: Fifth Edition. | New York : Oxford University Press, [2017] |
   Revised edition of the author's The sociologically examined life, c2008.
   | Includes index.
Identifiers: LCCN 2016048727| ISBN 9780190620660 (pbk.) | ISBN 9780190620677

  (e-book)
Subjects: LCSH: Sociology--Methodology. | Sociology--Philosophy.
Classification: LCC HM511 .S34 2017 | DDC 301.01--dc23 LC record available
   at https://lccn.loc.gov/2016048727

9 8 7 6 5 4 3 2 1

Printed by LSC Communications, Inc.

CONTENTS

....

PREFACE

....

The usual introductory text imparts a lot of facts and ideas but doesn't do a very good job of teaching students how to think sociologically, and that, more than anything, is what I try to get my students to do. My struggle in this respect has led me to write *The Sociologically Examined Life: Pieces of the Conversation*. I've half-jokingly called it an "anti-text," meaning that I want it to be everything that those ponderous hardcover texts are not: readable, provocative, personal, and ethically challenging. Through this book I'm trying to gently yet firmly teach readers how to think sociologically. In the tradition of Peter Berger (*Invitation to Sociology*) and C. Wright Mills (*The Sociological Imagination*), I believe that this requires not only a change in consciousness but also a change in how we live.

When standard introductory texts include a chapter on "the sociological perspective," the chapter usually boils down to either a list of concepts or a tip-of-the-iceberg account of sociology's conventional trinity: functionalism, conflict theory, and symbolic interactionism. I suspect that this standard fare leaves many students wondering how, if at all, everyday life looks different if you come at it sociologically. Here I try to get this across by deemphasizing the institutional discipline of sociology. Instead of saying "Sociologists think such and such about so and so," as if students should care about what sociologists think, I simply jump into the work of taking the social world apart sociologically. Rather than display the contents of our shiny intellectual toolbox, I try to put the tools to use.

The risk in this approach is that some teachers of sociology won't like how I've chosen to take things apart. Courting that risk—and I don't see how I could avoid it and still write an honest book—is another reason I've thought of *The Sociologically Examined Life* as an anti-text. Most texts play it safe, not pushing the implications of sociological thinking to the point of arousing much discomfort. My goal is certainly not to provoke for the sake of provoking, but neither have I tried to play it safe to make the book palatable to all political tastes. Many of the analyses here treat American society quite critically, and I'm sure this is going to bother some folks.

My hope is that the bother will be productive. I'd like this book to spark conversations between teachers and students and among students themselves. My examples and analyses are intended to stir thoughts and feelings that will impel discussion. In this sense, I think that *The Sociologically Examined Life* will appeal to teachers who want serious interaction with students, even if this means working through some disagreements. It seems to me that that's what intellectual conversation is about and that whatever gets us into such conversations offers us a chance to move toward better understanding of, and ultimately changing, the world we live in.

HOW TO USE THE BOOK
....

If you are reading this book to learn how to think sociologically, you have already figured out how to use it. Just continue to read. I suppose I could also suggest that you "keep an open mind," as the saying goes. But beyond that, no more instructions are necessary. Follow my sentences with reasonable care and you will do fine. If you are using this book to teach sociological thinking, your task is a bit more complicated, and so perhaps some suggestions will help.

Above all, I urge that this book be used to stimulate thought and conversation in the classroom. Inviting and posing questions about the meaning of what's in the book are good starting points. Beyond this, I suggest guided conversations that call for practicing and extending the kind of thinking being taught here. As an aid to doing this, I have created what I call Paths for Reflection, three of which appear at the end of each chapter. Each path sets up a situation, problem, or conundrum and then poses two or three questions that can be used to structure classroom discussion (or written work, such as keeping a journal). If you would like reflection to move along other paths, consider using mine as models for creating your own.

My other suggestions are about making productive use of reactions to the book. Reactions of pleasure and enthusiasm are not the problem; such reactions, and I hope they are not rare, will generate their own good results. It is predictable, however, that readers unaccustomed to looking critically at U.S. society will be irritated or made defensive by parts of the book. I do not think this is such a bad thing, since feelings, if handled well, can be great propellants to learning.

My suggestion, then, is that readers be taught to examine their feelings in a sociological way. Readers should be asked first to identify precisely what is troubling to them. For example, my remarks about "personal choices" (in Chapter 4) and violent sports (also in Chapter 4) are sure to anger some people. But exactly what is it I say or imply that arouses this feeling? Pausing to answer this question may clear up misunderstandings. It will also prepare readers for the next step, which is to see how their feelings are rooted in social life. To get at this link between self and social life, readers will need to be equipped with some questions. I suggest that they be encouraged to ask themselves, *What belief or practice that I value is being challenged here? How did I learn to value this belief or practice?* and *What relationships or privileges might be lost by giving up this belief or practice?* These questions, and an honest search for answers, can turn anger or irritation into a resource for fostering sociological thinking and for achieving self-knowledge. The goal is to help readers learn to see their feelings as data rather than as things that cannot or need not be analyzed.

By a defensive reaction I mean one that might, if articulated, sound like this: "Yes, I see what you're getting at with this sociological way of looking at things, but I'm not going to work very hard to get my mind around it, because it makes me feel guilty for being [white/male/middle class/straight/married]." This reaction is understandable. A critical sociological perspective can shine a discomfiting light on members of privileged groups, if only by making their privileges visible. It becomes harder, then, to teach sociological thinking when such thinking induces guilt and seems like putting one's self in for blame.

If this sort of reaction occurs, one point to make is that blaming individuals is contrary to sociological thinking, which sees social arrangements as the products of history and collective action. Another point is that racism, sexism, and capitalism are inheritances from the past and that sociology helps us understand how we are all shaped by and caught up in these oppressive systems through no fault of our own. It can also be said that a critical sociological view makes it possible to see why unjust arrangements persist and are hard to change, despite the humane and progressive intentions of some members of dominant groups.

These ideas can help open the intellectual doors locked by privilege and individualism. But then resistance can also arise from a desire to evade the moral pinch that comes with awareness of how one is implicated in reproducing oppressive arrangements. The internal logic now goes something like this: Okay, I see why I don't have to feel guilty for conditions

I didn't create. I also understand that inequalities persist when members of privileged groups simply accept the systems that provide those privileges. But there's nothing I can do about this. I'm just one person. And so I can't take sociology too seriously, or else I'll constantly feel bad about living my life in the way I've planned.

A reaction like this arises when conscience collides with individualism and fear. By way of response, you might point out that sociology rejects the notion of one person single-handedly slaying the dragons of oppression. If we think sociologically, we realize that change can't be accomplished that way, and so it makes no sense to berate ourselves for failing to do it. Sociological thinking, you might also say, helps us to see that power derives not from money or guns but from organization and cooperation. And so if we truly desire change, the best strategy, sociologically speaking, is not to work ourselves up to acts of heroism but to work with others who share our values and goals.

A second point to make is that while an individual acting alone cannot change society, an individual can be a catalyst for change. Both history and sociology tell us that, in the right time and place, even small acts of resistance—as little as saying no—can have huge consequences because of how others are inspired to think, feel, and act. Keeping this in mind can be an antidote to the despair-inducing notion that nothing one person does can matter. It might be added, once again, that acts of resistance are made more likely by the support of others.

A final suggestion is to apply the foregoing principle about individual action to the teaching of sociology, especially when progress seems slow. It is tempting sometimes to think that we are getting nowhere and that it doesn't matter anyway. The temptation arises for good reasons, too; considering the forces opposing it, critical sociological thinking will probably not take deep root in some places. But since we don't know ahead of time where those places are, we just have to keep planting. May these pieces of the conversation, if you will forgive the mixing of metaphors, be the seeds that grow.

About Dialogues, Notes, and the Fifth Edition

The first edition of *The Sociologically Examined Life* was a leaner book. The fifth edition, the edition you are holding, has grown by accretion. It might be helpful to explain how this happened.

I remember when I told a friend that I had been asked to produce a third edition of *The Sociologically Examined Life* (TSEL). She smiled and said, "That's nice. Will you be incorporating all the latest breakthroughs in how to think sociologically?" She was teasing me. We both knew that there were no such breakthroughs and that the real reason for producing new editions is to keep the book alive in the marketplace. But even as I laughed at my friend's joke, I wondered, What *am* I going to do for a third edition?

Some reviewers had suggested adding graphs and charts, or more references, or cartoons, or discussions of current events. A few people suggested adding a glossary of key terms. These ideas were well intended, but to me they seemed like gimmicks. I didn't think they would make *TSEL* a better book. I also didn't want to add material that would textbook-ify *TSEL*.

As I tried to figure out how to make a new edition honestly better and more useful, a student e-mailed me a question about religion. He had been reading *TSEL* in his class and wondered whether science wasn't based as much on faith as was his belief in God. (I said no, that what is sometimes called "faith" in science really means *trust* in science as the best way to answer empirical, not spiritual, questions.) After I replied to the student, I realized that I had found a solution to the problem of what to add to the third edition: Dialogues—responses to issues and questions raised by teachers and students—at the end of each chapter. By all reports, these Dialogues worked well to spark further conversation, so they became part of the permanent heft of *TSEL*.

Then there was a call for a fourth edition, and I faced the same problem again. What could I add that was of real value and not just cosmetic? And what could I add that would not substantially increase the length and cost of *TSEL*?

In reading reviewers' comments and looking over accumulated notes in my feedback file, I saw that people often asked me to say more about certain sociological concepts. In principle, I wasn't opposed to this; concepts are tools of thought, and sharpening them seemed like a reasonable thing to do, as long as I could do it in a way that didn't interrupt the flow of the book. I began by making a list of concepts that I thought I could usefully expand on, one concept per chapter.

At first I was going to call these additions "concept boxes," but I decided that I didn't like that term. It seemed too clunky and not befitting the essayistic spirit of *TSEL*. Eventually I decided to call each discussion of a concept a "Note," which struck me as a friendlier label. Thus the fourth edition included Notes on bias, common sense, the future, blind spots, emotion, deviance, theory, luck, passive voice, nonviolence, common wealth, and teaching others. These Notes, which follow the Dialogues at the end of each chapter, were well received by readers, and so they too have become part of the meat and bones of *TSEL*.

Which brings me to the present edition. Perhaps because I let so much time elapse between the fourth edition and the fifth, it was easier to think of what to do on this occasion. The statistics (even though there aren't many) in *TSEL* clearly needed updating, so I've done that. Some examples drawn from "current events" weren't so current anymore, so I tried to freshen those where I could. I also thought that I could say more about how to think sociologically in ways that I hadn't dealt with in previous editions. Hence there are two new chapters here.

One of the new chapters is about seeing the social in the natural. By this I mean seeing how human culture, organization, and behavior shape nature. I think of this as the "environmental sociology" chapter, even though it is not environmental sociology in the usual sense. This chapter also turns the equation around and suggests how to see the natural in the social. I show in this chapter that being sociologically mindful about the link between humans and nature means seeing humans as part of nature, not apart from nature.

The second new chapter is about unpacking process. In one sense, *TSEL* has always emphasized process, treating the social world as made of people doing things together in orderly ways on a regular basis. In this new chapter I go further and explain how to see process when it is obscured by surface appearances, ideology, or our limited perception of time. I also consider different kinds of processes that make human social life what it is. Here I show that being sociologically mindful includes seeing the elements of the social world not as static entities but as ongoing processes.

Given the updates, tweaks, and additions, it's fair to say that *TSEL/5* is a genuinely new edition. Instructors who have used the book in the past will find, I hope, that this version of *TSEL* is an even better tool for teaching students how to think sociologically. I also hope that a new generation of instructors and students will discover *TSEL* and draw on its content to critically analyze the social world, develop sociological self-awareness, and perhaps even live differently.

As with previous editions, I again owe thanks to the teachers, students, reviewers, and other readers who have taken time to send me their comments and questions. Each such message is a piece of the conversation that I originally hoped this book would become part of. Despite my grumblings about the challenges of doing new editions, I am delighted that the conversation is still going on and that *TSEL/5* will now become part of it. As long as readers keep talking back, *TSEL* will have reason for being.

ACKNOWLEDGMENTS

....

Much of the help I had in writing this book came before I sat down to do it. I could make a long list of the people who taught me—in the classroom, in print, and in conversation—and the list would be hopelessly incomplete (see Chapter 4 on the social nature of individual lives). Perhaps all I can do is to offer a wide, beaming gratitude to all the minds—within and beyond the sociological universe—whose thoughts have informed my own.

A subset of people in the sociological universe served as reviewers for the fifth edition of *TSEL*. If this edition is better than its immediate ancestor, it's in part because of comments I received from the following colleagues: Tennille Allen (Lewis University), Carl B. Backman (Auburn University), Denise Copelton (SUNY–Brockport), Martha Copp (East Tennessee State University), Sean Davis (MiraCosta Community College), JoAnna Howard (Langston University), Peter Kaufman (SUNY–New Paltz), and Michelle Wolkomir (Centenary College). My thanks to you all, and please see what I say in Chapter 13 about iterative processes.

If I were giving a Homeric account of this book's history, I would have to say that the gods of publishing have favored *TSEL*. Although no fortune has accrued, the book's fortunes have been good, as attested by its survival and effect. Yet the gods have been, if not capricious, at least somewhat mercurial, sending *TSEL* on a nineteen-year journey through multiple editors and three publishers. But in the end they have smiled, delivering *TSEL* to Sherith Pankratz and Oxford University Press. I count Sherith's faith in *TSEL* and her support for the book, in its new home, as prodigious blessings.

My deepest thanks go to my partner, Sherryl Kleinman, who helped me maintain a consistent voice throughout the text and a clear sense of purpose while I was writing. I am grateful, too, for her help in becoming more mindful of the patterns and connections that constitute our lives as social beings and, especially, our life together.

CHAPTER 1

....

Making Sense of the World Differently

Not much was happening in the shoe department. Elsewhere in the store people fussed over backpacks, tents, plastic kayaks, and other outdoor gear. But the two young men who sold hiking boots were enjoying a break. I was a few feet away, looking at hats, and could hear their conversation. One of them, leaning back against the counter, arms folded across his chest, was telling his coworker about college.

"It was a lot of fun," he said, "but I didn't learn anything I didn't already know."

"Yeah?" said his partner, a bit of wonderment in his voice.

"Yeah, my business communication class was good. We learned how to write memos. But most of the rest of it, pretty much all my classes—it was all just common sense. If it wasn't for getting the degree, it would have been a waste of time."

Hearing this took my mind off the hats. I imagined asking the young man how he had gotten so smart at eighteen that he could listen to professors and read books for four years and not learn anything new. I wanted to puncture his arrogance and scold him for wasting the time of those who had tried to teach him. Other college professors might have felt the same way.

My anger faded as I realized that the boaster could not have meant what he said. Surely he had learned *something* in college. So what was he saying? Perhaps he belittled his education because he was angry that it hadn't gotten him a better job. Or perhaps he was trying to say to his buddy, "I'm no better than you for having gone to college. Common sense is what matters." If this is what he meant, it was not such a bad message.

Still, I was sad that he spoke of his education as a waste. Even if he had learned more than he realized, he had also missed a lot. He had not learned how to look back on himself, how to see who he was, what he was becoming, and how he was connected to others. If he had, perhaps he could have explained, without making his buddy feel bad, how his education had benefited him.

I do not suppose that courses in memo writing or other technical subjects are likely to foster much self-awareness. That is not their purpose. But other kinds of courses, and whole fields of study, claim this purpose as their reason for being. My own field of study, sociology, is often justified on the grounds that it helps people gain insight into themselves and into society, so they can live more satisfying, self-determined, and responsible lives. If sociology, or any discipline, can do this for people, then I think it has good reasons for being.

Yet sociology courses sometimes foster less self-awareness and insight into society than sociology promises to deliver. This failure is most likely to occur, it seems to me, when courses aim primarily to teach about sociology as a discipline: "See how scientific we are? See all these theories and concepts and findings? You had better be impressed by all this!" No teacher says these things in quite this way, of course, but sometimes this is the message that comes through. Perhaps you have heard it yourself.

When sociology is taught as a body of work created by strangers, it can seem like an exotic and fanciful thing—something that one can take or leave, depending on how interesting it is to listen in on the sayings of sociologists. If this is how sociology comes across, most people will tune it out before long. After all, what sociologists say among themselves is less interesting than social life itself. Most people, sensibly enough, would rather pay attention to social life than to the academic study of social life.

And so it often happens that an encounter with sociology leaves only a faint impression. A few scattered facts and concepts are remembered, but there are no changed habits of mind, no well-learned ways of making a different kind of sense of the social world. It is as if, after so much telling about the pictures that others have made, we have forgotten that the point is to teach people how to make pictures for themselves.

If you would like a written portrait of the discipline of sociology, you can find one in many places—but not here. This book is not about the concepts, theories, and findings of sociology, although it makes implicit use of them. It is about how to think sociologically and about why this is worth doing. It tells and shows how to pay attention to and make sense of the social world in a sociological way. I call this the practice of being sociologically mindful. Once you master this practice, you can make the pictures for yourself.

Sociological Mindfulness

Do you recognize the typefaces used in this book? In what style is it bound? On what kind of paper is it printed? If such questions seem strange, it is because you have not learned to practice a certain kind of mindfulness with regard to books. It is the same with many things around us, familiar things that affect us deeply. We fail to see what they are because we lack the necessary kind of mindfulness. Fortunately, we can learn.

Mindfulness is more than paying attention. To be mindful of a thing is to see and appreciate its unique qualities. For example, to be mindful of a person is not just to be aware of and pay attention to that person. To be mindful of a person, as a human being, means trying to see and appreciate his or her uniqueness as a thinking and feeling being. When we are mindful of a person in this way, we see beyond stereotypes and prejudices.

Children often see things with amazing clarity because their minds are fresh and the world is new and wondrous to them. A child's mindfulness, however, is indiscriminate, as if one kind of grasp can get ahold of everything. As adults we learn to be mindful in ways that suit the things we encounter. We learn that people, for example, must be understood in terms of what makes them people: ideas, feelings, desires, bodies, and habits. Likewise, books must be appreciated for what makes them books: words, paper, design, binding, and so on. For each kind of thing, we learn a different way of grasping it.

Sociological mindfulness is the practice of tuning in to how the social world works. We are all tuned in to some extent, of course, just by being members of society. But to be truly mindful of the social world we must learn to see it for what it is. We must learn, in other words, the ideas necessary to see what makes the social world a unique phenomenon. These are ideas about *how to pay attention* to the social world. Sociological mindfulness is the practice of paying attention in these ways.

What do we see if we practice sociological mindfulness? We see, for example, how the social world is created by people; how infants become functional human beings; how we are interdependent with others; how people's behavior is a response to the conditions under which they live;

how social life consists of patterns within patterns; how contingencies shape our fates; how appearances are strategically crafted; how power is exercised; how inequalities are created and maintained; how the "things" of which the social world consists are actually processes; how the natural and the social are intertwined; and how we can create valid and reliable knowledge about the social world.

A Justification for Sociological Mindfulness

Why bother to be sociologically mindful? What is the point of all this analytic thinking about social life? My answers to these questions are based on three beliefs.

The first is that a good life—one that is stimulating, intense, joyful, purposeful, caring, and dignified—can be had only in a society that is peaceful, cooperative, egalitarian, and minimally regimented. My second belief is that everyone has an equal right to a good life, and so no one should enjoy power and privilege at the expense of others. My third belief is that because human lives are connected, we are all obliged to consider how our actions affect others, especially their chances of living a good life.

I hope you find these beliefs reasonable as starting points. If you want to mull them over, here is an angle from which to do so: Think of the people you love and the kind of life you wish for them. Is it a life of violence, deprivation, and suffering, or is it something more like my vision of a good life? If it is the latter, then I hope you will consider the possibility that mindfulness may be useful as a way to create better lives for more people.

Mindfulness is useful because it helps us see *how* our lives are intertwined and how our words and deeds help or harm others in nonobvious ways. Being sociologically mindful is especially important for helping us see that the consequences of our words and deeds often escape our intentions.

For example, a person who tells a racist joke may intend only to be funny. Yet what this person does is reinforce beliefs that some kinds of people are stupid, vain, immoral, or inferior. Even if no one is offended when the joke is told, in the long run people can be hurt. The sentiments expressed in the joke might decrease sensitivity to others' feelings and to their needs for help. Or it might be that the joke makes others seem unworthy of friendship, thus cutting people off from each other. The harm, in other words, can be indirect, subtle, and delayed. It doesn't matter that no harm was intended. It can happen nonetheless.

Harm can arise even when our actions seem honorable. For example, working hard at one's job is usually a good thing to do. But when people work for companies that make weapons, cigarettes, or pornography or when they work for companies that advertise, sell, or defend such products, violence, death, disease, and misery are the ultimate results. No one may intend others to be hurt, yet that is what happens, and those who make it happen are responsible. The harm could not happen if not for their hard work.

The kind of awareness that sociological mindfulness produces can be unsettling because it sometimes forces us to see things we would prefer not to. But by failing to be mindful, we can inadvertently damage or destroy what we would like to preserve. Or we might, through short-sighted action, diminish our own and others' chances of living good lives. By helping us see beyond our intentions to the consequences of our actions, sociological mindfulness can help us avoid traps like these, although it does not make them easy to escape.

Being sociologically mindful also means paying attention to the hardships and options other people face. If we understand how others' circumstances differ from ours, we are more likely to show compassion for them and to grant them the respect they deserve as human beings. We are also less likely to condemn them unfairly for doing things we dislike. By helping us appreciate the conditions under which others act, sociological mindfulness can help decrease the amount of hatred and conflict in the world.

Being caught up in our daily concerns, we often fail to see and appreciate all of our connections to others—to those who make our clothes, grow our food, clean up our messes, pay for the schools we use, use the schools we pay for, benefit or suffer from actions by politicians we elect, look to us as examples, and so on. Sociological mindfulness helps us see these threads of social life and how they sustain and obligate us. The main benefit of this awareness is that it can make us more responsible members of a human community. That seems to be as good a reason as any for learning a new intellectual practice.

The Rarity of Sociological Mindfulness

If sociological mindfulness were common, I wouldn't need to argue for it. You would simply take it for granted that we all need to be aware of and to think carefully about how the social world works. You would probably think it strange for anyone to make a big deal about doing so. But it seems that sociological mindfulness is actually quite rare in our society.

One reason might be that sociological mindfulness doesn't seem like much fun. Who wants more rules for how to think? As soon as there are rules, then we must worry about getting it right or wrong. So we might feel like saying, "Enough with fancy intellectual schemes! I'm doing just fine with common sense, thank you. Besides, I would prefer to *live* life rather than analyze it to death." This sentiment is not unreasonable in a society where we are constantly being offered ideas of dubious merit.

Another reason that sociological mindfulness is rare might be a belief that it won't matter. Why bother thinking analytically about social life if doing so won't make a difference? Some smart and caring people withdraw from the world because they do not believe they can do anything to change it. They feel powerless, as do many people in our society. I think this is what really impedes sociological mindfulness. We tend to be mindful of things that we feel responsible for and have some control over. But if we feel powerless to change a situation, we probably won't try to analyze it deeply. We might feel lucky just to avoid trouble.

American individualism also inhibits sociological mindfulness. As Americans we learn that it is good to be self-reliant, to achieve on our own, and to look out for ourselves. Under some conditions these are helpful ideas. But they can also blind us to our interdependence with others and keep us from seeing how our ties to others lead us to think, feel, and behave in certain ways. Ideas that lead us to think of ourselves solely as competing individuals, free to do anything we want at any time, can keep us from being mindful of the social world in which we are immersed.

It is also possible that a desire for money and status may so preoccupy us that we fail to think much about how society works or how other people experience it. Or we might fear the loss of security that can come from questioning the beliefs we grew up with. Or we might be so angry at those who abuse us that we lose all sympathy for others who are worse off. Or perhaps we prefer not to reflect on how we participate in oppressing others, because it would make us feel guilty or sad.

People resist being sociologically mindful for many reasons, but not because they are naturally selfish, competitive, or cowardly. If such feelings arise and inhibit sociological mindfulness, it is because of how people have grown up. In a less competitive society where good jobs were available for everyone, people could feel more secure and would probably be willing to spend more time reflecting on how society works. When it seems like life is a race, few people may want to stop to analyze what all the racing is about or where it is leading, lest they fall behind.

Being sociologically mindful goes against the grain in Western society. It may also go against many of the impulses that have been instilled in us as Americans. How can these resistances be overcome? With ideas, first of all, since people must think it is worthwhile to practice sociological mindfulness. I hope that the ideas I have offered so far have persuaded you, at least partly, if you needed persuading.

Here is one more idea that might nudge you toward more mindfulness: Even if you are young now, you will probably die in forty to sixty years; if you are older, you have fewer years remaining. The time will pass quickly. How do you want to use it? You could try to acquire as much wealth and fame as possible. That seems to be the main ambition for many people in our culture; there are, however, other goals for a human life. You could try to enrich the lives of others by teaching, creating art, restoring a piece of the earth, promoting health, resisting violence, or organizing for change. The question is, What kind of mark do you want to leave on the earth for having lived? If you would like to leave the earth a better place than you found it, sociological mindfulness will help you see what needs to be done.

A Continuing Conversation

No matter how carefully we study the social world, our knowledge of it is always incomplete. Even if you could read about everything, there would still be experiences that remained foreign to you. And even if you could read and experience far more than the average person, you would still be interpreting everything from your own point of view—a view shaped by your upbringing in a particular place, time, culture, and community. There is no way around this constraint on our knowledge.

Because people see and experience different things in life and have different ways of interpreting what they see and experience, people are bound to disagree about how the social world works and about how it ought to work. What then? If the disagreements concern matters of taste ("You *like* opera? Yecch!") or are trivial, then perhaps we can just shrug them off. "No big deal," we might say, as we wonder how it is that other people can embrace such odd notions.

Other times there is more at stake. One person might think that democracy is ensured by elections in which the candidate who gets the most votes wins a place in government, and the loser can try again next time. Another person might think that such a system is undemocratic, because it means that 49 percent of the people can end up with no voice in government. A disagreement such as this, when it involves a large number of people who have taken up sides, can lead to violent conflict.

Being sociologically mindful can help us to avoid the destructive potential of disagreements over matters large and small. If we are mindful, we will realize that our knowledge is always limited, that others know what the world looks like from where *they* stand, and that we cannot claim to have a monopoly on the truth. So at the very least we will want to listen to others and try to understand how and why they have a different view of things. We will also want to look back at ourselves and try to figure out where our knowledge has come from.

Being sociologically mindful is thus likely to engage us in a conversation aimed at understanding several important matters: how the social world works, how and why others are different from and similar to us, and how we can get along with others despite our differences. As long as we are engaged in such a conversation—as long as we are thinking, talking, and trying to understand each other and ourselves—we will not be beating anyone over the head and insisting that they do what we say. Nor will they be doing this to us.

The kind of conversation I am referring to can involve many people and can be carried on through print and other media, as well as through talk. It can also occur over long stretches of time—days, weeks, years. In fact, if we are lucky, this conversation will go on indefinitely, because that is the only way we can avoid violence and work together to create social arrangements that will allow as many people as possible to live good lives. Practicing sociological mindfulness is a way into this conversation and a way to keep it going.

This book is part of the conversation, and no serious conversation about how the social world works, or how best to make sense of it, proceeds without disagreements. And so I am sure that you will disagree with some things I say here. When this happens, please talk back to the book and raise questions, in your own mind and with others. Disagreement can move a conversation ahead if we take it as an opportunity to look more deeply into why others see the world differently. I hope that whatever disagreements this book might provoke can be used in this way.

At the end of each chapter I list a few sources at which you might want to look. These are not sources that "prove me right." They are relevant pieces of the conversation—pieces from which I have drawn and from which you might also benefit, if you care to consult them. If you do, you will see where some of my thinking comes from, how it is a response to what has been said before, and how my thinking goes its own way. This will give you a larger view of the conversation to which this book and its readers now belong.

All I can do in these pages is to invite you to consider a way of thinking that I believe holds great promise for making better sense of the social world and for living in it more humanely. I hope you will agree that sociological mindfulness is useful for these purposes. If I didn't believe this myself, I would not have written this book. But whatever you think, I will be satisfied if you are willing to keep the conversation going. Sometimes that is the best we can do, and sometimes it is enough.

Dialogue

Labels and Roots

I have heard that students who dislike parts of *TSEL* will proclaim, "Schwalbe is a liberal!" as if to thereby refute whatever I have said. The same thing sometimes happens in class. Students who call themselves "conservative," and who are bothered by an argument in a text, will sometimes try to dismiss the argument by labeling it, or its author, as "liberal." When I hear this, I ask, "Does applying a political label to an argument make the argument right or wrong?" I use this question to direct attention to the argument itself and away from distracting labels.

The problem is not that such labels—conservative, liberal, radical— are meaningless. The problem is that they are often used in a careless way. If we pause to define them, they can be useful.

In classic political theory, a conservative is someone who values tradition as an embodiment of accumulated wisdom. Conservatives thus believe in conserving existing social arrangements. As you might guess, conservatism tends to appeal to members of privileged groups because they benefit the most from existing arrangements. Note, however, that conservatism has, in principle, nothing to do with support for tax cuts, aggressive militarism, prayer in school, or forced motherhood.

In classic political theory, a liberal is someone who believes that we should use the power of human reason to continually improve society. Whereas a conservative might say, "If it isn't broke, don't try to fix it," a liberal might say, "We should always strive to improve our social machinery, whether it seems 'broken' or not." Liberalism thus appeals to people who have faith in human progress and who believe that tradition is often a barrier to progress. Note here that liberalism has, in principle, nothing to do with support for welfare, government spending, or reproductive rights.

Liberals are thus more suspicious of tradition and more congenial to change than conservatives. Even so, liberals usually agree with conservatives that the basic structure of society is fine. If there are problems, according to the liberal view, they can be solved without a major overhaul of society. A radical view is different from either the liberal or the conservative view. But radical does not mean far-out or wild.

The word *radical* comes from the Latin word *radix*, which means "root." Properly speaking, then, a radical is one who looks for the root of things. And so, when it comes to analyzing social problems, a radical will often try to see if those problems are rooted in the way that society is organized.

Here is an example. Let's suppose that we see a lot of children failing to do well in school. Let's also suppose that people of all political persuasions agree that this is a problem we should try to solve.

A conservative might say that we should not presume that the problem lies with the schools. After all, a conservative might say, our way of schooling is the result of many years of successful experience. This way of schooling has worked well in the past and still works well (or seems to) for most students. So let's not rush to trade proven methods for new educational fads. Perhaps we just need to encourage students to try harder.

A liberal might say that as society changes, old methods need to be reexamined. Perhaps students today are different somehow, a liberal might say, and so schools might need to adjust to this new reality. Yes, students ought to try hard, but we must also make sure that teachers are trained to work with students from diverse backgrounds. Perhaps schools also need more resources to ensure that all students, and especially those who are not members of privileged groups, are taught well.

In this example, the conservative view doesn't rule out looking at how schools work. It just doesn't look there first. The liberal view doesn't rule out looking at students' study habits or efforts. It just looks elsewhere first. Neither view, however, raises questions about how schools are organized, how they operate in the context of a capitalist economy, or how they serve the interests of powerful groups.

How is the radical view different? First, I should say that there is no one radical view. There are as many radical views as there are ideas about root causes. So there are alternative radical analyses of the problem of children not doing well in school. But here, in brief, are some possible radical views of the problem.

The first thing to ask is, Who does and doesn't do well in school? (We would need to define "doing well," but let's put that aside for the moment. I should also say that I am referring to public schools.) As it turns out, schools tend to work well for white students from middle- and upper-middle-class backgrounds and less well for students of color and students from working-class backgrounds. This is one clue telling us that we will need to take class and race into account. But this in itself isn't what would make a radical analysis radical. There is more to it.

A radical view might say that, in a capitalist society, the real purpose of schools is to reinforce and justify inequality. To expect them to do otherwise is, according to the radical view, naive. Yes, a few people will be able to use education as a way to move up the class ladder. But for the most part schools will operate as sorting machines that prepare working-class children for working-class jobs, middle-class children for middle-class jobs, and so on. To see this, all you have to do is to look at the results that schools produce and not confuse uplifting rhetoric (about education providing equal opportunity for everyone) with reality.

A radical might point out other things. For instance, in a society with vast economic inequality, many children will be poorly prepared—relative to kids whose families have greater resources—to succeed in school. And so it is predictable that many children will fail. A radical might say that if job opportunities are so limited that a lot of students doubt that school will pay off for them, then they probably won't accept the disrespect and boredom that school imposes just for the sake of good grades. Expecting to be discriminated against because of racism can also undermine people's motivation.

A radical might agree that schools could be tweaked to work better (e.g., anti-racism training for teachers, more resources for underfunded schools) and that some students might benefit from encouragement to try harder. Yet the problem of kids not doing well in school can be understood only by looking at basic features of the surrounding society: a class-based economy and pervasive white racism. It is in these basic features of our society, a radical would say, that the problem is rooted. And so, unless we pull up the roots, the problem will never be solved.

Which analysis is correct? It is impossible to say, without studying what's actually happening in the world, and that is a separate project. I can say, however, that being sociologically mindful requires taking the bigger picture into account and trying to see how one part of the social world—the economy, for instance—is related to other parts—schools, for instance. If we don't do this, we will fail to see important things about how our society works. I can also say that if liberal and conservative remedies have not worked, then we might reasonably suspect that the source of the problem lies deeper than either of these perspectives can see.

After saying all this about liberal, conservative, and radical perspectives, here is the upshot: The label put on an analysis doesn't matter much. What matters is whether the analysis is based on solid evidence and careful thinking. Trying to discredit an analysis simply by giving it an unpopular label is not intellectually responsible. All analyses are open to challenge, of course. But an intelligent challenge worthy of equal consideration must be in the form of a counterargument.

At the very least, an analysis of the social world, or of any part of it, must be sociologically mindful, or else important things will be missed. As for the perspective presented in *TSEL*, you are welcome to label it if you wish, but remember that a label by itself is not a thoughtful judgment, let alone a counterargument. A perspective should be judged based on the values it proceeds from and reinforces and based on the insight it can give us into whatever we're interested in. On those grounds, I welcome your evaluation of the perspective and arguments offered here.

A Note on Bias

One time a student in my gender course told me that he thought sociology was biased because it ignored the biological causes of women's and men's behaviors. I said that sociology did not ignore claims about biological causes, but that most sociologists find such claims to be based on faulty logic, dubious evidence, and poor understanding of how human beings are shaped by social life. He insisted that sociology was biased in focusing on social causes. In one sense he was right, but not because of anything peculiar about sociology.

To be biased is to have a mental inclination to see the world and things in it in a particular way. In this sense, the practitioners of all academic disciplines are biased. Biologists, for example, are biased toward seeing relationships between organisms. Psychologists are biased toward seeing the dynamics of perception, memory, and cognition. Physicists are biased toward seeing the law-like behavior of matter and energy. Sociologists are biased toward seeing how social behavior is patterned and how these patterns shape us as individuals.

If your way of seeing the world is pretty much the same as that of the people around you, then your view won't seem biased. In fact, your perspective might seem objective to them, just as their perspective might seem objective to you. Charges of bias (or nonobjectivity) often arise when people use different perspectives, or different "conceptual lenses," to make sense of the world. In everyday life, the views we define as objective or unbiased are, in other words, the views closest to our own.

Bias, then, is unavoidable and not necessarily a bad thing. We need perspectives to make sense of ourselves and of the world, and every perspective entails a bias, or slant, although we usually become aware of this only when we encounter unfamiliar perspectives. So when is bias a problem? First, when we fail to recognize that it affects us all and thus mistakenly imagine that our perspective is neutral and objective, while the perspectives of others are biased. Second, bias is a problem when it is so rigid that it keeps us from considering new evidence and new ideas. So the problem is not having biases, but being held captive by them.

Paths for Reflection

1. Think of a group of people about whom you know a lot. It could be a clique, a club, or a team to which you belong; it could be people you work with or used to work with; or it could be your family. In any case, think of a group about which you are an expert. Now imagine that an outsider takes a quick look at this group of yours and says, "These people seem like fools. Why would anyone act in such ridiculous ways?" You would probably think that this outsider was ignorant and unfair. But suppose that this outsider really wanted to understand the people in your group. How would you guide the outsider toward this understanding? Of what would the outsider need to become mindful?

2. Some people think that education happens when students are sent to school and made to listen. Another way of thinking is reflected in this old saying: "When the student is ready, the teacher will appear." This means that until we are intellectually and emotionally ready to hear certain messages, no one can get those messages through to us, but that when we are ready, we will find the teacher we need. How does this idea help to make sense of the young man who (at the beginning of Chapter 1) claimed not to have learned anything in college? Presuming we are ready to learn, what might we do to better our chances of connecting with people who can teach us?

3. Another professor who uses this book asked her students to answer my question about what kind of mark they wanted to leave on the world for having lived. When she showed me what her students wrote, I noticed that many had said something like this: "When I die, I want to be remembered as someone who cared about and helped others." That is a fine aspiration; we would all do well to strive to be known as caring and helpful

people. But being concerned with how others think of us is different from being concerned with how we might affect the world through our actions. So it seems to me that my friend's students misinterpreted the question. Then again, I suppose that many people would interpret and answer the question in the same way. How would you explain this tendency? Is there anything about our culture that might lead people to answer the question in the way my friend's students did?

Related Readings

Berger, Peter. (1963). *Invitation to Sociology*. New York: Anchor Doubleday.

Krause, Elliot. (1980). *Why Study Sociology?* New York: Random House.

Lee, Alfred McClung. (1978). *Sociology for Whom?* New York: Oxford University Press.

Mills, C. Wright. (1959). *The Sociological Imagination*. New York: Oxford University Press.

Nhat Hanh, Thich. (1975). *The Miracle of Mindfulness*. Boston: Beacon Press.

Zerubavel, Eviatar. (1997). *Social Mindscapes: An Invitation to Cognitive Sociology*. Cambridge, MA: Harvard University Press.

CHAPTER 2

Inventing the Social World

A dollar bill is just a piece of paper. Although it is nicely printed, it is not a precious work of art. So how can a dollar bill have value? Why should anyone trade a cup of coffee for a piece of paper? It can only be because people with coffee believe that paper money can be traded for things they want. If people did not believe that paper money could be traded for things they want, such money would be worthless.

The power and reality of money derive from shared belief, nothing more. People who have lots of money are powerful because they can use their money to get others to work for them. If no one would trade goods and services for money, having money would bring a person no power. For money to bring power, people must create and share a belief in its value— and then they must act as if that belief were true.

Think of the diplomas you have or will get. You probably hope that these pieces of paper will help you get a job. But why should anyone give you a job because of a piece of paper? A diploma is no proof that you are competent, honest, or hard-working. If a diploma helps you get a job, it is only because an employer believes that in getting the diploma you acquired skills and habits that will make you a good worker. If employers stopped believing this, diplomas would be worthless in the labor market, and many schools would be empty.

Wars could not happen without shared belief. If a teacher said to you, "The students in the back row are evil, and you must kill them before they kill you," you would probably not rise up and attack anybody. But suppose the president went on television and said, "The people in Oceania are evil and want to destroy our way of life, so we must bomb them before they attack us." What then? Would you volunteer to fly the planes and drop bombs? Would you cheer as the bombs fell? Many people would, even though they knew nothing about the people in Oceania.

For wars to happen, people in one country must believe that ordinary people in another country are a serious threat; that politicians tell the truth; that it is okay to kill if an elected official says so; and that there is no peaceful way to resolve conflict. When these beliefs are plainly stated, they seem so unlikely to be true that it is astounding that wars ever occur. Yet wars involving millions of people have occurred, and still do. We can see from this that shared belief is enormously consequential.

To talk about the power of shared belief is to talk about the power of ideas. In America, where many people like to think of themselves as down-to-earth, the power of ideas is often not grasped. Sociological mindfulness helps us appreciate this power more fully. As the examples of money, diplomas, and wars show, ideas matter a great deal. (When a person says, "Ideas are just talk; they don't matter," s/he is misled by a dangerous idea.) But we should also see that money, diplomas, and wars are not special cases. Every part of the social world exists only because of the ideas people embrace and act upon.

What the Social World Is Made Of

To say that the social world exists only because of ideas does not mean that it is an illusion. Bodies are not illusions, nor are their tendencies to act in certain ways. Families, schools, banks, churches, clubs, corporations, towns, governments, armies, and nations are not illusions, either. You cannot wish them away. They consist of people doing things together in recurrent orderly ways. That is really what the social world is made of: patterns of activity.

We don't usually put it that way. Usually we talk about families, schools, banks, churches, clubs, corporations, towns, governments, armies, nations, and so on. But these are just names for patterns of activity that involve lots of people. It is because people share ideas about how to do things together that these patterns persist.

Ideas let us get things done together, in familiar ways, day after day. Without ideas to guide, inspire, and justify what we do, we would have no society. Ideas do not grow on trees, of course; we cannot just pick one to help when we are confused, disorganized, or in conflict with others. If we lack the ideas we need to solve certain problems, or to inspire or justify certain actions, then we must create those ideas. Humans have a wonderful and sometimes frightening capacity for doing this. We can interpret, imagine, or justify almost anything.

The social world is no less real because its existence depends on ideas invented by human beings. Its reality is different, however, from that of stars and trees and bacteria. Humans did not create stars and trees and bacteria, all of which existed long before hominids evolved on earth. On the other hand, there were no families, schools, churches, governments, and so on until humans came along. These things exist only because of ideas and ways of doing things devised, ages ago, by human beings struggling to survive.

To say that the social world is a human invention sounds strange because this makes it seem arbitrary and flimsy, and that is not how we usually perceive it. The social world usually seems solid and durable, as if it existed apart from us and could be touched. It also seems compelling and real, at least most of the time.

One reason the social world is durable is that people refuse to doubt the ideas that hold it together. Suppose, for example, that you thought your parents were alien shape-shifters. If you told anyone of your belief, you would seem crazy. People wouldn't believe you, because to do so they would have to doubt many of the ideas on which their sense of reality depends. Most people, even those who act crazy at times, dislike this kind of disorientation. Every human mind strains in the opposite direction: toward making sense.

People also hold tightly to ideas because those ideas tell them what is right and wrong. "Thou shalt not kill" is just an idea, but it is a good one for guiding behavior, since it makes it safe to live with others. To threaten such a basic idea is to threaten society itself. There are many other such ideas about moral behavior, ideas that people see as essential to hold society (as they would like it to be) together. It is no wonder that people resist changing these ideas and even insist that such ideas be respected as sacred.

Ideas like this also allow people to feel good about themselves. How do you know that you are a good person? Because you have learned a set of ideas for judging yourself and your behavior. You have probably learned, for example, that kindness, generosity, and forgiveness are qualities of a good person. If you see these qualities in yourself, you can feel worthy of esteem in your own eyes and in the eyes of others. All of us relish these feelings of self-worth and resist changing the ideas on which such feelings depend.

The ideas that hold society together or help people feel good about themselves are often protected by other ideas. For example, some people might say, "These principles on which our society is based come from God and must never be changed." Other people might say, "In ancient times our wisest elders devised these principles, and we must not change them or else our society and everything we hold dear will perish." In either case, the attempt is to make society durable. To the people in it, a society thus will seem solid and real, for as long as it lasts.

Ideas shape people's feelings, too. When people settle into a way of understanding the world, they are also settling into a way of feeling about it, about others, and about themselves. Perhaps these feelings are pleasant, perhaps not. Either way, people can feel as if they are being pushed around emotionally—perhaps pushed toward feelings they don't want to have—when their ideas are challenged. So it is no wonder that people resist giving up familiar ideas and try to keep the world as they know it intact.

Habits and Invisible Ideas

You might wonder where all these familiar ideas can be found. Are they in books? Some are. But most exist only in people's heads, or are embodied in habit, and have never been spoken or written down. None of us is aware of all the ideas we hold and act upon. This is because many of our ideas are deep assumptions so taken for granted that, under ordinary circumstances, we do not think to question them.

You probably assume, for example, that this book is not a radio transmitter beaming messages into your brain. You probably do not suspect that the paper is coated with a drug, absorbed through the skin, that causes ringing in the ears. You probably also assume that this book will not explode when you reach page 67. Yet you have not been conscious of making any such assumptions, because they were so deep that you never became aware of them. A lot of our behavior is like this, rooted in places we never look.

The invisibility of the ideas that hold the social world together is part of what makes it seem so real. It's as if the social world were held together by invisible threads that wrap around us. Only when we try to pull away, to break from the pattern in some way, do we experience the realness, the tangible force, of the threads. If we are sociologically mindful, we can see these threads being spun by ordinary people in everyday life.

Many of the ideas that hold the social world together are invisible because they are built into habit. For example, as a child you were probably taught to brush your teeth before bed. Perhaps you asked why and your parents explained about cavities and dentists. You still know all this, but now you brush your teeth as a matter of habit. The idea "I should brush my teeth to avoid painful dental work" is built into your habit; you don't have to review the ideas that originally led to the formation of the habit. This is true of all habits. Once upon a time we were told why we should do a certain thing, or maybe we figured it out for ourselves, and now we do it without thinking. The guiding ideas are still there, although visible only as habits.

Teeth-brushing is a dull example, but it makes a useful point: some seemingly personal habits are part of a culture. Before you were born, someone devised teeth-brushing as a way to avoid tooth decay. This was a solution (or a partial one) to a problem that existed before you did. Today almost all children are taught to brush their teeth. This is the sense in which teeth-brushing has become part of the culture. People now do it routinely.

Culture is created in this way. Someone finds a solution to a problem, other people see that it works and adopt it, and eventually the solution becomes "what everyone does." For a time people remember the idea behind the practice, but then, after a while, they forget. "This is just how we do things," they begin to say. When children come along they are taught the practice as a matter of course, perhaps with little explanation of the ideas on which it was originally based. It is as if the practice—the behavior that solves the problem—becomes part of a sediment that constitutes culture.

One time a student talked in class about her career plans. She expected to work hard after graduation, get promoted fast, and make lots of money. Then she said she would slow down when it came time to have babies. I asked her why, if she wanted to pursue a career with such zeal, she would impede her upward climb by having babies. She looked at me and didn't say anything for a moment. Then she said, "I don't know. I guess I never considered *not* getting married and having babies." Now there is a powerful cultural habit! It is so ingrained that many people do not even think about behaving differently.

Confronting the Social World as Ready-Made

Think about your first experience of school. There you found a set of arrangements worked out before you arrived. No one asked if you liked having teachers, principals, and other students around; no one asked if you liked homework, tests, and grades; no one asked if you liked meeting indoors, sitting in hard desks, and having only a half hour for recess. All this—the social world of school—was there waiting for you, and you had to deal with it, like it or not. What you were facing were other people's habitual ways of doing things together.

When you take a new job it is much the same. Your boss says, "This is how we do things here. This is what your job consists of." Your coworkers say, "You can bend the rules a little, but not too much." Again you face a set of arrangements and must adjust to a reality that seems to exist apart from you. We go through life like this, repeatedly adjusting to habits and expectations formed by people who preceded us. Experiencing this time and again makes the social world seem very real—and of course it is, as long as everyone carries on as if it is.

The social world seems so real in part because it confronts us as ready-made. As children, we're taught the ideas and habits that our parents and teachers found useful. We don't have much choice about this. Although we might question some of what we're taught, we mostly accept it because it's hard to get along otherwise.

Every society is built on a set of practices through which people meet their needs for food, clothing (usually), and shelter. To change these practices—especially those that seem to work well—is risky. People are reluctant to abandon an old but workable system and thereby risk being unable to provide for themselves. Those who benefit the most from the old system will of course be least likely to want to change it. Anyone who tries to do so may discover that the social world is maintained not only with ideas that affect minds, but also with tools, such as guns and bullets, that affect bodies.

Making People Disappear

It is not easy to become and remain mindful of the social world as humanly made. For many reasons the social world seems to be "just there," as if no one were responsible for making it. So what? What difference does it make if we forget that the social world is a human invention? The difference it makes is like that between using one's tools with an awareness of what they are good for and letting those tools—as if they had minds and will of their own—take charge.

The failure to see the social world as humanly made is called reification, which can also be defined as the tendency to see the humanly made world as having a will and force of its own, apart from human beings. For example, someone might say, "Computer technology is the major force behind changes in our economy today." In this statement, computer technology is reified because it is spoken of as having a will of its own, independent of human beings. It is technology that appears to make things happen.

"Computer technology," however, is only metal and plastic. People forge these materials, turn them into computers and other devices, and then decide how to put such tools to work. All along the way there are people who choose what to build and how to use the results. But if we talk about technology as if it were a force in its own right, the people who do the building and choosing disappear. It thus seems as if technology is like gravity or the wind—a natural force about which we can do nothing.

Reification keeps us from seeing that the force attributed to technology comes from *people* choosing to do things together in certain ways. If we don't see this, we may forget to ask important questions, such as, Who is choosing to build what kinds of devices? Why? How will our society be changed? Who stands to benefit and who stands to lose because of these changes? Should we avoid these changes? Who will be held accountable if these changes hurt people? Should we decide to use technology in some other ways?

Here is another example of reification: "The market responded with enthusiasm to today's rise in interest rates, although economists predict that this could have unfavorable consequences for employment." You've probably heard this kind of statement before. It sounds like a report about a flood or some other natural disaster. Yet a market is just a lot of people doing things together in a certain way; interest rates are established by people; and employment results from choices by employers. Reification makes these people and their choices disappear.

In a large, complex society the tendency to reify is strong because it can be hard to see where, how, and by whom decisions are made. And so it is easier to say that technology, the market, or a mysterious *They* is making things happen. Even people who ought to know better get caught up in this. When sociologists say things like "Trends in inner-city industrial development are causing changes in family structure," they too are guilty of reification. Such language again makes it seem as if no one is responsible for choosing to act in a way that hurts or helps others.

Reification thus keeps us from seeing who is doing what to whom, and how, such that certain consequences arise. This makes it hard to hold anyone accountable for the good or bad results arising from their actions. Usually it is powerful people whose actions are hidden and who get off the hook.

Reification can also make us feel powerless because the social world comes to seem like a place that is beyond human control. If we attribute independent force to abstractions such as "technology," "the market," "government," "trends," "social structure," or "society," then it can seem pointless even to try to intervene and make things happen differently. We might as well try to stop the tides. People who think this way are likely to remain passive even when they see others being put out of work, living in poverty, or caught up in war, because they will feel that nothing can be done.

When we reify the social world we are confusing its reality with that of stars and trees and bacteria. These things indeed exist (as material entities) independent of human ideas and action. But no part of the social world does. To reify is to forget this; it is to forget to be mindful of the social world as a humanly made place. As a result, we forget that it is within our collective power to re-create the world in a better way. If we are sociologically mindful, we recognize that the social world as it now exists is just one of many possibilities.

Inventing Categories and Inventing People

Even if we believe that one way of schooling, churching, or governing is best, we can still admit that these ways of doing things together depend on ideas and habits invented by people. It can be harder to accept that the same principle applies to social constructions that have to do with who we think we are.

For example, many people think that they belong to a "race" and that races are visible, biological realities. But races, too, are human inventions. When people talk about distinct races, as if there were significant genetic differences among human groups that produce differences in intelligence and behavior, they are mistaken. "White" people, "black" people, and so on had to be defined into existence. Such groups were invented, once upon a time, largely for political reasons.

Race is, of course, a social reality. Based on skin tone and place of ancestral origin, people are defined as belonging to races, and such labels can affect how people are treated, whom they live with, the customs they learn, and how they think of themselves. But, again, all this results from the invention of schemes for sorting people into groups. We could sort people according to eye color, height, or warmth of heart. If we acted on these new schemes, they would be just as real and consequential as our current ideas about race.

Just as some people think they can see race when they see a person's skin, others think they can see gender when they see an infant's genitals. "Ah, this one has a penis—it's a boy. And this one, with a vagina, is a girl," people say. But it is a mistake to equate genitalia with gender. Although penises and vaginas are plainly part of human bodies, gender is something that humans must be taught.

If we did not assign the meanings we do to penises and vaginas, if we did not have the cultural habits of treating the possessors of these organs differently, we would not produce girls and boys, women and men. Such creatures are the results of many people embracing and acting on similar ideas. Other ideas and behaviors would produce different kinds of people. Men and women, as we know them, are just one set of possibilities.

Seeing race and gender as social constructions can be troubling because it makes it seem as if we have no substance as individuals, as if our sense of who we are could melt into air at any time. There is a grain of truth in this fear, even though people do not dissolve so easily.

It is true that if you had been born into a different social world, you would be a different person. You might never have learned to think of yourself as, for example, a man or a woman, as black or white, as European or African, as gay or straight. All these identities derive from invented categories; they are not part of nature. In fact, all your ideas about who and what you are come from the social world in which you were raised.

Perhaps you can see here another reason why a humanly made world seems so real: It gets inside us. The ideas that hold the social world together tell us who we are. If we didn't keep believing in the reality of the social world, we might lose a sense of our realness as individuals. Fearing such a condition, many people refuse to study the making of the social world, preferring instead to believe that it has supernatural origins and follows a blueprint devised in the heavens.

Inventing the Truth

If any of my ideas run counter to ones you hold, you might wonder whose are true, mine or yours. That's an important matter to consider, but I will let you do it on your own. Here I want to make another point about the constructedness of the social world. The point is this: The rules we use to decide which ideas are true are also invented.

You could, for example, follow a rule that says, "Accept as true what is written in books that are widely believed to be divinely inspired." Or you could follow a rule that says, "Accept as true only those things you can verify for yourself." Or your rule could be "Accept as true only what has been proven by science." You can find people who embrace these and other rules for deciding what is true.

Whichever rule you prefer, it will be one that you learned as a matter of growing up in a particular place and time. It will be a rule invented by people and passed on to you like any other notion about how best to do things. Figuring out what is real and true is as much a matter of cultural habit as teeth-brushing. We can do it almost without thinking, which is helpful in some cases and harmful in others.

This is how it is with humans: first we make rules for believing, then we follow our rules as a matter of habit, settle our beliefs, and presume to know how things really are, as if the truth had come to us through no effort at all. It might seem self-evident, for example, that the moon is not made of green cheese. To accept this claim as true, however, we must share understandings of what is meant by "moon," "cheese," and "is made of." We must also agree on what would constitute evidence for or against such a claim (must we have a sample of the moon? what if the sample is 99% mineral and 1% cheese?). If we can agree on these matters, we can create a true idea about the moon, just like we create true ideas about other things.

If we practice sociological mindfulness, we pay attention not only to how the world is socially constructed, but also to how we invent ways to decide what is real and true. If we do this, we may be more open to understanding how other people arrive at different ideas about what is real and true. We might also be less likely to insist that other people accept our picture of the world as the only true picture. We might even be more open to considering the pictures other people create.

The point of being mindful about the invention of truth is not to discover the best rules for deciding what is true. There are no best rules, only rules that are more or less useful, depending on our purposes. So the point is not to get at truer truths, but to better understand how social reality is created by paying attention to how people decide what is real and true. You will see two things if you pay attention to this process: Not everyone has an equal say in deciding what is real and true, and truth often bends toward power.

How to See the Social World Being Made

How can we see the social world being made? All we need to do is to pay attention in the right way to what is going on around us all the time. Instructions for how to pay attention to the social construction of the world can be put in the form of admonitions and questions. It is a matter of knowing what to look for and what to ask.

First, look for people solving problems together. Here you will see habits and routines being formed. When two or more people confront a common problem, arrive at a similar view of it, and devise a solution for it, they are creating a piece of social reality. When their solution is taught to other people, and when that way of doing things becomes a matter of habit for them, a piece of culture is formed. If this routine way of doing things involves lots of people coordinating their actions day after day, an institution is formed.

Ask who benefits from certain ways of doing things. Solutions for some people can create problems for others. For example, putting people out of work (downsizing a firm) might increase profits for employers, but it hurts workers. Certain ways of organizing school might be good for teachers because students are kept under control, but this might not be so good for students. So in looking at any social arrangement, ask, Who benefits and who suffers? You will find that there is often a great deal of conflict underlying the construction of the social world.

Watch for the invention of labels and categories, especially ones applied to people. Pay attention to disputes over the meanings given to these labels and categories, which often become the basis for people's identities. Observe how people are put into one category or another, how they are labeled in one way or another, and how they come to accept or reject certain identities. The meanings given to these labels, categories, and identities determine whether people will be respected, ignored, or abused. If you watch as these meanings are created and negotiated, you'll see social reality being constructed and people's lives being shaped.

Be mindful of the labels and categories you use to know yourself and others. Ask who invented these labels and categories. Ask who benefits from them and who is hurt. Ask how the meanings of these labels and categories affect people's behavior. The answers will not always be easy to find, but they must be sought if you want to be a responsible participant in the making of social reality. How else can you understand what you are doing and what you are a part of?

Watch for the assumptions people make when they claim that something in the social world is real. Look to see what people take for granted. Look to see what they refuse to doubt. Look for these things and you'll find the bedrock on which people build their sense of reality. It is good practice to inspect your own foundations as well.

Also pay attention to how people create among themselves a version of the truth. To see this you have to watch what goes on between people when matters of truth are being decided. Who says what? What sorts of arguments are accepted as plausible and convincing? What kinds of evidence are accepted as compelling? What assumptions are rejected right from the start? If you can discern these things, if you can learn to see the process as it unfolds, you will be able to see how groups of people create the different truths and social worlds in which they live.

Remaking the Social World

Although I have said that the social world seems to exist as if it were a hard and durable thing that could survive on its own, that is only how it seems. In fact, the social world could not continue to exist if we did not reenact it every day. We are part of it; our thoughts, feelings, and behaviors keep it going. Part of being sociologically mindful is paying attention to how we do this. Which ideas do we pass on to others, perhaps inadvertently? Which habits, routines, and institutions do we support with our actions? Which ones do we oppose? If we are to understand the making of the social world, we have to see how we contribute to its making.

Part of being sociologically mindful of the constructedness of the social world is seeing the possibility of changing it. This means recognizing the possibility of acting differently, of choosing not to support arrangements that are harmful or unjust. The consequences of not conforming might be severe, but we should not pretend that we do not have a choice. The only time we really do not have a choice is when it never occurs to us that we do. Once we are aware of the possibility of acting differently, it is dishonest to say, "I had no choice. I had to do what I had to do." What we're really saying is, "Because the consequences of doing X were more than I could bear, I chose to do Y instead." It is harder to say this, because it means taking responsibility for what we do.

What we do as individuals might not seem to have much effect on the world. Often our acts of resistance seem to go unnoticed. But it is through small acts that the world is remade. Suppose you realize that a certain cultural habit (e.g., throwing away usable glass bottles) harms the environment. That is a problem for you, so you find a way around it, a way to act differently. You offer that solution (a way to recycle) to others who share your concern. Pretty soon quite a few people are acting differently, and the social world is being changed, if only gradually and in a small way. Perhaps at some point a balance is tipped and more dramatic changes occur suddenly. History unfolds like this sometimes.

The making of the social world is always a collaboration; we can neither make nor remake anything *social* by ourselves. Our ideas, our solutions, must be communicated to and must appeal to other people. Only by paying attention to others' unmet needs and showing them how to do things differently so that these needs can be met are we likely to make any big changes. Our power lies, in other words, in our ability to communicate with others, through words and deeds, so that they can see the benefits of doing things differently.

It might seem as if there is a contradiction here. On the one hand, I have said that everything about the social world is a result of shared belief and of people doing things together in recurrent orderly ways. This seems to leave little room for individuality. Yet in talking about world-making and change, I have emphasized individual responsibility and initiative. How can it be both ways? If people must adjust themselves to established cultural habits and other social arrangements, if they are so thoroughly shaped by these habits and arrangements, how can they ever resist?

For one thing, human minds are unruly. They are not like computers that do only what they're told. Minds generate images and longings and strange, unpredictable impulses. These products of mind are the seeds of dissatisfaction, resistance, creativity, and change. No doubt you can conjure images of desirable objects, situations, and experiences—ones that do not exist in your life today. Your mind can always reach beyond everyday life and create longings for something more—more pleasures, challenges, satisfactions—than you now enjoy. Your mind, and everyone else's, tends to generate dissatisfaction with what exists, if only because you can imagine things being better.

When people share their feelings about what exists and share their imaginings about what might exist, they often begin to recognize problems where they saw none before, perhaps because of what they took for granted. This sort of conversation can create awareness that a problem is in fact widely shared, even if no one had seen it clearly before. If people then say, "Let's see if we can solve our common problem" and go on to devise a new way of doing things together, the social world is indeed remade.

So while it is true that for the most part we must adjust to the social world that precedes us, even as we learn to adjust—in part by developing minds and the ability to get along with others—we also acquire the inclination and power to remake the world, to force it to adjust to us, if only a little at a time. Being sociologically mindful, we thus see that human beings are both social products and social forces. Though we are shaped by the world, we are still, each of us, a place on earth where ideas and feelings clash inside a body that can act to affect other bodies. And that is how change is made to happen.

A student once said, "Seeing the world as humanly invented takes all the magic and mystery out of it, like the whole thing is nothing special." To him the world could be mysterious and special only if supernatural powers were behind it. I said that I wondered why some people needed to believe in the supernatural. I said that I marveled at the human capacity to invent ideas about such things. I said that it was a mystery to me how people, in a scientific era, could sustain belief in gods and ghosts. My point was to say that the social world becomes fascinating in new ways if we pay attention to its making, especially to the ironies and contradictions in which people entangle themselves.

We can be intensely mindful of how the social world is made and still not see all there is to see. There is always something new around the corner, behind our backs, or under our feet. And often we are so busy living that we don't see what we're making happen. This means that we can always spend tomorrow trying to understand what we did today. There is always more analytic thinking to be done about social life, since life always runs ahead of our ability to make sense of it.

Being sociologically mindful is thus not a way to see everything, as if everything could be so easily seen. It is a way to see more deeply into the process of world-making and to appreciate the nature of the social world as a human accomplishment. Even if we never fathom it fully, by trying to do so we can live more interesting and responsible lives. We can also see better how we might remake the world into a place where more people can live good lives.

Dialogue

Overcoming the One-Dimensional View

I have heard that some people are bothered by the idea that the social world is humanly made. One student, I was told, refused even to entertain the idea that gender is socially constructed. I suspect that this resistance comes from a wish to believe that our social arrangements—perhaps especially those concerning gender, sexuality, race, and social class—are divinely ordained. I'm sure it is also frightening for some people to think that their ideas about supernatural beings are no less social constructions than their ideas about clothes, movies, and music.

All of the above is said or implied elsewhere in *TSEL*. Here I would like to make a point about why the invention of the social world is hard for some people to see. I will also suggest a way around this problem.

Suppose you lived your entire life within a single culture and never visited a country different from your own. If this were the case, it might seem as if human culture is the same everywhere. It might also be hard to appreciate the variety of beliefs and practices that people create to help them survive in diverse environments. In other words, if you hadn't seen, or learned about, the range of human cultural diversity, it might seem that there isn't much. This lack of information would probably make it harder to see your own culture as an invention, just like all the others. Many people, if they haven't traveled or read widely, are stuck in this kind of narrow view.

How many human cultures have there been? We can't know for sure, because many were never documented. An answer would also depend on how we define a distinct culture. If we look back across the span of known human history, a safe answer would be "thousands." Today we have information on 330 distinct cultures that have been studied by anthropologists in modern times (look up the *Human Relations Area Files* in the library or on the Internet). Just knowing that so many different cultures exist, or have existed, should give pause to anyone who thinks that his or her own culture represents the full range of human possibility.

Some people might thus be led to underestimate cultural diversity simply by a lack of information or experience. But sometimes power has a lot to do with it, too. Consider the case of Native Americans, or the peoples often called North American Indians.

If I asked most non-Indian people in the United States to tell me what Indian culture was like in pre-Columbus days, they would probably mention feathered headdresses, bows and arrows, hunting buffalo on horseback, and living in tepees. For many non-Indians, this image is all they know. Yet this is a stereotypical image based on Hollywood portrayals of eighteenth-century Plains Indians. Even white people who claim to respect the ecological or spiritual wisdom of Native Americans often mistakenly lump all Indians into one group.

There was and is far more cultural diversity among North American Indians than most non-Indians ever grasp. A widely accepted estimate is that in pre-Columbus times there were about three hundred separate languages spoken by the indigenous peoples living in the area that is today known as North America. Each language could be said to reflect a different culture. We also know that across the continent the economies, religions, governments, and other customs of indigenous peoples varied considerably. This diversity was at least as great as that among Europeans, yet it all disappears under the label "Indians."

Suppose I asked how many Indian tribes exist today. Many non-Indians might guess a dozen, even if they couldn't name that many. Others might guess higher, perhaps 20. A few people might go as high as 100. But even that is too low. There are 567 tribes officially recognized by the U.S. government, plus about 400 unrecognized bands and clans. Not all of the tribes are large, but, as of the 2010 Census, more than 39 tribes had over 8,000 members.

I have asked these questions in classes, and so I know that many non-Indians guess too low. Even people who claim Native American ancestry often guess too low. So what does all this have to do with power?

In Chapter 10, I will say more about power, but here it will suffice to say that I am referring to the political and economic power of groups. European peoples, those collectively defining themselves as "white," have had far more power than any other group in U.S. history. This matters, in the present example, because one privilege that comes with being a member of a dominant group is not having to learn much about those who are less powerful. Historically, then, whites have often been oblivious to differences within groups of people who are not categorized as "white."

It is thus no surprise that most whites know little about diversity among North American Indians. Beyond what might be learned, inadvertently, from television and movies, whites are not otherwise compelled to study Native American cultures. This isn't about individual white people being lazy. It's about what typically happens when one group dominates another. The humanity of the powerless group often gets erased, and a whole people—as internally diverse as any other—gets reduced to a stereotype. And because the culture of a dominant group tends to shape society as a whole, everyone is affected. That's why most people, not only whites, have so little knowledge of cultural diversity among the indigenous peoples of North America.

The point of this example is to illustrate why it's hard for some people to see the social world as humanly made. What it comes down to is this: members of powerful or privileged groups, because they have little incentive to study people other than themselves, often end up with a limited view of human diversity. It comes to seem that everyone, or everyone who matters, is like them. The result is not merely a lack of knowledge about others, but a lack of perspective on one's own culture. It is this lack of perspective that supports the illusion of one's own culture being a gift of the gods rather than a design for living invented by previous generations.

The example of North American Indians is just one of many. Whenever we see enormous power differences between groups, we should suspect that a similar process might be at work. Consider how little Americans typically know about the thoughts and feelings of people in Third World countries. Here again we can see how power (or being at the center of a powerful empire) breeds ignorance. Being sociologically mindful, we recognize this tendency and make efforts to compensate for it. Doing this is how we can claim our power to invent a different kind of social world.

A Note on Common Sense

I've heard it said, and not as a compliment, that sociology is just common sense. The claim is that anyone who has common sense already knows how to think sociologically. In my observation, this isn't true (see pp. 5–7. in Chapter 1). People can have the kind of practical intelligence that helps them solve problems in their daily lives—and this is usually what we mean when we say that someone has common sense—yet not see the world in a sociological way.

For example, many people who grow up in U.S. culture learn the common-sense ideas that equal opportunity is available to everyone and that all it takes to succeed are talent and hard work, because individual merit will be recognized and fairly rewarded. I often hear this from students at the start of the semester when I teach about inequality.

But as we study inequality sociologically, students learn to see how children start life equipped with vastly different levels of resources, depending on the social class of their families; how the pyramidal shape of the job market makes it impossible for *everyone* to get ahead; how powerful groups hoard opportunities; how networks limit access to information crucial for getting ahead; and how chances to develop one's abilities, to display competence, and to be recognized depend on conditions and processes over which none of us has much control.

Thinking about inequality in these sociological terms is, for many people, a challenge to their common sense. Looking at the constructedness of the social world, as I did in the foregoing chapter, can pose an even greater threat. So while sociological thinking and common sense can overlap, they can also conflict. By definition, being *mindful* about anything means going beyond knowledge that is *common*.

Once upon a time, common sense told us that the earth was flat and was at the center of the universe. Today we know better. But the displacement of entrenched common sense didn't happen easily, because common sense is often embraced more for its comfort value than for its truth. This means that strain and strife are inevitable whenever an empirical, analytic perspective—like sociology—puts common sense to the test.

Paths for Reflection

1. Earlier I cited the idea "thou shalt not kill" as one that makes it safe to live in the company of others. But things are not so simple. Even in societies where people claim to accept this idea, there is killing. Sometimes this happens in moments of crisis, when people feel their own lives are threatened, or in moments of passion, when people "lose their heads," so to speak. In the United States, it also happens in a cold and calculated way when a person convicted of a crime is put to death. What ideas are used to justify violation of the commandment not to kill? Why do some people believe that it is okay for the government to kill, even when their religion would seem to tell them otherwise?

2. Many people still see gender as naturally rooted in differences between male and female bodies. There are, of course, bodily differences that lead to differences in function: Only females can have babies. Such a basic fact of human biology is bound to affect how some parts of social life are organized. To consider how this might be the case is not inconsistent with being sociologically mindful. Yet we must be careful about this, because many common ideas about links between biology and social behavior were invented to justify domination and exploitation. How do popular notions about the biological basis of gender (or race, or sexuality) function in this way? Who benefits if such notions are widely accepted?

3. Scientists once believed that when an object burned, it gave off a substance called phlogiston, visible as flame. Physicians once believed that sickness was caused by an imbalance of humors (sort of like emotional energies) in the blood. Biologists once believed that species could not go out of existence, nor could new species come into existence. Geologists once believed that the continents did not move. Most people used to believe that the sun revolved around the earth and that the earth was the center of the universe. We now know that all of these ideas, once accepted by many intelligent people, are untrue. Which currently popular ideas about "human nature," social behavior, or the social world seem likely to be discarded over the next hundred years? How do you suppose this will happen?

Related Readings

Becker, Howard S. (1986). *Doing Things Together.* Evanston, IL: Northwestern University Press.

Berger, Peter, & Luckmann, Thomas. (1966). *The Social Construction of Reality.* Garden City, NY: Doubleday.

Fausto-Sterling, Anne. (2000). *Sexing the Body.* New York: Basic.

Fenstermaker, Sarah, & West, Candace, Eds. (2002). *Doing Gender, Doing Difference.* New York: Routledge.

Lorber, Judith. (1994). *Paradoxes of Gender.* New Haven, CT: Yale University Press.

Omi, Michael, & Winant, Howard. (2014). *Racial Formation in the United States* (3rd ed.). New York: Routledge.

Schutz, Alfred. (1932/1967). *The Phenomenology of the Social World.* Evanston, IL: Northwestern University Press.

Zerubavel, Eviatar. (1991). *The Fine Line: Making Distinctions in Everyday Life.* Chicago: University of Chicago Press.

CHAPTER 3

....

Seeing Connections

One time a student said, "I believe in tradition and think that in the home the man should be dominant." Earlier this student had said that she wanted to be a corporate attorney, so I asked if she expected to be treated as an equal at work. "Absolutely," she said. Then I asked, "Do you think it might be hard for men to see you as an equal at work if they are used to treating women as subordinates at home?" She looked puzzled, but another student saw my point and said to her, "Think about your husband. If he's used to you being subordinate at home, that's what he's going to expect from the women he works with." Another student said, "If you raise boys in a home where a man is dominant, they'll expect to be dominant themselves when they go out into the world, and that's going to hurt other women." Another student tried to sum it up: "If women settle for inequality at home, they're never going to get equality in work or politics."

Part of being sociologically mindful is seeing how our actions in one part of life are the causes and consequences of what happens elsewhere. In the example above, the first student didn't see how accepting inequality at home could keep her and other women from achieving equality at work. She was not sufficiently aware of how home life and work life are connected, such that her actions in one realm could produce unintended consequences in the other.

Here is another example. For various reasons, some people don't want to pay taxes to support programs that help the poor. And so they vote for politicians who say they will lower taxes by cutting spending on welfare, education, public housing, and school-lunch programs. You might or might not think that cutting aid to the poor is a mean and selfish policy. But without judging it in those terms, we can ask whether it is mindful or not.

The first thing we should note is that the Federal Reserve Board sets interest rates so that unemployment stays, according to official figures, at about 5 percent (it is really about twice as high). This means that there will be millions of people without jobs, through no fault of their own. If there are not enough jobs to go around and public aid is eliminated, what is the result likely to be? Probably more crime, illness, and despair—all of which have costs: higher taxes to pay for more police and prisons; higher rates for health insurance to cover the cost of emergency-room care for the poor; higher rates for insurance to cover the costs of more burglaries; greater resentment and fear between the poor and the middle class. So where are the savings? Because of how our society works, there would probably be no savings, and in many ways there would be higher costs and more suffering for everyone, except the very rich.

Sociological mindfulness does not tell us how to make tax policy. But if we pay attention to how different parts of society are connected, we are less likely to make wasteful and destructive choices about how to collect and use our common wealth. Being sociologically mindful, we can see that when we pay less for one kind of thing, we might be creating conditions that will force us, eventually, to pay more for another.

Sociological mindfulness means taking a larger view of things. For example, in the case of taxes and public aid, it would be wise to look at how much of our federal budget is spent on Temporary Assistance to Needy Families, which is still commonly known as welfare (about 1%), and how much is spent on the military (about 30%, depending on what is counted as military). We might thus see that there is plenty of wealth to provide food, housing, education, health care, and so on to all who need it—if only we did not spend billions of dollars a year to build weapons.

Although it is sometimes helpful to study one problem at a time, it is also important to see how problems are connected. Consider the example of failure in school. Why do so many children and teenagers do poorly in school or drop out? Only part of an answer can be found by looking at what happens inside schools. To understand why students do badly in school, we must look at how schools are connected to the larger society.

Students who are hungry or tired probably will not do well in school. Why are they hungry or tired? Perhaps because their families can't afford adequate food and quiet housing. And why is this? Perhaps because there aren't enough good jobs to go around. And why is this? Perhaps because employers want a high rate of unemployment to keep wages down and profits up. A lack of jobs can also dampen motivation. If school is boring and doesn't seem likely to result in a job, why stay? To make another connection, school might be boring because teachers are underpaid, overworked, and worn out. Why is this? Perhaps because so much money is spent on machines for killing, instead of on education.

The problem of failure in school is more complicated than I have made it out to be. But that is precisely the point: The problem is complicated because it arises out of a web of connections between schools, students, teachers, families, corporations, and government. To understand the problem, in a complete way, we must trace out these connections. Simply attributing the problem to something inside schools or, as some do, to a deficiency inside students is not helpful. The point of tracing out connections is to find the roots of whatever problem we are trying to understand and solve.

Consider again the link between equality at work and equality in the home. Women cannot compete as men's equals at work if they are doing a second shift of cleaning, laundry, and child care at home. A man whose wife does these chores for him, or a man who doesn't do his share, is freer to devote himself to a job. As this freedom translates into higher earnings, a man expects and gains more power in the home because his job becomes the chief source of family income. The connection now runs two ways: a little extra power at home, arising out of old ideas about gender, can give a man an edge at work, which can in turn, over time, amplify his power in the home. Seeing things in this way implies that to reduce inequality between women and men we must tackle inequalities in different but deeply connected realms of life.

Awareness of Unintended Consequences

Perhaps you are thinking, "The household inequality problem is not so complicated. If two people are busy pursuing their careers and are doing well, they can hire a maid." This is a good example of a solution that is not a solution, as we can see if we are mindful of how unintended consequences can come about. To see these consequences we must first see connections.

There is clearly a connection between a couple's income and the act of hiring a maid. Only people who have high incomes can afford to do this.

There is also a connection between the lack of job opportunities and the availability of maids. If there were lots of jobs offering good pay and working conditions, few people would choose to clean others' toilets for a living. These are obvious connections; others are harder to see.

To see these connections we must note first that most maids are women and, second, that when a couple hires a maid it is usually because the woman in the couple has decided she does not want to do so much housework. This situation typically arises, as suggested earlier, because the man in the couple resists doing a fair share of the work. If he did his share, chances are that a maid would not be needed.

So what is going on here? Is any real change being made? Not much. There is no challenge to the idea that housework is primarily a woman's responsibility. It is just a different woman who ends up doing the work. The couple simply uses some of its income to put the burden of inequality on the back of a poorer woman. The result may be a little more equality in housework within the couple, but inequality in society as a whole is reinforced. This is doubly true if the couple is white and the maid is not.

The situation is not much different if the housecleaner is a man. In this case the idea that housework is a woman's responsibility is less obviously reinforced (though it is still typically the woman in a couple who hires a housecleaner). But what is still reinforced is the idea that inequality is okay. Once again, a person with few job opportunities cleans the toilets of others, who are then freer to do more enriching things. The message conveyed by such an arrangement is this: "I am too busy making money and having fun to be bothered with cleaning up my own messes. Other people, those who have less money, should do that work for me."

We can see here a connection to a set of ideas that make inequality seem acceptable. One such idea is that a person with money is entitled to have others do his or her dirty work. To use such an idea, if only implicitly, to justify hiring a housecleaner affirms the rightness of inequality. It is as if to say, "Wealth determines human worth, and it is thus okay for a person of my wealth and worth to hire a person of lesser worth to clean up after me." Parents who hire a housecleaner teach this principle to their children, who learn that people who are rich enough do not have to take responsibility for cleaning up the messes they make.

Men can use these same ideas to argue that they should be free from doing dirty work and have more time for "serious" work and for play, because, after all, they make more money and are thus worth more than others, usually women, who earn less. The connection here is between the perpetuation of two seemingly different kinds of inequality, one having to do with economics, the other with gender. Both kinds of inequality are connected because a similar belief—about what determines the relative worth of human beings—underlies and supports them.

Sociological mindfulness brings these connections to light. What we are trying to see is how our actions, and the ideas we use to justify them, can have intended and unintended consequences because of how the social world works. If our society were not so fraught with inequalities, the meaning and consequences of hiring a housecleaner might be different.

Analyzing Moral Problems

The need to be mindful of connections increases when the problem at hand evokes strong feelings. Abortion is a good example. To see the point I will try to make about sociological mindfulness, it will help if you can set aside, for a time, your feelings about this issue. Try to shift into an analytic frame of mind.

Opponents of abortion believe that a fetus is an unborn child and that abortion is akin to murder. Others believe that until a fetus can survive outside the womb, it is part of a woman's body. In this view, abortion is the exercise of a woman's right to sovereignty over her body and her life. A point that is often missed is that abortion is not just about the rights of individual women to control their bodies. If we are mindful of how our society works, we can see that there is more at stake: restricting abortion makes it unlikely that women will ever achieve equality with men.

If women are forced to be mothers, they cannot compete as equals with men who need never worry that pregnancy, or the obligation to care for a child, will impede their striving for success in work and politics. A lack of freedom to decide whether to give birth and care for children puts women at a disadvantage. Forcing women to be mothers by restricting abortion also reinforces the idea that being a mother is a woman's most important role, implying that it is best if women make babies and homes rather than laws or economic policy.

There is another connection to see here. If women cannot get safe, legal abortions, they will get them under unsafe conditions, risking injury and death. This has always been the case when abortion is restricted. What this means is that not only women's wishes but also their safety is ignored when abortion is restricted. Such a policy thus conveys messages about women's role and worth. It says, in effect, that women should not resist motherhood and that women are less important to society than the fetuses they carry.

Denying women the option of ending a pregnancy is connected to inequality in another way. A policy of restricting abortion implies that women are incapable of making wise choices in these personal matters of life and death. If that is so, then women are surely incapable of dealing with the larger matters of life and death that concern men, matters such as whether to wage wars and kill millions of fully grown people. Restricting abortion thus not only impedes women's ability to compete with men; it also reinforces the idea that women are not men's moral and intellectual equals when it comes to dealing with the vital affairs of society.

Perhaps this sounds like an argument for abortion. Not necessarily. It is an attempt to practice sociological mindfulness with regard to the abortion issue, so as to see more of what is at stake. This way of seeing does not inevitably lead to the conclusion that abortion is right. You might believe, for example, that abortion is an undesirable practice because it reinforces a view of inconvenient life as disposable and that such an attitude will have harmful consequences in the long run.

Differences in values may also lead to different conclusions. You might believe, for example, that a zygote or a fetus deserves no less moral consideration than a fully grown woman and that restricting women's freedom is a reasonable price to pay for protecting a fetus's "right to life." If so, then you may think it is fine to restrict or outlaw abortion. But to arrive at any sound and responsible conclusions either way, one must be mindful of the connections between abortion and women's freedom and equality.

Sociological mindfulness can help us see more of what must be taken into account in seeking solutions to moral problems. This is mostly a matter of trying to see connections between our acts and their consequences, in light of how the social world works. The example of abortion shows that being mindful in this way requires a willingness to look with some detachment at how the social world works, whether we like it or not. This does not mean ignoring our hearts when making moral judgments. It means also using our heads.

Reading Indexes

The social world is full of signs called indexes. Like all signs, indexes point to, refer to, or represent something else. Learning to see and read indexes is part of learning to be sociologically mindful. To read or interpret an index sociologically is to see its connection to some aspect of how the social world works.

Imagine, for example, an unpaved road in an area where many poor people live. The road is an index. It points to the poverty and powerlessness of the people who live nearby. That is an interpretation, of course; we would want to check to see if it was true. But it is a plausible interpretation, given how our society works. We know that people usually like to have nice, paved roads and that officials who control road-building are usually more responsive to people who have money. The unpaved road could thus also be seen as an index of how government works in this country. If we know how to read it, the road can point us to many other things.

Some indexes attach to people. For example, we learn to read cars, clothes, and houses as indexes of a person's wealth. We learn to read behavior as an index of character. We can do this because we have ideas about how society works and why people act as they do. These ideas allow us to see connections between indexes and other conditions. In general, the more such ideas we possess, the more connections we can see. If people don't see the same connections, it is probably because they have different ideas about how the world works.

Sociological mindfulness does not tell us precisely how an index is connected to some other condition. Nor does it tell us what is an index of what. Being sociologically mindful simply means trying to see how conditions, customs, and events might be signs that point to other things. We can do this by making a habit of asking, "What does this condition, custom, or event *mean*? What other realities does it *point to*? What does it *say* about the nature of our society?" The answers we arrive at depend on our knowledge of how the world works.

Nonobvious Indexes

Most people learn to read the behavior, appearance, and possessions of individuals as indexes to their character and wealth. This is a basic interpretive skill. But sociological mindfulness can take us further. Things that once didn't seem meaningful are examined more closely and probed for their meaning. In this sense, sociological mindfulness amplifies our powers of interpretation.

Here are examples of arrangements, customs, and conditions that can be read as indexes. My interpretations are based on my understanding of how the social world works. Your ideas about how the world works might be different. If so, some of my interpretations will seem strange. That's fine. You do not have to interpret a sign the same way I do to appreciate that it *is* a sign. What matters is forming the habit of seeing parts of the social world as indexes.

I have already mentioned the vast share of our common wealth that is spent on tools for killing and on training people to use these tools. You might think this situation is atrocious, merely unfortunate, or quite all right. For the moment it doesn't matter. I ask you just to think about what it means that we use so much of our common wealth to kill or prepare to kill other human beings. What does this say about our society? What does it say about us as a people?

I think it says that we live in a society where the rich and powerful use a large part of our common wealth to become richer and more powerful by creating well-equipped armies to control workers, gain access to raw materials, and keep trade markets open. It says that we live in a world where many people feel they have no choice but to violently resist oppression and exploitation. It says we live in a world where some people feel entitled to exploit others, as long as they have the power to do so. I think it also says that most of us are afraid to protest the use of our common wealth to create a huge apparatus of violence.

"Military spending" could be read differently. You might not agree that it points to what I think it does. Again, that is fine. What matters is not taking it for granted but instead seeing it as an indicator and a consequence of how our society works. Being sociologically mindful, we look at "military spending" as a doorway to other social realities. Once the door is opened, we can trace out connections and talk about what else they might lead us to see.

Here is another example. Today the conditions in many of our inner cities are wretched. Many industries have moved to more profitable locations. Good jobs are thus scarce and unemployment is high. Because so many people cannot find steady work, inner-city housing is deteriorating, drug use and street crime are rampant, rates of infant mortality are extremely high, schools are in bad shape, and good health care is hard to find. Many of the people living in these areas are members of racial minority groups.

In this case we could say that conditions in inner-city areas are indexes of how our economy works. When it is more profitable to move a factory elsewhere, that is what will be done, regardless of the effects on those who are left behind. But there is a different kind of index that appears in this situation. We can see it if we look beyond the cities themselves. Consider how most white Americans react to conditions in inner cities.

What is the reaction? The most visible reaction is to blame the poor, insist that they work harder, and cut off public aid. But the most widespread reaction among white Americans is disregard. The majority of white Americans are not demanding that more be done to help people in inner cities. Most white Americans seem to wish the problem would just go away.

What is the meaning of this lack of compassion? What does it say about white Americans? It can be read as an index of racism, although I think it points to more than that. It also points to white Americans' insecurity about their own economic status; to their desire to believe that their achievements are of their own doing; and to their feelings of powerlessness when it comes to solving problems that require generous use of our common wealth, over which we do not exercise democratic control. In this case the index is *action not taken*. If we are sociologically mindful, we can see that the absence of something can be a sign, too.

Social Organization as an Index

The ways we organize ourselves to accomplish tasks can also be read as indexes. In other words, our customary ways of doing things encode messages about us; they can be read as signs of what we value and what we fear. Consider, for example, our ways of schooling.

We give grades to individuals and insist that individuals do their own work. We separate school from home life, make teachers act as surrogate parents and bosses, break the school day into blocks of time, give students breaks and vacations, make students follow rules of order (raise your hand if you want to speak!), and punish students for violating these rules. What do these practices say about us? I think they say that we, or at least the people who organize schools, are mainly concerned with turning students into good workers.

Schooling does more than transmit knowledge and basic skills. Our *form* of schooling teaches students to be competitive individualists, to accept hierarchy and authority, to follow rules, and to get up every day and do meaningless work. Students who learn to accept this regimen adapt quickly to the world of work, which is organized in much the same way. If school were organized differently—with less hierarchy and authoritarian control, less regimentation and regulation by the clock, less competition, and more respect for students' real concerns—then students might not adapt so well to the demands of employers.

Do we really value creativity, independent moral judgment, and critical thinking as much as we say? The answer encoded in our form of schooling is no. Even though some people, including many teachers, may value different kinds of knowledge, skills, and habits of mind than do employers, most schooling is organized to create good workers, rather than artists, social critics, and political activists. This fact can be seen as an index of the power of employers, and of business in general, to influence how we conduct seemingly non-economic activities in our society.

Let me suggest some other things that can be seen as indexes. You can try to read these on your own. Ask what they mean, what other realities they point to, and what they say about the nature of our society.

- The popularity of violent movies and sports
- The small percentage (<5%) of chief executive officers of *Fortune 500* firms who are women
- The refusal of TV stations to run ads for condoms, even in the midst of an AIDS/STD epidemic
- The intense interest many people have in the lives of actors and other celebrities
- The addictive way that many people use smartphones and social media
- The continuing widespread belief in religion, even in a scientific age
- The use of mood-altering drugs by many people who are *not* poor or marginalized
- The acceptance of surveillance cameras nearly everywhere
- The presence of police in schools
- The incarceration rate in the United States (about 700 people per 100,000—the highest rate in the world)
- The percentage (28%) of Americans who do not read even one book a year

You could see these items as mere curiosities and not give them another thought. Practicing sociological mindfulness, however, you can see them as doorways behind which lie interesting and complex connections to other aspects of the social world.

Connections to the Past

If you care to muse about the past, or about its connections to the present, you need not go to a museum. You are already in one. The past is all around us. Our clothes, the language we speak, the houses we live in, the ideas we embrace, and the customs we practice are all bequeathed to us from the past. We do change these things, of course, but we do not start from scratch.

When we are sociologically mindful we try to see how the past delivers us into the present moment and what the present moment tells us about the past. We could call this "trying to see historical connections," or "looking backward to try to see how things today got to be what they are." It is like seeing things in the present as indexes to the past, although things in the present do not merely point to or refer to the past; they carry it with them.

This seems most obvious if we consider material objects, such as clothing and buildings. The clothes we wear and the ways we wear them are clearly matters of tradition. It is the same with our buildings and the ways we build them. Food is a good example too—at every meal the past is served up to us. These solid objects seem to hold the past firmly in place. We can look at them and say, "This is how it was done long ago. And see? We are still doing it much the same way today." In these instances, evidence of the past is plain to see.

Knowledge itself is the past living in our minds and habits. We know what we know and do what we do—today—because of what others learned before us, thousands of years ago. This is evident right now, even as I am writing and you are (somewhat later) reading. Our language—each word, each grammatical rule—connects us, not only to each other, but also to a common human past.

The idea that the present is connected to the past might seem obvious. Yet people often fail to see historical connections, sometimes because they don't want to. For example, many white people in the United States will say, "Racism is a problem of the past. Discrimination is illegal now. Everyone is on an equal footing. So we don't need affirmative action or special programs for racial minorities." Statements like these erase connections to the past—as if all the power and privileges white people accumulated while enslaving blacks for hundreds of years do not exist.

Here is another example. In the past, women gave up their family names upon getting married and took the last name of their new husband. This practice served to indicate that a woman, as a piece of property, had been transferred from one male (the father) to another (the new husband). Men did not change their names. Men were owners, not property.

Today we reject the idea of women as property, yet this name-changing practice persists. Why? Perhaps because many young women do not see the connection between this practice and the past. If so, they fail to see the significance of changing their names. They fail to see that giving up their names—when few men would consider doing such a thing—helps perpetuate the same idea on which an older form of patriarchy was based. The idea is that a woman's identity is determined by her relationship to a man. If we want to affirm the value and equality of women, it would seem wise to reject practices that keep an oppressive past alive in the present.

The example of name-changing suggests how to be sociologically mindful about connections between past and present. It is not enough to say, "The past shapes how we think and act today." That is an important recognition, but we must go further. Being sociologically mindful, we should ask, How did this practice originate? and What problems did it solve for whom? These questions can be answered only by looking into the past. To seek answers is not merely to satisfy curiosity about times gone by. It is to try to better understand what is going on now.

Deepening the Present

Being sociologically mindful of connections between past and present can also lead us to ask better questions about the present. For example, we can ask—about any traditional idea, custom, or social arrangement—Does it serve the same purpose today as it did originally? Has it become dysfunctional in some way? If so, why has this tradition been preserved? Who benefits from carrying on this tradition—the same people as in the past? How has the tradition been changed over the years? Why?

Asking these kinds of questions makes the present more complex and interesting. Finding answers can also help us to appreciate the constructedness of the social world. By looking at connections between the past and present we see that what people intend to construct, once upon a time, can diverge greatly from what comes about over time. Looking backward also helps us see how *contingency* (a peculiar mix of fateful circumstances) affects the making of the social world.

Earlier I used the example of slavery and the consolidation of political and economic power by whites. I said that this past shapes our present and that it is foolish and wrong to deny it. But there is still room for argument and for the weighing of evidence about exactly how this past shapes which parts of our present. Undertaking this kind of inquiry and conversation is part of being sociologically mindful.

Another way to be mindful of the past in the present involves listening to others here and now. Specifically, we should be mindful of the meaning of the past and the feelings these meanings evoke. The question is not whether people's ideas about the past are correct. Rather, the question is, How do people's feelings about the past, whatever those feelings might be based on, affect how they behave in the present?

Consider again the example of slavery. We might analyze how it has affected the balance of power between blacks and whites in the United States today. That is an important kind of analysis to do. But we must also consider the meaning of slavery as a part of our past. We must consider what this part of our past means to people today. We must take these meanings into account if we want to understand the present, because these meanings affect how blacks and whites get along. If my people were enslaved by yours for hundreds of years, and then you tell me, less than 150 years later, "Oh, that's no big deal, and it certainly doesn't have any bearing on the present," you can be sure that this will affect my feelings toward you.

Understanding how people define the past and how they feel about it is part of being sociologically mindful of connections between past and present. It is to see another way in which the past lives on inside us and affects what goes on between us. Here is one more example.

One time a few professors were talking about Atlanta, Georgia. We were all going to a conference there soon. Everyone spoke well of the city. One person said, "It's amazing how they rebuilt the city after it burned in the Civil War." Another person in the group, a woman from Georgia, then said, "Honey, Atlanta didn't burn in the Civil War; it *was burned*." She wanted to remind us that a horrible event didn't simply happen, but that a Northern army had savaged a part of her home state. Her remark surprised me, since I had grown up in the North and had never met anyone with strong feelings about the Civil War. Our interaction on this occasion was affected by feelings arising from the meaning given to events that had happened more than 120 years before.

We can argue about whether it is good or bad, useful or not, to hold on to certain parts of the past. But that is a different matter. The point here is that we can't deal well with others without being mindful of how the meanings they give to the past affect the meanings they give to things in the present. We must also be mindful of how people learn about the past and come to define it as they do. To know these things we must connect a person to his or her own past, as we must do with ourselves.

If we can't see these connections, the present will seem to just tumble into the future. The present itself might seem like a random configuration of circumstances. Practicing sociological mindfulness is a way to dispel this illusion and to find orderly connections between present and past. It is a way to avoid repeating mistakes of the past and to see when old dangers arise in new forms.

Dialogue

Little Things and Big Things

I have been told that the practice of a woman taking her husband's name is a "little thing" about which one should not get too bothered. I have also heard this said about sexist language. For instance, when I have objected to use of the term *freshmen* to refer to a group of first-year students that includes women and men, I have been told that this is a little thing that I should not make an issue of. After all, no one uses this term with sexist intent. So why make a fuss?

The main reason for making a fuss has already been mentioned: practices can be harmful regardless of people's intentions. So it doesn't really matter if people who use sexist terms do not *intend* to cause harm; most people don't. What matters is whether the practice is likely to have harmful consequences. If so, perhaps we ought to make a fuss.

You might wonder how name-changing or the use of male generics (e.g., mankind, chairman, freshman, or "you guys" to refer to a mixed group of people) can cause harm. Earlier in this chapter, I said that the name-changing practice is a vestige of a patriarchal era in which women were treated as property and that even today the practice carries this connotation. I also suggested that repudiating the practice would be a way to symbolically affirm the equality of women. Still, you might think, "What does it matter if a few old practices persist? Nobody literally thinks of women as property anymore."

It is not so clear, however, that no one thinks of women as property. Many men still think of wives and girlfriends as *theirs*. If another man expresses interest in the woman, this is perceived as a form of *trespassing*— a violation of the first man's property rights. Some men may even use violence to try to enforce their imaginary ownership claims.

You have probably seen the headline MAN KILLS WIFE, KILLS SELF. These stories often involve a woman trying to escape a bad relationship. What kinds of ideas lead some men to act so violently? Probably ideas like this: If she wasn't going to be *mine*, if I couldn't have her, then no man was going to have her. How do such ideas persist? Might they be subtly reinforced by the name-changing practice?

Violence against women is not limited to a few tragic cases. Sexual harassment, sexual coercion, sexual assault, and rape are epidemic in U.S. society, and these problems are not going away. Why not? A complete answer would be quite long, but it is safe to say that these problems stem in part from some men feeling entitled to control women, from the willingness of some men to treat women as objects, and from the fact that men can often get away with treating women badly. Nonviolent acts of discrimination share these same origins in the thoughts and feelings of men.

Just to be clear, I should say that not all men are violent or abusive, or treat women as objects, or try to get away with mistreating women. But many men do fit these descriptions, and many more men treat women in demeaning ways without realizing it. The key issue, however, is how it is possible—after decades of struggle for women's equality—for problems of violence and discrimination to persist. Why isn't the full and equal humanity of women so deeply entrenched by now that violence and discrimination are unthinkable?

Again, a complete answer would require a separate book. Here I want only to suggest that sexist language, one of those little things, has something to do with it. To see this, we need to be mindful about connections.

Throughout *TSEL*, I say that ideas are important for shaping behavior. I do not claim that any one idea causes any one behavior. That would be too simple. It makes more sense to say that a widely shared set of ideas guides people as they act and interact and that as long as these ideas remain stable, the result will be stable patterns of behavior. To put it another way, we each have a worldview that guides our perceptions and leads us, often without our being aware of it, along certain paths of action.

A good question to ask, therefore, is this: How does a worldview get stabilized? Part of the answer has to do with the ordinary, everyday use of language. Our ways of using language to represent and define reality reflect a particular worldview. But these ways of speaking and writing do more than reflect a worldview. They also bind us to it and reinforce it.

So, then, what if our habitual ways of speaking and writing make certain groups of people invisible? What if our ways of speaking and writing imply that certain groups of people (men) are standard and normal—representative of all humanity—while other groups (women) are different, deviant, or inferior? Perhaps you can see what I am getting at. Language is not merely a window to a sexist worldview; it is the main tool with which both the world and the view are continually rebuilt.

To get back to examples, the name-changing practice and the use of male generics make women invisible. To refer to a group of first-year college students, half of whom are women, as fresh*men* is to say, symbolically, that the presence of women doesn't matter. It is also to say, symbolically, that human = male. This linguistic practice thus reinforces a worldview in which women are not as important as men, not as fully human as men, not equal to men. What sorts of behavior might follow from this? The answer has already been given: if women are not seen as fully human, as the full equals of men, then it becomes easier to ignore them, abuse them, discriminate against them, restrict their freedom, and so on.

The larger point here is about the need to be mindful of connections between "little things" and things that most people acknowledge as serious. We live in a society where many large-scale patterns of behavior are harmful to women. These patterns of behavior are upheld by a sexist world view that is in turn upheld, millions of times a day, by sexist language habits. Which is why those habits are not too little to worry about. They are part of what helps to perpetuate bigger problems.

Some people get defensive when they are asked to change their language habits. "You shouldn't bug me about *that*," they will say. "It's a little thing. You should worry about bigger things." But then I wonder, if it's truly little, why resist changing it? In fact, why not change the little things first? Shouldn't that be easiest?

Perhaps the defensiveness arises because people feel accused of being intentionally oppressive. If so, they are failing to see how easy it is, in a sexist and racist society, to pick up the unconscious habits of speaking and behaving in ways that reflect and reinforce sexism and racism. None of us is to blame for picking up such habits as children; it's part of what happens in a society fraught with inequalities. So there is no point in feeling guilty about it, as long as we are willing to reflect critically on the habits that have been instilled in us and on the consequences of those habits.

So, if we are sociologically mindful about how parts of the social world are connected, we will pay attention to how seemingly little things can reinforce bigger problems. If we desire to change the social world, we can decide to work on little things that are easy to change (e.g., our language habits) *and* on bigger things (e.g., sexual violence against women) that will be harder to change. There is no contradiction between working on both at the same time. We should also keep in mind that little changes, if they challenge a worldview in which inequality is accepted as normal, can lead to much bigger changes.

A Note on the Future

Connections between the present and the past already exist and can be studied by anyone who wants to do so. But how can we see connections between the present and the future if the future hasn't happened yet? On the one hand, we can't; all we can do is to speculate about or imagine what those connections might be. On the other hand, this is something we can't avoid doing, either.

Whenever we make a choice in everyday life, we try to see connections between the present and the future. This is what it means to try to envision the likely consequences of our actions. When we think, "Will doing X or Y lead to the best results?" we are trying to figure out how a choice in the present will lead to some outcome in the future. People who don't engage in this kind of thinking are said to be impulsive or to lack foresight.

As suggested in the foregoing chapter, being sociologically mindful entails thinking about the consequences of our choices in a way that goes beyond calculating what will benefit us the most as individuals. Being sociologically mindful means thinking about how the choices we make today might affect other people, perhaps even society as a whole, in the future.

According to Native American folklore, one of the governing principles of the Iroquois Confederacy was that, when making decisions, tribal councils were supposed to take into account the possible consequences of the decision for seven generations to come. Admittedly, this is hard to do in a modern society, because the rapid pace of change means that we can barely predict how things will turn out even one generation into the future. Yet the principle seems wise.

As individuals we can try to be mindful about how our actions in the present are connected to our own future and that of other people. The Iroquois principle goes further. It says that this kind of mindfulness can be built into how a society operates. We might thus look at how our government, or our form of economy, encourages or discourages taking the future into account. If it seems that a lack of foresight imperils us as a society, perhaps something can be done. What would be needed is a collective effort by people who are mindful of how the world we are creating today will affect the lives of our children, and their children.

Paths for Reflection

1. Years ago I took a poetry course in which the teacher asked us to look up the meaning of our names. He wanted to raise our awareness of the meaning of the language that we attached to ourselves. I already knew that Schwalbe was German for "swallow" (i.e., the bird). But then I learned that Michael meant "God-like" or "with God" in Hebrew and that Louis, my middle name, meant "warrior" in French. For me, the assignment was fun; I enjoyed seeing how my names linked me to old cultures. Why might African American and Native American students have experienced the assignment differently? How might a student's experience of the assignment be connected to past and present inequalities in our society?

2. Adolf Hitler was Germany's leader during World War II. After the war, as the extent of the atrocities committed under his orders came to light, Hitler was defined as one of the most evil men of all time and as a

man who had to be stopped. Even though Hitler killed himself near the end of the war as Allied soldiers closed in on Berlin, there is a sense in which "Hitler" is still alive. Where and when is Hitler, as a symbol or image, still used today? What other historical persons or events have been turned into symbols that are invoked to shape the present?

3. In this chapter, I said that how an activity is organized can be read as an index. I used the example of how schooling in the United States is typically organized and what this way of schooling says about how our society works. The same principle of mindfulness can be applied to any organized activity. Consider, for example, a single course in school (perhaps the one for which you are reading this book). Note how class time is used, the kind of assignments that are given, the type and frequency of exams, the kind of books and other readings that are used, the number of students in the course, the kind of students in the course, and the kind of feedback students get on their work. To what other social realities do these things point? Why might your interpretations of these indexes differ from those of your teacher or fellow students?

Related Readings

Barabási, Albert-Lászlá. (2002). *Linked: How Everything Is Connected to Everything Else and What It Means for Business, Science, and Everyday Life.* New York: Penguin.

Chandler, Daniel. (2007). *Semiotics: The Basics* (2nd ed.). New York: Routledge.

Coates, Ta-Nehisi. (2015). *Between the World and Me.* New York: Spiegel & Grau.

Dunbar-Ortiz, Roxanne. (2015). *An Indigenous Peoples' History of the United States.* Boston: Beacon.

Ehrenreich, Nancy, Ed. (2008). *The Reproductive Rights Reader: Law, Medicine, and the Construction of Motherhood.* New York: New York University Press.

Kadushin, Charles. (2011). *Understanding Social Networks.* New York: Oxford University Press.

Kleinman, Sherryl. (2002). "Why Sexist Language Matters." *Qualitative Sociology* 25(2): 299–304.

Moraga, Cherrie, & Anzaldúa, Gloria. (2015). *This Bridge Called My Back* (4th ed.). Albany, NY: SUNY Press.

Postman, Neil. (1996). *The End of Education.* New York: Vintage.

CHAPTER 4

....

Relationships, Groups, and Interdependence

Sometimes I run through an area where there are huge houses, an exclusive country club, and a private golf course. The roads in this area are wide, traffic is tight, and the spaces between the houses are wooded and green. On the golf course there are ponds where ducks and geese swim and chat. In some ways it is a very pleasant place. But it can also be troubling.

As I run, I wonder why we allow some people to live in mansions while others live in shacks or tenements or on the street. I get angry at the self-indulgence and waste that I see reflected in houses that are bigger than anyone needs. When I see children in this area I think of how they will grow up accustomed to comforts and privileges that few people in our society will ever know. And when I see new houses being built I think of the workers who build these houses but can't afford to buy them.

One time, while running through this area on a hot day, I said hello to two Latino men who were cutting grass in a front yard. They nodded to me but did not return my greeting with any enthusiasm. I thought about my own privileges and how I must look to them. In the middle of the work day, while they cut grass, I was running five miles for my own pleasure. They would still be cutting grass when I was home, showered, and in my recliner reading.

A few blocks later two gray-haired men passed me in a golf cart. We were going in the same direction, I on the sidewalk and they to the left of me in the street. Just after they passed me they turned onto the golf course—right into my path, forcing me to jog around them. They were gabbing away, not seeming to care that they had almost run me over, so I yelled at them, "Wake up and watch where you're going!" They looked surprised and angry. These well-to-do white men were probably not used to being scolded for their misbehavior.

I had gone another mile and was now running in the road, facing traffic, when a car coming toward me slowed and the passenger-side window began to open. I could guess what was about to happen. "Where is the country club?" someone would ask, without even apologizing for interrupting my run. In either direction, the same quick answer sufficed. "Keep going straight. Turn on Lancaster," I would say, without slowing down.

I didn't like being interrupted while running, and, having nearly been hit by the men in the golf cart, I did not feel charitable toward lost country clubbers. So when the car slowed, I just waved and kept going. "You aren't really lost," I thought, "just keep driving and you'll find your stupid clubhouse in a minute."

The driver realized that I wasn't going to stop and started to pull away. I glanced inside the car and saw that the driver was a middle-aged black man; the passengers were three plainly dressed black women. It was unlikely that they were country club members. I felt ashamed for not helping them. Thinking that to them I must have seemed like one more white man treating them with disrespect made me feel worse.

When I got home, I thought about how my feelings depended on what had happened during my run. My experience of the run was affected by these brief interactions along the way. I realized that much the same thing occurred whenever I went out. Whether it was to the post office, the grocery store, the coffee shop, the movies, or wherever, interactions always shaped my mood. No doubt my behavior—a hello, a scolding, a snubbing—affected others' moods as well. How might this in turn affect the rest of a person's day? Much could depend on these brief encounters between strangers.

The interactions that occurred during my run were not the products of personalities. Inequality intruded in each case. The Latino men reacted to me as they did in part because of inequalities in our economic positions and in part because of inequalities between Anglos and Latinos in this society. The men in the golf cart might have been merely careless, but I suspect it was their social class that led them to expect others to yield the right of way without complaint. My impulse to yell at them, and the pleasure I took in doing so, can probably be traced to my own working-class roots.

Inequality also made a difference when I did not stop for the people who needed directions. If the people in the car had been white, or if I had been black and they were white, or if the neighborhood had been different, my passing by would not have had the same meaning. But because I was white, and because of how whites have mistreated blacks in U.S. society, my behavior could be interpreted as another instance of disrespect. Knowing that my behavior may have hurt the people in the car is what made me feel bad.

Sociological mindfulness can help us see how our feelings depend on what happens in encounters like those on my run. It can also help us see how our emotional responses to these encounters are affected by history, culture, and current social arrangements. We connect with others as we do, in other words, because of the context in which we do it. If we are sociologically mindful, we see that we cannot go through the world disconnected from others, no matter how alone we might feel at times. Even loneliness is a feeling that depends on the state of our relationships with others.

As I've told it, the story of my run is about emotional interdependence, though it also illustrates other kinds of interdependence. I would not have been running at all if I hadn't learned from someone that running is good for my body. I also depended on shoes that let me run without injury. The briefs, shorts, socks, T-shirt, glasses, sweatband, and watch I wore also helped make my run possible—as did the sidewalks and roads on which I ran. And if there had been no clean water coming out of my faucet afterward, I might never have run again. Even though I was running "by myself," I was still connected to others.

We are able to do what we do because of what others have created for us to use. Not only our special activities but our everyday survival depends on getting things through our relationships with others. Even our most creative acts build on, or make use of, ideas and materials that we get from others. Likewise, others depend on us for what they need to live and thrive. Part of being sociologically mindful is paying attention to how these connections are made and to what happens because of them.

Beyond Individualism

People in Western society often fail to see their interdependence. We like to imagine ourselves to be self-reliant individuals, making our way through the world by the strength of talents that are ours alone. Being sociologically mindful, we can see that this notion is rather silly. If we are going to live as human beings in the modern world, we can no more get by without others than we can get by without air.

Consider the matter of achievement. Typically, we think of achievement as resulting from individual effort. We think of people striving to do great things. We then attribute such achievements to the person's special qualities. This way of thinking is seductive because it allows us to create heroes, to take credit for our successes, and to blame others for their failures (rather than noticing our contributions to those failures). But if we are sociologically mindful, we will see that individual achievement is an illusion.

Certainly there are instances of what we call individual achievement. It is just that the achievement is not really individual; it always grows out of a person's ties to others. Suppose that a person from a poor family works hard, overcomes many hardships, and becomes a justice on the U.S. Supreme Court. Isn't this a matter of individual achievement? Not really. It is the result of many relationships and interactions, and it could happen only as a result of many lucky accidents.

To see this, we must not forget the obvious: Every judge in black robes was once a baby in diapers. None of us would be alive today if not for the adults who cared for us when we were infants. So there is the first blow to the illusion of individual achievement. We must remember, too, that as children we depended on adults to teach us, encourage us, set examples for us, and help us develop good habits. If they had not done these things, we would not have grown up to be the intelligent, kind, hard-working people we sometimes are.

Achievement also depends on others giving us opportunities to develop and display our abilities. It depends on others being able and willing to recognize the results of our efforts. It depends on powerful others not going out of their way to keep us down. Along the way it depends on others nurturing us, opening doors for us, and giving us time on stage to prove ourselves. If these things don't happen, and happen at the right times, we can't achieve.

Gaining a high social position also requires the existence of institutions. For anyone to become a justice of the Supreme Court, there must be schools, universities, law schools, a federal government, a criminal-justice system, and so on, or there would be no such position to achieve, nor any paths to get there. These institutions exist only because many people continue to do things together in orderly ways. Any individual's achievement thus depends on many other people doing their parts to keep the whole show going.

Achievement also depends on collectively created ideas and values. Why, for instance, would anyone think it worthwhile to strive for power and status in the first place? Why would anyone value such things? How would people know what to do to attain such things? These ideas and values also had to be created, once upon a time, and instilled in individuals. Ambition and cunning are social constructions too.

People who achieve status and power often do not see what enables their achievement. Perhaps they think, "Yes, I suppose I did get a few breaks along the way, but mostly I have achieved because I am smarter and more determined than others. I am truly a splendid human specimen." This is an illusion fostered by individualism. It is like saying, "See how good I am at climbing this rope? I can do it all by myself"—with no awareness of who taught you to climb, who made the rope, who let it down for you, or who built the place you are climbing to.

Perhaps you would like to believe in genius as a power that springs mysteriously from inside individuals. There are, of course, people whose minds develop rapidly in certain ways. Mozart, for example, wrote symphonies when he was a child and went on to become a great composer. We can marvel at this but still see the need to look beyond Mozart. If Mozart's world had not included pianos, music, and music teachers (especially his father, Leopold Mozart), he would not have become what he did, at any age.

The same point applies to all instances of genius. A capacity for any kind of performance turns to nothing if the context does not enable its development. No doubt many potential Mozarts have lived and died without ever having seen a piano.

Mindfulness of Interdependence

Students who are striving for success, if only in the form of finding decent jobs when they finish school, are often unmindful of their interdependence. Sometimes they will say, "I am here because of my own merits and will achieve whatever I desire because of my merits. Nothing can stop me." While it is good to be self-confident, it is even better to be self-confident and also to see how we depend on others—past and present—for the nurturing, recognition, and reward of our merits, whatever they might be.

Mindfulness of the social basis of achievement can help us avoid being egotistical, selfish, and ungrateful. It should also help us to feel compassion for those whose chances to live good lives are limited. If we can see how our own achievement depends on ties to others—parents, teachers, friends, life partners, mentors, employers—we should also be able to see that not everyone starts with or can make the same connections and thus may not be able to develop, display, and get rewarded for their abilities. If we can see this, the next step is to look for patterns, that is, to try to see how groups of people are denied chances to do well.

Later I will talk about "seeing patterns." Here I want to say more about being mindful of how social life makes us human. That is what this chapter and the next are about—how our relations of interdependence make us what we are. Even to understand this principle of interdependence depends on our relationships with others.

Consider your reactions to this book. You have probably liked some parts of it and disliked others. Why? It might be hard to say, but it must be because of the ideas and feelings you brought with you to this book. Where did these ideas and feelings come from? The source must be your relationships with others, extending back into your childhood. The implication is that where we stand today—the standpoint from which we react to books or try to understand the world—is a result of our prior and current connections to others.

Philosophers put it this way: "All knowledge is perspectival," which means that we can know about the world only from some point of view. Part of being sociologically mindful is trying to understand how our point of view is a result of our relationships with others. If we are sociologically mindful, we can also see that these relationships are what they are because of the families, schools, social classes, workplaces, ethnic and regional communities, gender groups, nations, and historical times in which we grew up. All this is to say that *what* we know and *how* we know are the results of our ties to others.

Because our knowledge of the world and of ourselves arises from the relationships we have experienced so far in life, we are limited in what we can know about the world and about ourselves, unless we move around a bit. We can literally move around—that is, live in different places, meet new and different people, and learn how they see the world—or we can use our minds to move around. We can read about other people's experiences and ideas. Looking back on ourselves from these other points of view, we might see things we never imagined.

Perspectives and Groups

Sociological mindfulness means recognizing not only that there are other points of view but also that these points of view are linked to groups and to the position of groups relative to each other. Consider teachers, for instance. They come to share ideas, a way of talking, and a general outlook because they do similar kinds of work and face similar problems in doing it. Teachers also learn from each other about how to deal with students, parents, secretaries, principals, school boards, and so on.

Teachers face similar problems because of how schools are organized and how teachers are positioned relative to the other groups that are part of the scene. If schools were reorganized so that teachers were in charge, that would change the way groups relate to each other and would no doubt lead teachers and others in the system to develop different perspectives. A perspective thus takes shape because of commonalities (in this case, among teachers) and differences (between teachers and others in the education system).

To take another example, as long as doctors relate to patients, nurses, administrators, and each other in ways that are determined by how hospitals are organized, doctors will tend to face similar problems and develop a shared perspective. It is not that all doctors, any more than all teachers, think alike in every detail. The point is that people who do similar kinds of work, solve similar kinds of problems, earn their money in similar ways, and relate to others in similar ways will tend to develop a shared outlook on the world.

When I want students to think about the dangers of masculinity, I will say, "Every man in the room can probably imagine circumstances in which he would feel compelled to kill another man, so as to prove his own manhood." The men look grim and nod their heads. Then I ask the women, "Can you imagine having to kill another woman to prove that you are a woman?" They just stare back because the question makes no sense in light of how we define womanhood in our culture. Where is the interdependence here? It is between women and men. We can see this if we recognize that men are constructed to be what women are not.

In our culture, men are supposed to be capable of violence; women are not (even though, in fact, some women can be quite violent). To be a respected member of the category "men," it is necessary, under some conditions, to threaten or to commit violence. Men know, even if they do not say it, that violence may be necessary to avoid being treated like a woman—which would mean being dominated by other men. When I ask for examples of times when a man might have to fight to prove he is a man, someone usually says, "If, like, another guy called you a woman."

What is important to see here is the interdependence between the gender categories that give rise to different perspectives. "Men" and "women" are complementary categories, usually fashioned as opposites. In this sense the categories are interdependent—neither would make sense without the other. If we did not create the categories women and men and enforce the idea that, to be a man, one must not show the weakness, softness, and passivity defined as womanly traits, then men would not know what they know about manly honor and killing.

If we did not create groups of people called women and men, and if we did not segregate them and teach them different ways to be human, they would not be much different at all. But our society is organized so that women and men typically experience different kinds of tasks, hardships, and pleasures. Men thus know and feel things that women do not, and women know and feel things that men do not. These differences in knowledge and feelings are not natural, but rather the results of how the categories women and men are defined and of how the people in these categories are taught to think, feel, and act.

Again, it is not that all men think alike, feel alike, or agree with each other, nor that all men are totally different from women. These things are obviously not true. Yet it is true that knowing one's self as a man, and knowing the world from the standpoint of a man, is possible only because of the interdependent categories *men* and *women* to which males and females are assigned. What sociological mindfulness helps us to see in this case is that our "individual" point of view—as a man or a woman—is really a result of how we learn to relate to others.

Understanding Ourselves by Understanding Others

The nature of our ties to others can keep us from understanding important things about ourselves and others. Consider the example of blacks and whites in the United States. Which group is likely to know more about the other? It seems likely that blacks will know more about whites than whites know about blacks. Why? Because whites have been more powerful (politically and economically) than blacks, so blacks have had to watch whites carefully, just to survive.

It is like this: If you are a worker, you must pay attention to what your boss is thinking and feeling, because your job depends on being able to anticipate his or her behavior. Good bosses will pay attention to what workers think and feel, but that is not the point. Because of a boss's power, a worker has more incentive to study the boss than the boss has to study the worker. After all, if a worker doesn't do a good job of anticipating what the boss wants, the boss can fire a worker. A worker can't fire the boss.

In the history of the United States, blacks have not been able to "fire" whites who enslaved, abused, or disrespected them. Blacks have not had the power to do that. And so, to survive and avoid trouble, blacks have had to study whites more closely than whites have had to study blacks. The average black person is thus likely to know more about whites and about "white culture" than the average white person knows about blacks and about "black culture." This is an example of how inequalities between groups can shape, or limit, the knowledge that people in those groups come to possess.

To push the example, consider this question: Do blacks know more about whites than whites know about themselves? The answer is most likely yes, because learning about ourselves requires taking the perspectives of others. We must, in other words, be able to see ourselves as others see us. If we have a great deal of power—relative to other persons or groups—then we are unlikely to concern ourselves with how others see us.

Most white people do not try very hard to see themselves through the eyes of black people. This is not to say that whites willfully ignore the perspectives of blacks. More likely, it never occurs to most whites to look at themselves from the perspectives of blacks, since whites have no compelling reasons to do so. Likewise, most Americans rarely look at themselves through the eyes of people in other countries. The economic and military power of the United States allows Americans to ignore what people in other countries think.

The principle here concerns power and knowledge. If groups are unequal to each other, this affects what members of those groups are likely to know about each other and how hard they will try to know each other. Those in more powerful groups will generally know less about people in less powerful groups. Powerful people are even likely to know less about themselves, in some ways, than the powerless know about them. It is as if the cost of power is ignorance about one's self and others.

Relations of inequality are also relations of interdependence. One group may be stronger than another, yet still depend on the other. Masters need slaves just as capitalists need workers. As people in dominant and subordinate groups struggle to survive—recognizing that the struggle may be much harder for one group than for the other—they create the conditions and experiences that lead some people to know what others do not. The knowledge that individuals acquire depends largely on which group they are in and how their group cooperates and competes with other groups.

A second principle is thus that "individual" knowledge is always a social product. What we know depends on the nature of our relationships with others. Part of being sociologically mindful is getting beyond individualism and appreciating how those relationships make us what we are.

By doing so we can discover the limits of our knowledge and see how to increase it in ways that will allow us to live more responsibly in the world.

"Personal Choices"

If you had younger brothers or sisters, your parents probably urged you to set a good example for them. In telling you this your parents were trying to make you mindful of a kind of interdependence. They wanted you to be aware that your behavior could affect others who learned from watching you. Otherwise you might have thought that your behavior was purely a matter of "personal choice," with no sense that your choices could help or harm others.

Sociological mindfulness, in contrast, means paying attention to how our behaviors affect, and are affected by, others. We might thereby see that many of our choices are not so personal, in that they have significant bearing on others, directly or indirectly. It is not always easy to see how this is so, and in some cases we may not want to see.

I said earlier that being mindful of the consequences of our actions does not mean trying to imagine all possible consequences. That would keep us from acting at all. The best we can do is to imagine the consequences that are *likely*, in light of how the social world works. Sociological mindfulness does not prescribe or prohibit any particular choices. Being mindful is a matter of taking more things into account before we act. If we do that, we may very well decide to act differently, depending on what we value.

In Chapter 1, I used the example of working in destructive jobs. Sociological mindfulness, I said, can help us see the harm that arises from working in such jobs, perhaps leading us to try to earn a living differently. Below are several more examples of that kind, although not about jobs. In each case I am suggesting what we might see if we are mindful of our interdependence with others.

Smoking

If you are a smoker, you might defend your habit on the grounds that it is a personal choice. Perhaps you think that even if smoking harms your body, it is *your* body to do with as you please. Perhaps you think that as long as you bear the costs of your addiction and do not blow smoke in anyone's face, then it is no one's business but your own. That is the kind of thinking encouraged by individualism, which inhibits a mindful assessment of how your habit affects others.

As a smoker you are setting a bad example for children and others who might look up to you. Your behavior says that smoking is okay and not really harmful, or else why would you do it? If you smoke outside and drop your cigarette butts on the ground, as most smokers do, you are also communicating a disrespect for public space and for the earth. And if you smoke in an enclosed space where others are present, you are harming other people's health, even if they do not complain.

There is more to consider. For example, when you buy cigarettes you are helping to get others addicted—not only because of the example you set, but also because you provide tobacco companies with funds for advertising. This is like donating money to drug dealers to help them persuade children, especially teenagers, that drug use is sexy, glamorous, and a sign of adult sophistication. Your choice to smoke thus has, as one consequence, the harm done to others who are duped into becoming users themselves.

Even if you smoked stolen cigarettes in a closet, you could not avoid harming others. Consider that health insurance costs more for everyone because smokers require extra care to treat their various smoking-related diseases. Your choice to smoke imposes these costs on others. And if you are disabled by emphysema or die early because of lung cancer or a heart attack, your family and friends may be deeply anguished. In this way you force them to pay for your choice, which, if you can see it mindfully, is not personal at all.

If you think that I think smoking is a bad idea, you are right, although what I have said here is not an argument against smoking. It is an illustration of what sociological mindfulness calls us to consider when we presume to make personal choices. If we are sociologically mindful, we see that it is possible, sometimes, for our choices to have effects that travel far beyond us. Part of being mindful is trying to discern the effects that arise because of our interdependence with others.

Violent Sports

Here is another example of a harmful choice, one that might strike you as strange: watching football. Perhaps you are thinking, "Football? He has gone too far! What could be wrong with football? It doesn't cause lung cancer or heart disease. It's just fun!" It is true that, other than injuries to players, football doesn't cause physical disease. But it does contribute to several diseases of social life: authoritarianism, militarism, and sexism.

If we say that football is just another game in which athletes compete for prizes, we are ignoring the crucial particulars. Football is not just any game, but one that calls for violence and thus places a premium on size, strength, and force. Yes, it also calls for strategy and skill, and in this sense it is like many other games. But then we should ask, To what ends are strategy, skill, and force put in the game of football? The answer is in the game itself: the goal is to penetrate the farthest limits of the opposing team's territory (achieving a touchdown or field goal). It takes no great interpretive skill to see this as a metaphorical enactment of war.

So, then, what does sociological mindfulness lead us to see when we watch a football game? We could say, "Ah, we see a metaphorical enactment of war." But we could say, more simply, that what we see are groups of beefy men striving to dominate each other. Then we can widen our view and note that we also see women on the sidelines, cheering for the men as they perform the serious action; we see fans shrieking and yelling in delight when "their team" crushes the other; and we see that the action is directed by a few male commanders—coaches and quarterbacks.

Seen in this way, football is not only a metaphorical enactment of war; it is also a microcosm of social life on our planet. Men struggle with each other for power, a few elite men ordering other men to do the violent dirty work; women keep out of the way, providing support and decoration; most people, lacking any power themselves, just watch and cheer; and highly paid commentators explain why the game is wonderful and no sensible person would want to change it.

You might accept all this and still enjoy football. Really, what could be the harm? The answer is that participating in the spectacle of football, if only as a casual viewer, reinforces the same values and impulses that underlie war and men's domination of women. It does so by implying that a violent struggle for masculine power is fine entertainment. People may not intend to imply any such thing; they may intend only to be amused by the game. Their behavior nonetheless signifies the acceptability of the values encoded in the game.

Imagine, in contrast, what a conscientious objector to football might say: "I will have nothing to do with this game—not even lend it legitimacy by watching it—because football makes violence and domination, and the devaluation of women, seem normal and acceptable." The objector is mindful of how deeds can reinforce ideas and values, because deeds, such as watching football, convey messages. And so the objector chooses not to convey to others the message that the values encoded in football are okay.

Having Babies

Here is another example that pushes even farther into the territory of what we usually consider personal choice: women having babies. I do not propose to consider all the circumstances under which women might choose to have babies. I have in mind the case where an educated young woman, perhaps a college graduate, gets married, works for several years, and then quits working to have babies and live primarily off her husband's income. This is a common pattern among heterosexual women in the United States.

If such a young woman wants to get married, work for a while, and then quit to stay at home and raise children, isn't that a choice she should be free to make? Yes, of course—just as people should be free to smoke and to watch football if that is what they want to do, after considering the consequences as fully as possible. Sociological mindfulness demands only mindfulness, not any particular course of action.

So what should a young woman be mindful of if she is considering having babies? Consider how her situation might unfold. Because women tend to be channeled into lower-paying, lower-status jobs than men, it is likely, first of all, that her job will be less rewarding than her husband's. Her paid work may not feel especially meaningful, either. Under these conditions, the option of raising children may be attractive. It is a way to avoid the hassles of the workplace, a way to do something meaningful, and a way to achieve adult status as a woman. It may also be a way to end nagging by parents: "So, when are you going to have children?"

If she quits her job to have babies, several consequences are likely to follow. One is that her boss, who is likely to be a man, will think, "Yes, this is what I feared would happen. We invest time and energy in training these women, and after a few years they quit to have babies. I guess that is just their nature. In the future I will try to put men in these jobs and promote them faster, since men are likely to be more committed to their work." This kind of thinking on the part of an employer could have bad consequences for other women in the workplace.

A woman who quits her job is also likely to lose power in the home. This happens in part because she becomes economically dependent on her husband. Now her husband can say, "I go out into the world every day to earn the money that keeps this household afloat. I take my lumps out there. So I think my preferences deserve extra consideration when it comes to making decisions around here." Even if he doesn't say exactly this, it would be surprising if he didn't believe it. And whether we think this belief is right or wrong, it is not crazy, economically, to give extra weight to the needs of the person whose income supports the family.

So now she stays home to cook and clean and raise the children. He may help out occasionally, but because he is the breadwinner for the family, he must work all the harder at his job. He may thus have little time for what he sees as the trivia of housework. "Besides," he might think, "isn't that supposed to be *her* contribution to the family? If I earn the money to support us, she ought to keep up the house and tend to the kids. I have more important things to worry about." Perhaps the woman accepts this arrangement because it helps her husband get ahead at work, which means more money for the family. It is an arrangement that has other costs, but she sees it as her personal choice.

To begin to see the unintended consequences of this choice, consider her husband's workplace competitors. Who are the ones least likely to have wives providing support at home? Women. Lacking wives, women are less able to dedicate themselves fully to work. Bosses thus get the impression that men are better employees, especially at higher ranks, because they will be more dedicated—more willing to "stay late and get the job done." One consequence, then, of a woman's choice to stay home, raise kids, and nurture a husband is the perpetuation of gender inequality at work. To say it another way, one consequence is to limit women's chances of getting ahead.

You might think, "If a woman does not want to impede her career by having children, she should just not have children, and perhaps stay single as well. Then she will be able to match the men at work." Of course. Suppose, however, that most of the men with whom a single or child-free woman works have economically dependent, stay-at-home wives. If these men are used to dealing with their wives as "junior partners," will they be able to accept women as equals and superiors at work? Or are these men likely to think that a woman's place is in the home, where her job is to service a man's needs? Under such conditions, men may come to presume that the workplace is a man's domain. They may also come to presume that the service and deference they get from their wives at home is what they are entitled to receive from women in general.

A husband and wife are obviously interdependent, emotionally and financially. That is easy to see. It's harder to see how *women* are interdependent, such that the "personal choices" of women who stay home to have babies have consequences for women who are striving for equality in the workplace. If we are mindful of how our society works, we can see that when women give up their economic independence and stake themselves on a relationship to a man, they are perpetuating disadvantages for other women. What's more, when a woman wishes to return to work, out of need or desire, she will find those disadvantages waiting for her.

I have heard women students say, "I really dislike it that feminism says that if you stay home and raise children, you are bad." When I ask why they think any feminist would say such a thing, these students say, "It's because they see housework as demeaning." This is quite wrong. It is actually men who see housework as trivial and demeaning, which is why they don't want to do it. Nor do feminists say that women who take care of homes and children are bad (actually, feminists have argued that caring and nurturing are valuable and important).

What feminists have done is to urge women to be mindful of how their choices affect other women. To opt for having babies simply because that is what women are expected to do, or because of a stalled career, is not to make a mindful choice. It is to be pulled back to a deeply rutted path that most likely leads away from equality for women in our society. Again, to be sociologically mindful about these matters does not preclude choosing to have children. It means recognizing the interdependencies that make this a choice with far-reaching social, rather than merely personal, consequences.

A Scientist's Dilemma

Suppose that you are a scientist who needs money to do a research project. Suppose that a foundation is willing to fund your project. Suppose that this foundation is associated with a tobacco company, such that its money comes from selling cigarettes. Would you take the money? Before deciding, you would probably want to consider why the foundation gives money to support research and what it hopes to gain by doing so.

Why does a company "give away" some of its money? The answer is, to make the company and its products appear legitimate. It is really a form of advertising. If you take the money, you are helping the company appear respectable. Taking the money would mean that it is no big deal if it comes from selling a drug that injures and kills people. You would be saying, in effect, that this is not worth worrying about. You would thus be helping the company stay in business by aiding its claim to be a useful corporate citizen.

If you were the scientist in this case, you might find it hard to be sociologically mindful. You might be inclined to exaggerate the possible benefits of your project and rationalize taking the money: "If I don't take it, someone else will. At least I'll do some good with it." That may be true; some good might come of your project.

But is it realistic to expect this possible good to offset the harm done to millions of people whose health will be damaged and who will die prematurely because they are tricked into smoking? Making tobacco companies seem legitimate and respectable is part of the trick. Being honestly mindful of this, you might work harder to find money for your project from another source.

Reexamining Our Choices

When we call smoking, watching football, having babies, or taking money from any legal source a "personal choice," we mask our interdependence with others. It is as if to deny that these behaviors have any effect on others and to say that no one has a right to challenge us about these behaviors. Sociological mindfulness is in part the practice of reexamining our choices, paying special attention to how our choices have consequences for others.

When faced with choices, people sometimes look at the option toward which they are inclined and say, "Why not? I don't see any reason why I *shouldn't* do X, so I guess I will, since X is most appealing to me." But what this often means is, "I don't want to, or don't know how to, think any more about the consequences of doing X, so I'll go ahead with X." This is not a mindful way to proceed.

We always come to a point, in any case, where we have considered all that we know how to consider. If we are sociologically mindful, it will take longer to get to that point because we will be considering more connections and interdependencies. We will also be trying to look at our choices from a range of perspectives. This will take extra time, too, since we need to talk to others, or read what they have written, to learn how to examine our choices from new perspectives.

Being mindful may slow us down, but it does not diminish our choices. It may in fact lead us to see choices that we previously missed. It also equips us to make well-considered choices that reflect our best values. Being mindful of connections and interdependence can thus help us make real individual choices, not the kind that merely seem to be individual because they are conveniently defined as "personal."

Then again, individuals are not solely responsible for the results of their acts. Interdependence means that our acts have the consequences they do because of how the social world works. Women ought to be able to have babies without reproducing gender inequality. Scientists ought to be able to fund their projects without aiding rapacious corporations. If these things are not possible, it is not because individuals are immoral, but because of the conditions under which they act. Being sociologically mindful is a way to see more clearly what these conditions are and to see how we can act responsibly despite them.

Dialogue

Emotional Investments and Opinions

My remarks about "personal choices" have caused trouble. As I expected, some readers are upset when I say that smoking, watching football, and having babies (under certain conditions) can have harmful consequences that often go unconsidered. One time when I visited a class that was using *TSEL*, a student said that readers would "take me more seriously" if I used less provocative examples. A teacher told me that one of her students dismissed my remarks about smoking, football, and having babies as "just Schwalbe's opinions." I have heard both kinds of comments more than once.

Yes, I could have used less provocative examples. Many other actions have harmful consequences that we fail to consider. Leaving a light on in an empty room, or tossing out a recyclable can, is wasteful of energy and contributes to pollution and global warming. Many people are oblivious to these consequences. But if I had written about light bulbs and cans, would anyone remember?

By now most people are not terribly resistant to thinking about the environmental consequences of wasteful consumer habits. In this realm, many people are willing, with a little prodding, to be *ecologically* mindful and even to behave differently. Recycling cans doesn't strike a nerve for most of us. Mindfulness and behavioral change are much harder, however, when people are emotionally invested in a practice.

Strange as it might seem, many people in the United States are emotionally invested in watching football. They have come to rely on the game to provide occasions for having fun with friends. Or they have come to find pleasure, perhaps even a sense of power, in seeing their team win. Men might be invested in football because being a fan is a way to signify one's affinity for things that are defined as tough and manly.

I could analyze smoking, having babies, and taking money from dubious sources in the same way. In each case there is something at stake that is emotionally important for people: an image of themselves as cool, acceptance by a group, achievement of adult status, or career success. Because people want to feel good about themselves, it can be difficult to think critically about practices that produce such feelings. Yet it is precisely in these areas where we need to be on guard. Unmindfully taking "paths of least resistance," as sociologist Allan Johnson says, allows us to be comfortable, but doing so often leads to harmful results in the long run.

The sociological point here is that harmful practices often persist because people are taught to derive feelings of pleasure and self-worth from those practices. Being sociologically mindful can help us to see how this process operates and how we get caught up in it. But the deeper our emotional investments, the harder it is to look critically at ourselves and our practices. Then again, if we can learn to be mindful in the hard cases, we can surely do it in the easy ones.

One further suggestion: Examine your reluctance to think critically about certain practices—smoking, watching football, having babies, playing violent video games, listening to sexist rap music, supporting U.S. militarism, wearing makeup, or wearing scanty clothes. If you are reluctant to think critically about these things, ask yourself why. How might you be invested in these practices? Are they in some way a source of good feelings about yourself? After you answer these questions, try to consider the unintended consequences that result from your choices. Perhaps, then, you will be led—by your own powers of critical thought—to choose differently.

*   *   *

Is what I say about "personal choices" just an expression of my idiosyncratic opinions? If so, then you could just dismiss me by saying, "Well, Schwalbe dislikes smoking and football. He's entitled to his opinions. But mine are different, so the heck with him." I would guess, based on what I've heard from some teachers, that this is how some students interpret my remarks about smoking, watching football, and so on. Readers who do this are, I think, missing the point.

My point isn't to condemn any particular practices, but to say how we can be more sociologically mindful about all of our practices. If there is a central message in what I say about personal choices, it is this: *Please think about how your actions might have unintentionally harmful consequences for others, because only by doing this can you make morally responsible choices.* So my point isn't really about smoking, watching football, having babies, or taking money from dubious sources. It's about how to be mindful of our interdependence as social creatures and why we should strive to do this.

An ornery reader might say that it's still only my opinion that people ought to be mindful in the ways I prescribe. This is true. It is only my opinion, though it is one I share with a tradition of philosophers going back as far as Socrates. So it is not exactly idiosyncratic. I am merely urging the examination of one's life, including one's choices, in a sociological way.

I should add a point here about the nature of opinions. You have probably heard it said that opinions are cheap, because everybody has one. This implies that all opinions are of approximately equal worth, which is close to zero. I don't believe this, and here is why.

Opinions are conclusions. Ideally, we arrive at them by weighing all the relevant evidence and then reasoning carefully. In other words, *we need to formulate a sound argument to arrive at an intelligent opinion.* Of course, not everyone does this all the time, and so some opinions are based on bad information, incomplete information, or illogical reasoning. In which case they are indeed of little value.

On the other hand, some opinions are based on solid and extensive evidence and careful thought. We are lucky to find such opinions, because they can save us a lot of work. But it's even better to be able to see how the work was done and to be able to do that work for ourselves. This is a large part of what *TSEL* aims to teach: how to do a good job of forming opinions about the social world. And so you should, of course, cast a critical eye on all opinions expressed here. Examine their foundations. Then try to see how they were built.

A Note on Blind Spots

Trying to be sociologically mindful all the time can seem like a daunting task. In fact, it *is* a daunting task, one that nobody succeeds at all the time. Not even me. But after a while, with practice, being sociologically mindful can become "second nature," so to speak. This means that being sociologically mindful becomes part of who we are and requires less conscious effort. Even so, we are still likely to have blind spots in certain areas.

A blind spot is part of a person's field of vision where s/he can't see clearly or can't see at all. If we were talking literally about people's eyes, we might note that blind spots can be caused by, for example, damage to or degeneration of part of the retina. But I'm using "blind spot" here in a figurative sense to refer to a person's inability or unwillingness to think critically about, or even perceive, some aspect of the social world.

Consider this example: A white male from a low-income background works hard, stays out of (serious) trouble, goes to college, and eventually achieves upward mobility. He might find it easy to be sociologically mindful about the social class system and how it advantages some people and disadvantages others. This is easy because he has experienced some of the disadvantages.

It might be harder, however, for him to be sociologically mindful about white privilege and male privilege. Why? Because seeing these social realities would mean acknowledging that, despite facing obstacles because of his class background, he had unearned advantages because of his race and gender—and this would threaten a view of himself as having achieved success through nothing but talent and effort. In this case, we might say that he has blind spots when it comes to race and gender.

We all have blind spots when it comes to seeing things that might threaten cherished views of ourselves. The best we can do is to try to become aware of these blind spots and make extra efforts to face what might be unsettling truths. This isn't something we can learn to do once and for all and then be done with. Being sociologically mindful is a life-long process. It requires practice to see not only what is easy to see, but also what we might prefer not to see.

Paths for Reflection

1. Even if we recognize the harm that can arise from certain of our choices, we might refuse to change our behavior because of how those choices ben-efit us (or seem to). For example, in response to the section about football, some students have said that they do not really like football and would be happy never to watch another game, but they watch it because of the occa-sions it provides to have fun with friends or to bond with a parent, usually a father, who likes the game. But why is it that so many people feel they must rely on football to provide these pleasures of companionship? How else might people choose to seek these pleasures?

2. Imagine that a young woman—call her Mara—is hired to tend bar. She makes it clear to male customers that while she enjoys bantering with them, she won't tolerate sexist remarks or jokes. For the most part, the men change their behavior. Then another young woman—call her Christie—is hired. The men test her and find that she doesn't mind their sexist remarks. She just smiles and plays along. Soon the men fall back into their old habits. When Mara confronts one of the men, he says, "Hey, Christie doesn't mind. Why should you?" Then Mara talks to Christie about the problem, and Christie says, "I don't care how the men talk. It's my choice to put up with it or not, and it's none of your business." What makes it hard for Christie to be sociologically mindful in this situation? How might Mara get Christie to think differently and perhaps make a dif-ferent choice about how to interact with the men?

3. According to one view, emotions are determined more by biochem-ical events in the brain than by social interaction. Being sociologically mindful, however, we would at least suspect that goings-on in the brain must somehow be linked to goings-on in social life. In fact, you can

demonstrate this by picturing in your mind a painful injury that you witnessed, a kind of food you hate, or a sexual fantasy. When you do this, the mental image evokes a reaction in your body, a reaction that arises because of how the image affects what goes on, biochemically, in your brain. Consider how these images, and their meanings, arise out of social life. How do emotionally powerful images get formed in our minds? How do we learn to use these images to manage our own emotions?

Related Readings

Bellah, Robert N., Madsen, Richard, Sullivan, William M., Swidler, Ann, & Tipton, Steven M. (1985). *Habits of the Heart: Individualism and Commitment in American Life*. Berkeley: University of California Press.

Berry, Wendell. (2003). *Citizenship Papers*. Washington, DC: Shoemaker & Hoard.

Callero, Peter. (2013). *The Myth of Individualism: How Social Forces Shape Our Lives* (2nd ed.). Lanham, MD: Rowman & Littlefield.

Collins, Chuck. (2016). *Born on Third Base: A One Percenter Makes the Case for Tackling Inequality, Bringing Wealth Home, and Committing to the Common Good*. White River Junction, VT: Chelsea Green.

Dewey, John. (1908/1932). *Theory of the Moral Life*. New York: Holt, Rinehart and Winston.

Gilligan, Carol. (1982). *In a Different Voice*. Cambridge, MA: Harvard University Press.

Nhat Hanh, Thich. (1987). *Interbeing*. Berkeley, CA: Parallax Press.

Schwalbe, Michael. (2014). *Manhood Acts: Gender and the Practices of Domination*. Boulder, CO: Paradigm.

Wilkinson, Richard, & Pickett, Kate. (2009). *The Spirit Level: Why Equality Makes Societies Stronger*. New York: Bloomsbury.

CHAPTER 5

Becoming Human

To do the experiment I am going to describe, we would need a pair of newborn identical twins. We would also need a large box in which one of the twins could live without contact with other humans. The box would have to deliver food and water, and remove waste, mechanically. It would also have to be opaque and soundproof, so that there could be no interaction through its walls.

The experiment is simple: one child is raised normally and the other is put in the box. After eighteen years we open the box and compare the two children to see if they are any different. If they are, we can conclude that being with other people matters. If both children are the same after eighteen years, we have to conclude that socialization (learning from being with other people) makes little difference and that personality is genetically programmed.

You might think, "Of course socialization makes a difference. We don't need to raise a child in a box to prove that!" But there are many people who argue that what a person becomes depends on his or her genes. If that's true, then it shouldn't matter if a child is raised in a box. Genetic programming should turn the child into whatever s/he is destined to become, inside or outside the box.

It would be wrong, of course, to do the box experiment, since one baby would be denied experiences that we value in our culture: intimacy, physical affection, and mental stimulation. We value these things precisely because we know how crucial they are to creating decent human beings. Merely imagining the box experiment shocks us into remembering this.

But not everyone is mindful of how social life makes us human. One time, after a discussion about how children are taught to be girls and boys, a male student said, "My mom taught me to sew and cook, and my dad taught me to hunt and fish. My sisters learned to do all these things, too." His point wasn't clear, so I asked, "Are you saying that you were biologically wired to become the man you are, regardless of what your parents taught you?" He said yes, that's what he was getting at.

At the next class meeting I told this student about his twin brother, Fester, who had been sold to unscrupulous experimenters right after birth. "He lived the first eighteen years of his life in a box," I said, "and when the box was opened, it was a sad sight. Fester cowered like a helpless, terrified animal, unable to speak or reason. You did not know about the comparisons that were made between you and him because they were done secretly, by video. The judgments were made by a team of scientists who reviewed the tapes and determined that—" At this point another student chimed in, "There were no differences!" Even poor Fester's brother laughed.

The joke made the point that it is absurd to think that anyone could "just turn out" to be a well-functioning adult. If that were so, parents could save themselves a great deal of trouble by raising their children in boxes.

In real life the nature-versus-nurture debate is unresolvable. Every person develops as s/he does because some potentials are nurtured while others are not. Without social life, no potentials would be developed; a different social life would develop different potentials; and if the potentials aren't there, nothing can develop them. So there is really no separating the contributions of nature and nurture to making us what we are (see also Chapter 12). Everyone is a result of the interaction between these two influences.

To be sociologically mindful of how we become human, we need presume only this: everyone has more potential than will be realized. This means that what we become as individuals—the abilities, desires, and habits that make us who we are—is just the realization of one set of possibilities. We can't really know what all our potentials are; we can only know, late in life, which ones have been realized. What we can know, or at least be mindful of, is how social life turns us into certain kinds of people.

To see this, we must be mindful of our interdependencies. But there is more to it. We must also pay attention to how society is organized, where we fit into it, and how our place in it gives rise to experiences that make us what we are. This "socialness" includes all that makes us more than other animals: the workings of our minds, the possession of self-consciousness, our desires and hopes, and our feelings about ourselves. All of these things about us, these qualities that make us human, arise out of social life.

Not everyone wants to know how this happens. Some people, like Fester's brother, resist being sociologically mindful of how we become human. Why? Perhaps because we are taught, in American culture, that our worth depends on being unique individuals—while being mindful of how we are shaped by social life makes us seem less special. Since a lot of other people have been shaped in similar ways, to reflect on this fact may make us feel like undistinguished members of the common horde.

Are we just like others? In some ways, yes. We have had similar experiences, hold similar attitudes, values, and beliefs, and do similar things. This is what we would expect when people grow up in the same culture. In some ways we are slightly different from others—not a lot different, just a little. And in still other ways we may be unique. No one else has had exactly the same experiences we have had, no one else has been shaped in exactly the way we have, and no one else lives inside our skins.

It is the case, then, that we are both one of a kind and of a kind. We are both different from and the same as others. Often in U.S. culture we exaggerate our differences and fail to be mindful of what we have in common with others.

An old Chinese proverb says, "The first step to becoming an individual is to recognize that you are not one." This means that as long as we cling to an illusion of individuality—without examining how we are like and unlike others—we will fail to become all that we could become as individuals. It is as if the illusion of being unique is so satisfying that it stops us from doing the kind of thinking that helps us grow as people. The proverb also reminds us that our similarities with others are essential to being human.

The point of being mindful of these matters is not to help us strive toward individuality, as if that were the highest goal of a human life. The point is to be mindful of how we make ourselves and others human, as a step toward doing it with more wisdom and compassion. Being sociologically mindful is a way to see how what we become as people depends on the nature of our ties to others. We can thus see, perhaps, how we can do things together in ways that make human beings abler and more willing to create good lives for themselves and for others.

Gathering Meanings

You are lucky not to have grown up in a box. Instead you have learned from other human beings a language that allows you to get a mental grip on the world. For you the world is not a confusing blur but a place that makes sense, a place full of meaningful events, situations, and objects (including yourself and other people). Without language, all this would be lost. You would be trapped in a world without meaning.

What makes us able to live together as humans? It is our ability to solve problems peacefully and creatively; our ability to build elaborate institutions and traditions; our ability to share experiences with each other; our ability to preserve knowledge over time; and our ability to imagine and talk about the future. We couldn't do these things without language, which gives us the power to develop our individual humanity and to connect with others in distinctly human ways. If you are mindful of the power of language, you will want to pay close attention to its nature and use. To do so is to be mindful of how human beings create themselves and a shared social world.

Taking on Identities

As an infant you did not know that the sound you heard over and again was your name, although eventually you learned that "Mal" or "Rosa" was a sound that referred to you and you alone. In learning your name you became aware of yourself as an object. You learned that you were a creature that could be talked about, thought about, praised, scolded, loved, hated, and so on. As soon as you were able to think "I am so-and-so," you began to gather meanings to yourself and become a complex being.

As we grow up, we gather meanings to ourselves from the culture in which we live. This means learning to define ourselves using the terms available in our culture. Others must teach us which terms to use and when. These meanings we gather—identities such as student, biology major, son or daughter, Democrat, liberal, Christian or Buddhist, black or white, gay or straight, baby boomer or millennial—give us a sense of who we are. This is part of becoming human, this process of coming to know who and what we are.

Being sociologically mindful, we see that the meanings we give to ourselves always arise out of social life. We depend on each other not only to define ourselves, but also to maintain a coherent and stable sense of who and what we are as persons. If others didn't help us sustain our identity claims, we would have a hard time knowing for sure who and what we really are.

Our identities—the meanings we give to ourselves and announce to others—locate us relative to others and tell them how to treat us. Announcing our identities allows others to interact with us in predictable ways. If others know you are a plumber, for instance, they will know how to treat you in certain situations—like when a pipe is leaking. Identities thus are not private meanings that rattle around inside our heads. Identities are public meanings that determine much of what goes on between people.

You might gather other meanings that work the same way. If others know that you are "short-tempered," or "rich" or "good-humored," they will know something about how to interact with you. In gathering meanings to ourselves we thus acquire many possible points of connection— that is, many ways that others can see who and what we are and thus interact with us predictably and smoothly. Social life not only gives us our identities, it also depends on them.

Identities let us interpret ourselves to others quickly. When you say, "I am a student," or "I am a biology major," or "I am an engineer," you are using a shorthand way of telling others who and what you are. Not everyone grasps the meaning of "student" or "biology major" or "engineer" in the same way. Even so, such an identity is a handy starting point. After claiming an identity, we usually go on to interpret ourselves to others. We try, in lots of ways, to influence the meanings others give to us.

Acquiring language and developing self-awareness are essential to becoming human and to being able to function in the social world. Gathering meanings to one's self—that is, becoming known to one's self and to others as a particular kind of person—is also part of becoming human. Being sociologically mindful, we can see that these processes happen only because of interaction. We cannot become human in a box. Who and what we become depends on the symbols and meanings, and the opportunities to use them, that social life affords. We are no less interdependent in becoming human than in being human.

Regulating Ourselves

Fester's brother might have taken offense at the joke about "no differences" and gone berserk. Fortunately, he laughed with the rest of us. How come? Why didn't he go berserk? He must have developed some ability that allowed him to regulate his behavior so as to be a safe and useful participant in social life. If people do not become self-regulating in this way, they can cause a lot of trouble.

Language and self-awareness are prerequisites to being self-regulating. But they are not enough. We must develop several other distinctly human characteristics. First, we must become attached to the meanings we gather to ourselves. We become attached to them because they provide a sense of coherence and continuity. You are today your mother's son or daughter, just as you were yesterday. This knowledge, along with knowledge of your other identities, keeps you sane by allowing you to be comfortably sure of who and what you are from one day to the next.

It is even better if you are attached to some identities because you (and others) value those identities highly. If this is true, these valued identities will be a source of self-esteem. This is another reason you might be attached to them. Perhaps, too, the more self-esteem you have staked on a particular identity, the more firmly you will be attached to it.

What does this have to do with self-regulation? If you are attached to your identities, you will try to act in ways that uphold them. If you think of yourself as, for example, an honest person and then have a chance to cheat on a test, you might decide not to cheat, so as to be able to continue to see yourself as an honest person. If you think of yourself as a good student, and this self-conception is important to you, you will tend to do things that good students do: read, think, ask questions, attend class, complete assignments on time, and so on. These behaviors say to you and to others that you are indeed a good student.

If we are attached to certain ideas about ourselves, we will tend to do things that affirm rather than contradict those ideas. We will try to behave in ways that lead others to see us as we would like to see ourselves. For instance, if "friendly person" is an important identity for someone, s/he will probably repress impulses to grouch at people or to remain aloof, so as to avoid discrepant feedback from others: "You grouch, you are not very friendly!" The identity, whatever it might be, and as long as we care about embracing it, becomes a device for regulating our own behavior.

Being self-regulating also depends on learning criteria for self-evaluation. Generally, we want to feel good about ourselves, so we will try to do things that attest to our competence and morality. What these things are depends on the culture, the situation, and the identity a person is claiming. For example, a man might learn that, when dealing with children, a good man is patient, kind, and generous. If he can exhibit these qualities he will be able to evaluate himself highly and thus maintain self-esteem.

Not all criteria for self-evaluation are so benign. In U.S. culture a man might also learn that a real man is powerful, aggressive, competitive, and in control. He may thus feel compelled to try to exhibit these qualities so as to feel good about himself as a man. If he goes too far, his behavior is likely to cause harm to others.

Fortunately, Fester's brother seemed to think of himself as the kind of man who was strong enough to take a little teasing and enjoy a joke at his own expense. If he had seen himself as the kind of man whose strength lay in using violence to punish anyone who affronted his dignity, the situation might have turned out badly.

You can see why it is necessary to be careful about the criteria for self-evaluation that we teach children—and why we should critically examine the criteria we apply to ourselves. The danger otherwise is that we will come to stake our feelings of competence and worth on being good at things that produce bad results for others.

We should be glad that for most people being a good person means being honest, kind, generous, compassionate, and peaceful. Having learned these criteria for self-evaluation, people are nicer and easier to get along with. To put it another way, most people avoid doing things that are dishonest, cruel, selfish, callous, and violent so as to avoid seeing themselves as rotten. This makes people self-regulating in a useful way. If people learn to seek self-esteem by treating others well, then they are more likely to behave like decent human beings.

Silent Knowledge

Self-regulation also requires being equipped with knowledge of how to interact with others in various situations. This knowledge is usually unspoken; it is a matter of knowing how to do something without necessarily being able to explain it. We rely on a great deal of this kind of silent knowledge to get through everyday life.

For example, you probably know how to go into a store, find the best deal on tofu and eggplant, make your purchase, and leave. You probably also know how to line up to buy tickets, how to behave at a funeral, how to make small talk at parties, how to dress yourself in the morning, how to behave on a first date, how to deal with your boss, how to ask for and give directions, how to blow your nose in public, and so on. These might seem like simple acts, but that is only because we forget how much knowledge they require.

Imagine programming a robot to mail a letter. At first it might seem that only two instructions are needed: "Put stamp on envelope. Put envelope in mailbox." But robots are stupid, so you'd have to provide more explicit instructions. You'd have to say what a stamp is, how to choose the right kind of stamp, what an envelope is, where to put a stamp on an envelope, what a mailbox is, where to find one, how to put an envelope in it, and so on. Your robot would need to know all this.

Eventually your list of instructions might run to hundreds, perhaps thousands, of lines. Even more amazing than the effort it would take to program a robot to do a job as "simple" as mailing a letter is the fact that you have all this knowledge in your head already. Imagine someone trying to program a robot to do all the things you know how to do. It is unlikely that all that knowledge—billions of lines of instructions—would be put into a form any less complex than the brain itself.

As one more example of silent knowledge, think of what you must know to be able to speak a sentence in the English language. Can you explain how to do it, how to get all the right words in the right order so that a coherent sentence comes out of your mouth? Probably not. But still you know how. Somehow.

Knowing how to interact with others is much the same. Just as we need to know the rules of English to formulate proper sentences, we need to know the rules of social life to be able to fit our actions together into coherent wholes.

Some of the rules we need to know are normative, such as, *Do not treat other human beings as objects*, or *Always respect other people's feelings*. These rules tell us what is right and wrong and how to behave morally. Other rules are procedural; they tell us how to make situations unfold in the ways we want them to.

If everyone knows the same procedural rules, we can smoothly go about our business of buying eggplant and tofu, lining up for tickets, driving in traffic, having conversations, falling in love, running universities, and so on. Each of us will have a rough idea of how to proceed when we try to do things together. Once we are equipped with the procedural rules needed to handle routine situations, we can carry on our lives without having to call home for instructions. In other words, we become self-regulating.

These rules do not control us from the inside. Rather, they are resources we use to get things done with other people. Sometimes we get things done by breaking a rule.

Suppose, for example, a rule says, "Do not stare at people." When walking down a busy street you use this rule to avoid attracting the attention of strangers. You hope that if you avoid eye contact, strangers will not feel invited to annoy you. Under other conditions—perhaps someone invades your space on the bus—you might break the rule against staring so as to say, "Please get away from me." In this case you stare as a way to send a message. This works because people know the rule against staring and know that breaking it is meaningful.

Keeping Things on Track

Basic rules of interaction will get us through most situations. But problems can arise when it's not clear, or not clear to everyone, exactly what the situation is or when people disagree about the rules that ought to be used in a given situation. For these and other reasons, interaction can go awry. Somehow we must be able to get things back on track.

We do this, most obviously, through talk. In cases of confusion or conflict—when someone doesn't seem to know what's going on, or doesn't behave properly, or rejects our understanding of what's going on—we can usually talk our way to some kind of solution. We have to do more than talk, however. We must also be able to take the perspectives of others. This means imagining what they are thinking, feeling, and likely to do.

It is crucial that we learn to read others in this way. We have to be able to look at others' circumstances and think, "How would I feel if I were in that kind of situation? How would I be likely to act?" Sometimes we must make inferences from others' speech and appearance. We might think, "She is slouching, unkempt, not looking me in the eye, and sounding tired and sad—she is probably depressed." I am exaggerating a bit here; the signs of a person's inner state are often more subtle. In any case, we must learn how to "see inside" others, so we can anticipate how they will behave and what they expect from us.

Doing things together requires us to be able to read people in these ways. Navigating our way through the social world requires not only that we be equipped with rules for interacting in standard situations. We must also be able to deal with unusual situations where it is necessary to figure out how strangers are thinking and feeling. Talk and perspective-taking are the best means we have of figuring out how to proceed.

Feeling for and with Others

Perhaps I have made it seem that self-regulation depends solely on reason, so that if people just think straight, they will be gentle and considerate. There is, however, more to it than that. Reason is not enough to keep us from hurting ourselves and others. As history has shown, human beings can always think of ways to make cruelty and violence seem reasonable. So logic and rational argument are not enough to ensure that humans will behave humanely. What is also necessary is the ability, and willingness, to feel for and with others.

I am referring to what might be called perspective-taking with the heart—allowing ourselves to respond emotionally to others. Our responses can be sympathetic (feeling *for* an other) or empathic (feeling *with* an other). If we feel sorry for a friend whose parent has died, that is a sympathetic response. If we feel some of the friend's grief, as if our own parent had died, that is an empathic response. In either case we experience feelings in response to the other person's feelings. Such responses are not automatic; we can refuse to have them.

Imagine you have a chance to steal a pot of money that has been donated to buy medicine for poor children. The money is right there, unguarded. You could use it to pay bills, buy a new stereo, and have a spot of fun. The chances of getting caught are slim. How will you decide whether to take the money?

You might try to imagine how stealing the money would make others feel. The people who donated and collected it would be angry. The children who expected to benefit from it would be sad, discouraged, and made to suffer for lack of the medicine they need. If you were caught and sent to trial, then your family and friends would feel shame and disappointment. You would probably also feel disgust for yourself. If you can imagine all this and let yourself feel what others would feel if you stole the money, you will probably leave it alone.

But suppose that your mind is quicker than your heart, and before you feel anything you think, "The people who gave this money are rich and just looking for a tax deduction; they don't really care about poor children. As for the kids, I'm sure they'll find help somewhere. Besides, most medicines don't do any good at all; you're better off not taking them. I doubt that much of the money even goes to the kids at all. It probably goes into administrators' pockets. Those folks already have more money than they need. I don't. I'm broke. This money will do me a lot more good than it will do them. I'll just scoop it up and be on my way."

In the second case you would have convinced yourself, quite rationally, that taking the money is a reasonable thing to do. There is even some perspective-taking involved: "The rich don't really care about poor children." That might be true, although it cannot justify taking the money, since other people's feelings are also at stake. It is only by ignoring these feelings that reason is allowed to proceed to a hurtful conclusion.

It is not just to deter hurtful acts that we must feel for and with others. Ordinary interaction also depends on emotional responsiveness. Consider, for example, the ritual greeting we usually enact when we pass someone we know: "Hi, how're you?" "Fine, how're you?" "Good." "That's good." "See you later." "See you." It seems that there is little thought or feeling in this exchange. So why do we do it? What purpose does it serve?

The greeting ritual is a way for people to acknowledge each other's presence. We do this because we know it feels better to have one's existence affirmed than to be ignored. We do it, in other words, because we respect other people's feelings, and they respect ours. It is a little ritual that uplifts and stabilizes us emotionally as we go through our days. Imagine how you would feel if everyone to whom you said "Hi, how're you?" either did not reply or said, "Bug off."

Small acts of politeness serve the same purpose. These small acts—the pleases, thank yous, pardon mes, and so on—signify respect for others' feelings. These acts show others that we can be trusted as interactants. If we signify respect in these little ways, we can probably be trusted not to act in ways that will damage others' feelings, especially their feelings about themselves. What this implies is that being emotionally responsive to others is necessary for getting anything done with other people.

We must also be emotionally responsive to others to protect our own feelings. Others can, if they wish, reject our identity claims (that is, they can refuse to accept us as the good people we claim to be) or treat us with disrespect. Of course, we can do the same things to others; we can, if we are so inclined, deny their identity claims and disrespect them. This is another way we are emotionally tied to others. We treat others respectfully not only so they can feel good about themselves, but also so they will feel obligated to treat us in a way that upholds our cherished identities and allows us our self-respect.

Most of our conformist behavior is based on our emotional responsiveness to and interdependence with others. In other words, our good or bad feelings about ourselves depend greatly on how others react to us and on how we imagine they are evaluating us. Consider, for example, the practice of leg shaving.

When I ask women in my gender class why they do such an odd thing, they usually say, "Oh that, well, that's just a personal choice; I do it because I think my legs look better shaved." This is a useful answer, because it is not at all mindful. To show this I ask, "Why is it, then, that every woman in the class makes this same choice? If it were really a personal choice, wouldn't there be at least 10 percent who chose differently, especially in a culture that supposedly values individuality?" After a minute, the answers come: "My boyfriend would hate it"; "People would think you are a lesbian"; "You couldn't wear shorts in public because people would stare." So what is really at stake are feelings about one's self, as affected by the real or imagined reactions of others.

You might think, "So what if our culture favors hairless legs on women and disfavors dresses on men? What's the big deal? Every culture has its fashions." This is true, but it is not the point, which has to do with why people feel compelled to conform to traditions. What is important to see is that the force of tradition arises in large part from our emotional responsiveness to others. This responsiveness arises, in turn, from our ability to imagine how others are judging us and from a desire to feel good about ourselves. It is hard to feel good about ourselves if we imagine that others think we are stupid, ugly, or immoral.

The Risk of Cutting Ourselves off from Others

Our emotional responsiveness to others gives us incentive to treat them with respect and to try to get along peacefully. Knowing that our feelings are in the hands of others, and their feelings are in ours, we have good reason to be kind and gentle with each other. It is possible, however, for our responsiveness to break down. Under some conditions we may cut ourselves off from feeling for and with certain others.

In war, for example, people in one country define those in another country as enemies. But that is not all. For war to be carried out, people in opposing countries must stop feeling for and with each other. This emotional cutting-off is what enables ordinary and otherwise decent people to kill in cold blood. If people on both sides could feel the anguish of those who were shot, cut, blinded, burned, and maimed, there could be no war. Politicians and generals who gave orders to kill might then be banished to a place where they could do no more harm.

Even in war, people remain emotionally responsive to *some* others: fellow citizens and comrades in battle. In the face of a common enemy and the prospect of death, emotional bonding can be intense. If people lack this kind of intense connection in everyday life, they may find war attractive. It is as if the price of temporarily loving one's neighbor, or fellow soldier, is the mass killing of others.

Part of the problem is that we become too responsive to the judgments of some audiences and thus feel compelled to do things we know are not right. Our desires to be accepted and liked by people in one group can lead us to hurt people in other groups. Being sociologically mindful, we are alert to this danger. If we sense that our allegiance to one group is leading us to treat members of another group as less than human, we can ask ourselves, "What will the consequences be if I disregard the humanity of others just to be accepted here?" That is a question that should be posed aloud to other self-regulating humans.

People do not have to be at war for a cutting-off of emotional responsiveness to occur. If members of one group feel there is no way to gain respect from members of another group, members of the disrespected group may stop caring about the feelings and judgments of members of the other group. Often this kind of situation arises between dominant and oppressed groups. For example, in the United States, centuries of white disrespect for blacks have led to contempt for white people, and a disdain for things defined as "white," on the part of many black people. This is not "reverse racism," but rather a rejection of a dominant, disrespectful culture.

Not responding emotionally to others can thus be an act of self-defense. It may simply be too painful to care about the judgments and feelings of those who will not respect us in any case.

There are, however, other reasons why this cutting-off might occur. It may be that members of a dominant group feel shame and guilt at the suffering they have caused others. To listen to and feel with those who have been abused and deeply hurt may be too painful to bear. Perhaps this is why many whites in the United States have such a hard time listening to people of color describe the pain caused by racism. It is too much for whites to feel this pain and sadness and to admit that they are partly responsible for causing it.

A similar thing can happen between people who love each other. If someone else hurts a person we love, we rush to be sympathetic and empathic. We try to feel for and with the person who is hurt. But if *our* actions are the source of the loved one's pain, we may be unresponsive emotionally. Perhaps we use reason to avoid dealing with feelings. We might say, "It's too bad that you feel hurt, but if you just think carefully about the situation, you will realize that you have mistakenly interpreted my actions; therefore, you should not feel the way you do."

Few of us want to feel the guilt that comes with knowing that we have hurt a person we love, so we might try to define them as irrational, overly sensitive, or wrong about our intentions. Ironically, we do this because we *are* so emotionally responsive to others. If we were not, we would not have to be so clever in using reason to avoid the unpleasant feelings that can be induced in us by others' suffering. Sometimes it is our fear of how others can make us feel, if we open ourselves to feeling for and with them, that pushes us apart.

Reason is not the enemy of emotion. Reason helps us sort through our feelings and choose the best course of action—perhaps the one that best respects the feelings of others. Precisely because we sometimes have impulses to lash out at others, we need reason to be peacefully self-regulating. I am using reason here, for example, to argue for the importance of being emotionally responsive to others. A problem arises only when we use reason to avoid listening to others when we don't know how to deal with their feelings or our own.

Mindful Resistance

All of us care more about some audiences than others. For all of us there is always some group that matters, whether we admit it or not. Even the teenager who strikes a pose and says "I don't care what *anybody* thinks of me" is cultivating an image to impress peers and annoy parents. The claim not to care what anyone else thinks is part of the performance.

There may, however, be good reasons to resist the judgments of certain others. Women might decide not to shave their legs as a way to oppose a sexist culture that insists on women being smooth and soft and pleasing to men. African Americans might decide not to straighten their hair as a way to resist a racist culture that imposes a Eurocentric standard of beauty. We might all decide not to care about the judgments of politicians and generals who tell us that to be patriotic we must hate and kill people in another country. In cases such as these, deciding not to care about certain audiences can be a way to resist oppression.

It is a serious matter to decide not to care about the judgments and feelings of any group of people. There will be costs, of course. A woman who does not shave her legs may have to work harder to find a partner who shares her anti-sexist values. In some places, a person who resists the power of corporate bosses can face job loss, jail, torture, and death. So we must be mindful in our acts of resistance. If we decide to ignore the wishes and feelings of one group, it must be because doing so will help promote justice and equality in the larger human community.

If we are sociologically mindful, we can see that our emotional responsiveness to others is greatly affected by the conditions under which we live. For example, in a society where there is much suffering because of inequality and injustice, it may be hard to stay open to feeling for and with others. We might feel overwhelmed by all this distress and thus try to shut it out. It may also be hard to feel the distress of others if we are the victims of injustice and inequality ourselves and are thus eaten up with suffering of our own.

Inequality can affect emotional responsiveness in other ways. Members of powerful groups may be unresponsive to the powerless because power fosters a lack of regard for others' feelings. At the same time, members of oppressed groups may develop a defensive lack of regard for the feelings and judgments of the powerful, since it seems that respect cannot be earned in any case. And in extraordinary times, times of war, many people in a society may try to cut themselves off emotionally from those with whom they are fighting.

Perhaps you can see how the boundaries between groups are important. These boundaries determine who are the insiders—people like us—who deserve care and respect, and who are the outsiders—people who are different—who deserve less care and respect. Of course, we do not *have* to believe in such boundaries and the illusion of difference they create. Being sociologically mindful, we will question all boundaries and categories, since they can diminish our emotional responsiveness to others, thus making disrespect and abuse more likely.

Sociological mindfulness helps us see more than just the importance of socialization. Most of us know that producing kind, gentle, intelligent people requires careful nurturance. If we are sociologically mindful, we can see something more: how we organize ourselves to live together also affects the creation of human beings. A great deal of inequality in a society generates fear, abuse, distrust, disrespect, anger, and even hatred and cuts people off from each other. In such a society it is as if many of us grow up in boxes.

Being sociologically mindful, we will pay attention to how social life shapes us as human beings. We will ask, Do our beliefs and our ways of living together aid or inhibit our ability to be peacefully self-regulating and emotionally responsive to others? Sociological mindfulness is not an answer to that question, but rather the practice of seeking an answer—a practice that is crucial to seeing how we might create a better social world. By being sociologically mindful, we can see not only how we become human, but also how we might live more humanely.

Dialogue

Brains and Minds in the Social World

Two questions have come to me in response to what I say about "becoming human." One question has to do with how our experiences shape us in ways that we cannot change later. A student put it this way: "You make it seem as if people can become whatever they want to be, at any time. But isn't it possible for people to be damaged in ways that can't be fixed?" That is an important question.

The first thing I should say is that I do not think people can become whatever they want to be, at any time. Things are not so simple. People can certainly change themselves. But depending on the kind of change we are talking about, the process can be arduous and complex. This is not just because of how we are molded in childhood; it is also because of how we fit into the world as adults.

Part of becoming human is acquiring ways of seeing, ways of thinking, and ways of feeling. By the time we are nearing adulthood, these ways have become *ingrained* in us—much like a piece of wood develops a grain as a result of how a tree grows, how it is nurtured, and how it is stressed during its life. We are not wooden planks, of course, so change remains possible. But after a while, it requires much greater pressures.

Such pressures are not mysterious. You can probably imagine what they are: fresh ideas that alter our worldviews, experiences that induce disturbing emotions, people who demand that we act differently, a new environment that renders old habits unworkable. Sometimes when we face such pressures we don't realize how much they change us until we look back, years later. Sometimes we *seek* such pressures, in hopes of changing ourselves in a short period of time.

What makes change difficult is that—even when we seek it—we must also resist it in part. We do so to preserve our sanity. If from day to day we did not maintain coherence and stability in our views of the world and ourselves, we would lose our grip on reality. Too much change too fast would disrupt us in unhealthy ways. And so we must always keep one foot on the brake, so to speak.

Sociological wisdom holds that the best way to change a person is to put him or her into a new environment that brings new people, new relationships, new ideas, new kinds of work, and so on. By implication, people who claim to want to change, but who can't or won't change their circumstances, are not likely to change very much. This is often the case with people whose troubles stem from having adapted to bad circumstances. Unless they can get into different social worlds, they are likely to remain troubled.

Perhaps, then, you can see why it is too simple to say that people can become whatever they want, at any time. As we struggle to make sense of ourselves and the world around us, we will naturally resist pressures for dramatic change. What's more, the orderliness and stability of the world around us—how other people think, feel, and behave; and the steadiness of the physical environment—conspire to keep us the same.

So far I have ignored the second half of the question: can people be so damaged that they are unfixable? Or, to ask it a bit differently: can people be so hurt by their experiences that they cannot later function as intelligent adults able to get along peacefully with others? The student who asked the question was thinking of men who grow up under conditions of abuse and deprivation and who later go on to commit one impulsive violent crime after another, often ending up in prison.

Are such people *irreversibly* damaged? I don't know. But if we look at this matter in a sociologically mindful way, perhaps we can arrive at some useful thoughts.

One thing to keep in mind is that behavior is a product of circumstance, not merely personality. I will say more about this in Chapter 6. Here I will just point out the obvious: most of us have the potential to act violently—under certain conditions. So we should not be quick to assume that people who have a history of violent behavior are any more damaged than anyone else. Perhaps they have simply been caught, more often than other people, in circumstances conducive to violence.

Remember, too, that there are many people who turn their lives around. Sometimes people who have behaved in mean, selfish, and violent ways for many years experience an awakening, a radical change of heart and mind, that leads to very different behaviors. The fact that this kind of thing occurs at all implies that the *possibility* of change can exist even when it seems unlikely. So here again we should be wary of assuming irreversible damage. Perhaps some people just need the chance to develop compassion.

Still, early experiences can affect later growth. For example, if children do not learn to use language during the crucial "developmental window" that exists when they are very young (when their brains are forming neural networks), they may never develop normal verbal skills. In other words, extreme deprivation at key times early in life can make it hard to learn certain things later. But does this mean there is irreparable damage? It's not clear. The human brain is amazingly plastic and, here again, surprising cases of psychological change or late-blooming genius suggest that the brain is capable—with the right environmental stimulation—of more growth and self-repair than we now realize.

And so there are good reasons to be skeptical about claims that people are damaged beyond repair. This seems unlikely, unless there is injury, disease, or deprivation severe enough to cause organic damage. Yet it is reasonable to be concerned with how the social environment affects individual development. Doing this in a sociologically mindful way, however, suggests taking a further step. Instead of asking only about damage caused by deprivation or cruelty, we must also ask how to create a world in which no one is deprived or abused and in which each person's best human qualities are developed to the fullest.

*   *   *

A student who was taking a biological psychology course asked a question about the influence of genes on behavior. "Isn't it true," she asked, "that scientists are learning more and more about how genes influence behavior?" Yes, that is true. But they are not learning that genes directly influence behavior, apart from the environment. In fact, they are learning just the opposite.

If you want a technical explanation, you will have to consult a different book. Here I will use a metaphor to explain what genes are and what they do. What they are is a kind of recipe, encoded in molecular form, for creating proteins and assembling them into a living organism. But the genes that guide this process, like any recipe, do not ensure a particular outcome. Much depends on how the environment—think of the cook who mixes ingredients, sets the temperature of the oven, and decides when the baking is done—interacts with what the recipe says to do. Scientists have also learned that environmental conditions can activate some instructions and deactivate others.

So even if we are speaking of how *bodies* develop, genes alone do not rigidly determine the process or its results. If we speak of *brains*—and especially of the neural networks that form in response to environmental stimulation—there is even less genetic determination. If we go further and speak of *minds*—patterns of thought and internal mental representation—then it is hard to see how genes matter at all. Genes guide the building of a brain capable of human thought. But they do not determine what those thoughts will be or what kind of behavior will follow from them.

Scientists who study these matters are learning that there is more interaction between genes and the environment than previously suspected. This supports my point about the futility of trying to disentangle nature and nurture as contributors to human development. In any case, our main concern here is with behavior, not anatomy. We must therefore be careful not to confuse the shaping of bodies, a matter that is most definitely guided by genes, with the shaping of minds. The latter process depends on culture and our relationships with others. People who strongly wish to believe in genetic determination of behavior often overlook this obvious fact of human existence.

A Note on Emotion

We usually think of emotions as rooted deep inside us, arising from psychological dynamics that are unique to us as individuals. The story of my run, told at the outset of Chapter 4, showed how, on the contrary, emotions arise from interactions with others—interactions that are in turn shaped by membership in social categories. But there is even more to the social nature of emotions than I previously suggested.

It's easy to see that in everyday life our emotions are affected by interactions with others. What's less obvious is that part of becoming human is learning what we are supposed to feel in different situations, how to properly display emotions, and how to manage our own feelings and the feelings of others. A person who did not learn these lessons would be seen as strange and would probably have a hard time getting through the day.

Imagine that you are driving along at high speed on the freeway and someone cuts you off. You swerve quickly to avoid a collision and nearly lose control of your car. When the moment is over, your hands are shaking and your heart is pounding. Now what? What emotion do you feel? Perhaps you don't yet know. You might decide that you're afraid, or angry, or sad, or grateful—or some mix of these. What you will have to do is to *interpret* your state of arousal and *put a label on it*. This, too, is something that we must learn to do as part of becoming human. We must learn, in other words, how to figure out what's going on inside us.

How we label our feelings matters. In the example above, a driver who decided s/he was angry might try to catch up to the other driver and retaliate. Such action would of course be extremely dangerous. To forestall such a response, the offended driver might try (one hopes) to calm down by imagining how bad s/he would feel if innocent people got hurt or killed as a result of such an action or by imagining the good things that would be lost if the worst were to occur.

Thinking aimed at changing how we feel is called *emotion work*. Learning how to do this kind of work is another part of becoming human. Social life can indeed knock us around emotionally. But culture also equips us to cope with the knocks, individually and together.

Paths for Reflection

1. One way to get at the meanings that people attach to themselves is to use what is called the Twenty Statements Test. The instructions for the test are simple. People are told to ask themselves the question *Who Am I?* and then to write down the first twenty things that come to mind. Try this yourself and see what you come up with. Your answers to the *Who Am I?* question will help you take stock of the meanings you have gathered to yourself. Looking over your list, which meanings would you say are most important to you, and why? How do these meanings depend on your relationships with others?

2. When we think of "socialization," we usually think of parents, teachers, and other grown-ups telling children how to behave. It's true that socialization often happens that way. Parents, teachers, and other adults often give children explicit instructions about what to say and not to say, what to do and not to do. But if we pay attention to how socialization actually occurs, we notice two things: much of it does not involve overt instruction, and much of it is accomplished as children interact with each other. Think about how you learned to conduct yourself as a girl/woman or boy/man. What lessons did you learn from your own observations? What lessons did you learn from interacting with your peers?

3. Part of becoming human and learning to get along in society involves forming adaptive habits, that is, habitual ways of responding to people and situations. Generally speaking, we form and retain habits that work. Problems can arise, however, when habits that are useful in one kind of situation spill over into situations where they are not. For instance, in a highly competitive society, many people might develop the habit of seeing every situation as a contest in which it is important to try to come out on top of everyone else. Where, how, and for whom might this habitual competitiveness cause problems? What is it about U.S. society that encourages a lot of people, perhaps especially men, to develop this sort of habit?

Related Readings

Erikson, Erik. (1950). *Childhood and Society.* New York: Norton.

Gerth, Hans, & Mills, C. Wright. (1964). *Character and Social Structure.* New York: Harbinger.

Goffman, Erving. (1967). *Interaction Ritual.* New York: Pantheon.

Hochschild, Arlie. (1983). *The Managed Heart.* Berkeley: University of California Press.

Lane, Harlan. (1977). *The Wild Boy of Aveyron.* Cambridge, MA: Harvard University Press.

Lewontin, Richard. (2001). *The Triple Helix: Gene, Organism, and Environment.* Cambridge, MA: Harvard University Press.

Mead, George Herbert. (1934). *Mind, Self and Society.* Chicago: University of Chicago Press.

Noddings, Nel. (1984). *Caring.* Berkeley: University of California Press.

Piaget, Jean. (1954). *The Construction of Reality in the Child.* New York: Basic Books.

Polanyi, Michael. (1958). *Personal Knowledge.* London: Routledge.

Shibutani, Tamotsu. (1961). *Society and Personality.* Englewood Cliffs, NJ: Prentice Hall.

....

CHAPTER 6

Behavior as a Product of Interaction

A fter a lecture a speaker might ask, "Are there any questions? Is there anything you would like me to clarify?"—and there is silence. Everyone stares mutely. This is a curious situation, since it seems unlikely that even a dull talk would produce no reaction from conscious adults. So how do we explain the silence? Perhaps it is that people who go to lectures, in college or elsewhere, suffer from a disorder called hyperquietism.

It might seem unlikely that everyone in an audience would have the same trait. And your own experience might tell you that the idea of hyperquietism is silly. Even though you rarely ask a question after a talk, it is not because you are naturally quiet. After all, in other situations you can be boisterous and loud. But this just deepens the mystery. How come people who are sometimes boisterous and loud, people like yourself, *still* sit silently after a talk?

Being sociologically mindful, we would try to answer this question by looking at situations rather than personalities. We would try to determine the conditions under which people stay quiet, even when they have a lot on their minds. Perhaps we would find that people tend to sit quietly when they feel that they are being evaluated for their intelligence, are not participating in a discussion as equals, and feel that, by asking a question, they risk appearing foolish. We might also find that these conditions exist in most places where lectures are given.

The point is that people act in response to the situation they think they are in, on the basis of what they think is at stake for them in that situation. Such a simple idea would seem to be easy to apply. Yet we often fail to consider others' perceptions of the situation they are in. If another person behaves badly, we might think, "That's awful! I would never do such a thing!" Perhaps not. But perhaps also we would be less quick to judge if we stopped to consider how the other person perceives his or her circumstances and choices.

As an outsider to a situation it can be hard to appreciate what people in the situation are seeing, thinking, and feeling and thus why they act as they do. For example, why do people often fail to give help in situations where it seems clear that someone needs help? As outsiders to such a situation, it is easy to say that those who fail to give help—people who just stand by or walk by and do nothing—are apathetic or cowardly.

It might make us feel good to suppose that cowardice or apathy underlies the failure to give help, because then we can imagine that we, as braver or more assertive people, would do better. Cowardice and apathy are no better explanations, however, than hyperquietism was in the earlier example of silence after a lecture. Again, we must pay attention to the context to understand what people do or fail to do.

The context in which people often fail to help, at least in the United States, is a society in which few of us know our neighbors well. In a big city, or even in a suburb, we can live near people for years and know little about them. So it might not be clear, on some occasion, if we should stick our noses into what seems like other people's business. We also live in a society in which there are angry and violent people, from whom the police cannot protect us every hour of the day. So it is not unreasonable to fear "getting involved" and perhaps becoming victims ourselves.

Situations can also be confusing. It might not be clear that help is called for or wanted. If a man in ragged clothes is lying on the sidewalk and people are casually stepping over him, should you bend down to see if he needs help? If you see smoke coming from under the hood of a car stopped along a busy freeway and hundreds of cars are speeding past, should you go back and help? Or suppose you see a woman rush out of a bar and a man come out after her, grab her arm, and jerk her around. Is this an assault in progress, a quarrel between drunken lovers, or an attempt to stop a thief?

Even if we think help is called for, we often prefer to imagine that someone else will give it. Perhaps when you see a man on the sidewalk, a smoking car, or a quarreling couple, you think, "Why should I be the one to get involved? I'm busy right now. In fact, I'm running late. Besides, if there's a *serious* need for help, I'm sure *someone* will give it." Of course, if everyone thinks this way, no one will help.

Recognizing that situations can be ambiguous, that giving help can be risky, and that we may innocently rationalize a failure to give help is not to offer excuses. Excusing or blaming is not the point; rather, it is to be mindful of how circumstances affect people's behavior. It is to try to understand why people do what they do, rather than to judge them for failing to do what we, as outsiders to a situation, imagine that we would do.

To understand people's behavior in context we must grasp the facts of a situation: who does what to whom, where, when, how, and under what conditions? If we can't answer these questions, we do not know enough to understand why people act as they do. We must also be mindful of how the situation appears to the people in it. We must try to see things through their eyes, a task that is made more difficult by prejudice.

For example, young African American women, especially poor women in inner cities, are often accused of having babies so that they can collect welfare. These claims are usually made by people who know nothing about job prospects in inner cities; about racial discrimination; about what life is like for poor, African American teenagers; or about how much money welfare actually provides. Despite this ignorance, accusers will boldly say, "They are irresponsible! They don't want to work! They would rather survive by having sex, having babies, and collecting government checks!"

Being sociologically mindful, we would ask, "How many babies are being had by whom? What does the world look like to these young women and to the men who impregnate them? How do they think of sex and of birth control? What does it mean to them to be a mother or a father? What options do they perceive for making a living and earning respect in their communities? Are jobs available for everyone who wants to work? What does it cost to live in these places, and how much money does the average job provide? How much money does welfare provide?" With good answers to these questions we might begin to understand what is going on.

It is also important to let people explain their own behavior. We might or might not accept their explanations at face value, since people can be unaware of all the social forces that act on them. But we should at least listen to how people explain their own behavior before presuming to judge them. If we have not listened, then perhaps we should keep quiet until we learn more.

It is much easier to rely on stereotypes and prejudices than it is to find out the facts about other people's lives. It can also make us feel good about ourselves to condemn what we see as others' misbehavior, rather than to see how the behavior we dislike grows out of circumstances beyond the control of individuals. Being mindful, we will resist the temptation to elevate ourselves at the expense of others. Certainly we want others to consider the circumstances that lead us to act as *we* do, especially when we fail to live as saints.

Cultural Context

Being sociologically mindful of context also means paying attention to culture—the beliefs, values, and practices that are shared and transmitted from one generation to the next among a group of people. Culture, too, has to be put in a larger context, since culture is a group's adaptation to the environment in which it exists. Beliefs and behaviors that might seem strange usually make sense when we consider the conditions under which a group is trying to survive.

If we take culture into account, we can appreciate how behavior that seems weird or wrong to outsiders is normal and proper to insiders. This is not to say that any behavior is okay merely because it is some group's traditional way of doing things or because it aids their survival. It is to say that we cannot *understand* what people do, and why, without considering what they have been taught to see as normal and correct in their world.

We must remember, too, that people do not choose the worlds into which they are born. If we are born into a world of calm and wealth, we might learn to get what we need simply by asking for it. If we are born into a world of scarcity, struggle, and despair, we might learn that our survival depends on being aggressive, even violent. The point is not to justify aggression and violence, but to say that understanding others' behavior in context requires understanding the nature of the world that has formed their survival habits.

Imagine growing up in a place where any sign of weakness made you prey to abuse. Imagine that your survival depended on swift retaliation for any threat to your dignity, especially in public. Now imagine that your first job is as a sales clerk. In this job you must put up with being bossed by your boss, teased by coworkers, and insulted by customers. Will you respond, day after day, with patience and good humor, or will you fall back on your old habits and one day give your boss, a coworker, or a customer a punch in the nose?

If you come from a different background, you might think, "All low-level jobs require putting up with some obnoxious people. You just have to bear it until you get into a better position." If you believe this, it is because you have learned different survival habits. Perhaps you have learned to mask your feelings and do what the boss says, so as to get along and prosper. This strategy pays off well in some worlds, but it doesn't work everywhere, and it has costs.

Suppose you have formed the habit of doing as you're told. Imagine that this habit has gotten you a nice job with a high salary. One day you realize that a product your company plans to make is defective in a way that will injure some of the people who use it. You argue that the product should be redesigned to be safer, but you are told, "That will raise production costs too much. We will make it as planned. If anyone gets hurt, insurance will cover it." So you rely on the habit that has helped you succeed: you do as you're told. Then, as you foresaw, some people are badly hurt by your company's product.

After all this is revealed to the public, outsiders say that you should have blown the whistle or quit your job in protest. You could have kept people from being hurt, but you didn't. Why? We could say that you are weak and irresponsible—like those women who supposedly have babies to collect welfare. Or we could try to understand your behavior in context.

We should be mindful of your options as you saw them. Did you think you would be fired if you protested any harder? Did you think you could find another job if you quit or were fired? Did you believe that your career would be ruined if you blew the whistle, because of how whistle-blowers are treated by other employers? Perhaps you had children to think about. If you'd lost your job, how would you pay for their food, clothes, shelter, medicine, school, and so on? So perhaps you felt compelled, for their sake, to keep your mouth shut.

We should also be mindful of what your job meant to you. Perhaps, like most people in U.S. culture, you learned to stake your identity on your job, so losing your job would have been devastating to you. Or perhaps you were taught that the boss who gives orders, not the worker who carries them out, is responsible for the results. That is a dangerous belief, also common in U.S. society, but we can't blame you for inventing it and putting it in your head.

To understand your behavior in this example we would have to be mindful of several contexts at once: the firm in which you had little power; the family and friendship networks of which you were a part; and the competitive, individualistic society in which you reasonably feared for your ability to make a decent living. In light of these circumstances, your behavior, though not admirable, would at least make sense.

Interactional Surprises

Being sociologically mindful does not lead to the view that "context determines behavior." There is a grain of truth in that phrase, but it is important to see that what happens in a situation is the result of people trying to figure out how to do something together—with no guarantee that things will turn out as anyone expects. We must pay attention, in other words, to how behavior arises, often unpredictably, out of interaction.

We must pay attention to interaction because people do not simply react to a context; they join with others to *create* a context and to figure out what kind of behavior it calls for. For example, suppose you are having coffee with friends. What exactly is going on in this situation? Is it flirtation, seduction, therapy, domination, education, arguing, gossiping, worship, scheming, competition, or theft of ideas? It could be any and all of these, depending on how the situation is defined and how the interaction unfolds.

Suppose that you and some friends are talking in a café. A great many things might happen, some of which no one could predict. Perhaps at some point two men walk by holding hands. Seeing this, Pat says, "Look at those faggots. I *hate* that." Everyone is surprised to hear this, since Pat has never before made such homophobic remarks. Then Robin says, sharply, "Maybe you say that because you wish you were as brave as they are." With this brief exchange, triggered by the two men walking past, the situation is altered. What will happen next? Depending on how the scene plays out, people's lives could be dramatically changed.

Many scenes in social life are fairly predictable. If you go to the store or to the movies, you have a pretty good idea of what will happen. Even so, things could happen that you don't expect. Perhaps the checkout clerk comments on your purchase of pickled herring and you end up in a conversation that leads to a date and a new relationship. At the movie the people behind you might throw popcorn in your hair—and then you end up getting in a fight and thrown in jail. Even in familiar situations we can never be completely sure what will happen.

Here is another example, in the form of a brief story (one that I have invented, though it is loosely based on a real incident). In this story, interaction leads to an outcome that no one expects or wants. The main character is Thomas, a young man who grew up in a public housing project in Chicago. He studied hard in school and won a scholarship to an Ivy League university. During spring break of his first year in college, while many of his friends went to Florida to play, Thomas visited his family. He knew that his mother could use help with the younger kids, if only for a week.

The night before he was supposed to go back east, Thomas got together with his old buddies Derek and Jamal, neither of whom was in college. Although Thomas had been a good student and never got in any serious trouble, he was hardly an angel. After all, he had grown up in a tough area and had to be tough to survive. Jamal and Derek teased him about going to college to become a "fat, rich, white man." Thomas accepted the teasing because he knew it was a way for his friends to vent some of their own frustrations.

Thomas, Derek, and Jamal joked and talked for hours. Now it was late and they'd all had a lot to drink. Thomas said he had to get going because his flight was early the next morning. As he and his friends walked home, a car full of slightly younger boys from a nearby housing project pulled up alongside them. Someone yelled from the car, "You muthafuckas better get your ass off our street." Derek yelled back, and the car accelerated, then turned at the next corner, half a block away.

The car kept going, and after a tense minute Thomas and his friends began to joke about "kids these days" and who would've won if there'd been a fight. But the mood was spoiled. Thomas and his friends now walked quietly and warily. In another block they came to the apartment building where Thomas's mother lived. Thomas and his friends stood on the sidewalk saying their good-byes when a car came speeding down the street. Four doors flew open before the car screeched to a halt in front of them. It was the same car as before.

Five boys poured out of the car and surrounded Thomas and his friends. Two of the boys were older and bigger than the others. One of the older boys said, "You muthafuckas need a lesson in respect." Jamal stepped up to the first boy and said, "There's gonna be a lesson, asshole, but you sure ain't the teacher." The first boy reached under his jacket and pulled out a gun that had been tucked into his pants. Jamal grabbed for it but was too slow and got shot in the stomach.

As Jamal fell to his knees, another shot was fired and the first boy's head snapped back. Thomas dove away, rolled, and in the next instant found himself crouched behind a car with Derek. "Take this," Derek said, handing him the gun dropped by the first boy from the car. Derek had a gun of his own. Thomas didn't want the gun but his hand seemed to reach for it automatically. Two bullets hit the windshield of the car behind them and pellets of glass rained in the street.

The boys who started the fight were trying to get back to their car, which was still in the middle of the street with its doors open. Thomas heard a siren in the distance and hoped it meant the shooting would end soon. Just then Derek stood up and fired at a boy who was trying to get into the driver's seat of the car. The boy pivoted and fired back. Derek fell into the street, clutching his neck and groaning. Thomas wanted to reach out to his friend, but he felt as if he'd been paralyzed.

Instead of getting in the car, the boy who shot Derek began to walk toward him as he lay in the street. Thomas stared in horror. As the boy pointed his gun at Derek's head, Thomas stood up and screamed, "No!" The boy was so surprised that he fired into the pavement. He was still staring wide-eyed when Thomas shot him in the chest.

The car in the street sped away, and after what might have been one minute or ten, the police arrived. Thomas was in shock. He barely understood that he was being arrested for murder.

*   *   *

If these were real events, the story would not end here. Thomas's life has been changed. Even if he is not convicted of murder, it's doubtful that he will be able to resume his college life. What will happen to him? And though the story is over for the boys who were killed in the fight, we can wonder what will happen to their families and friends.

This story shows the power of context to catch us up in events and actions that we do not expect. Thomas and his friends just wanted to visit and have a good time. They weren't looking for trouble. If not for what the other boys started, Thomas and his friends would have gone back to their usual lives the next day. Thomas would have been back at school, in a very different and much safer social world.

You might think, "Yes, but Thomas and his friends should have known better than to be out drinking, in a bad neighborhood, late at night. And they should not have yelled back at the car in the first place." It is tempting to think this way. We often try to make sense of people's troubles by blaming individuals instead of thinking about the context.

In this case, try to see the situation through the eyes of Thomas and his friends. To them this was not a "bad neighborhood," but the place where they had grown up and where two of them still lived. Hanging out and walking down the street at night were things they had always done. They were also young men who had learned that it could be dangerous to let an insult go unanswered. You might say that yelling back was a bad choice this time, but that is hindsight. If the other boys hadn't pursued the fight, you would think that Thomas and his friends just did what was normal in their social world.

Or perhaps you think, "Thomas was smart, successful in school, and had everything going for him. He should have known better than to get into a fight." Again, that is easy to say as an outsider. Thomas didn't want to get in a fight, but he was caught up in a situation where his life and the lives of his friends were at stake. He could hardly say, "Wait a second, guys, I'm a college boy on my way to a bright future. Leave me out of this." It is unrealistic to expect that sort of response, considering how Thomas grew up, his loyalty to his friends, his regard for his own honor, and the threat posed by the situation.

Being sociologically mindful, we can see that what happened to Thomas and his friends was not any one person's doing but a result of interaction. Everyone collaborated, so to speak, in making happen something that perhaps none of them really wanted. Events unfolded as they did because of how Thomas and his friends, and the other boys, perceived the demands of a situation that they had created together.

The story also suggests another way we need to be mindful of context. We need to look beyond the immediate situation and ask, Why did these young men have so little regard for their futures that they would get involved in deadly violence? Why didn't they all have good lives to look forward to? How did they come to think that violence was the proper way to prove they were men? And how did they happen to have such easy access to guns?

To ask such questions is to be mindful of the larger context within which the scenes of social life are played out. We must be mindful, in other words, not only of the action on stage, but also of how the props, the script, and the theater itself are created. Or, to hark back to Chapter 3, we must be mindful of the connections between a scene and the context in which it occurs. If we do this, we will see patterns where before we saw random events. Perhaps then all the stories that are in some way like Thomas's will begin to make sense.

Minding and Un-minding the Self

If there is a football field near you, go there and tear down a goal post. If the cops try to stop you, tell them to get lost. Here are some other things you can do when you have the time: run naked down a busy sidewalk; go up to a car at a stoplight and begin rocking it as if you are going to tip it over; find an area where there are beautiful old oak trees and throw rolls of toilet paper up into the branches until the trees are streaming with the stuff. While you're doing these things, chant loudly, "We're number one! We're number one!"

You might think these are crazy things to do. If you did them right now, by yourself, you would probably be arrested and forced to undergo psychiatric testing. But if you wait until your football team wins a big game and a few thousand other fans join you, you could probably do any of these things without getting locked up. Your behavior might be seen as obnoxious, but it would not be seen as evidence of mental illness or evil intent. Most likely you would be seen as "getting a bit carried away."

Just to be clear about this: I do not think you should do any of these things at any time, since they are hurtful to other people and disrespectful to the earth. The point in bringing them up is to offer another example of how to be sociologically mindful of context and its influence on behavior.

The usually temperate person who goes wild in a crowd might say, afterward, "I don't know what came over me. I just didn't seem to care what happened. It was like it wasn't even me doing that stuff." These might seem like hollow excuses, but they are probably close to the truth. The self-awareness on which we depend to control our behavior can be greatly reduced in a crowd.

One reason we do not usually wreck property, run naked in the street, and befoul trees is that we can imagine how others would react to us if we did. Most of us prefer not to be seen as destructive and foolish. And so, even if we sometimes have urges to do crazy and hurtful things, we do not usually act on those urges, because we can imagine the trouble we would cause ourselves and others.

But in a crowd, people may feel anonymous. They may feel as if they won't be recognized and held accountable for their acts. When people "act crazy" in crowds and do things they would not normally do, it is because they have stopped caring, for a moment, about how they will be judged, at least by any audience that is important to them. Or we might say that wildness results because people feel there is no chance that they will be held accountable for their behavior by any audience whose disapproval matters.

Defining the Situation

You might think, "It is not merely a crowd that makes the difference, since people don't automatically go berserk in a crowd, and most crowds are not rowdy." You would be right, of course. What matters is not merely the presence of others but also how a situation is defined. In the postgame situation, people want to bask in the reflected glory of their conquering heroes. It is a situation in which people are allowed, even encouraged, to show that they too possess the indomitable spirit of champions. How does one do this? Perhaps by ignoring the usual rules of public civility. Winners, after all, make their own rules.

Yet the same people who are rowdy after a football game will be solemn at a funeral. Again, what matters is how the situation is defined, which is to say, what matters is the idea that people share about what is supposed to be going on. People might feel anonymous in a funeral crowd, if the crowd is big enough. But they will probably not violate the mood of the occasion by dancing around the grave and singing, "Ding dong! The wicked witch is dead."

The presence of others can sometimes *raise* self-awareness. Perhaps you can sing "Amazing Grace" in beautiful resonant tones—in the shower. But suppose you were in a classroom and the teacher said, "Before we discuss the nature of the carbon bond in the benzene molecule, we will sing 'Amazing Grace' to help us get in the mood for learning." Would you sing boldly, or would you hold back?

You might worry about being exposed as a lousy singer. Or you might want others to see that you are too cool to do anything as silly as singing "Amazing Grace" in a chemistry class. Or, even if you had a sweet voice and *wanted* to sing, you might worry about singing louder than others and seeming to show off. In a situation like this, your self-awareness would be raised and you would probably try hard to control yourself.

Whether we feel anonymous and reckless or self-conscious and cautious depends on how a situation is defined. Is the situation one in which people expect to criticize each other for how well they perform or one in which people expect to be free from others' scrutiny and judgments? Being sociologically mindful of why people act as they do in any given situation means paying attention to how the situation is defined and to the degree of self-awareness it induces. This isn't easy to do, especially from the outside of situations that are unfamiliar to us.

Seeing the Bigger Picture

When the arteries that supply blood to the heart get clogged with fat, part of the heart muscle is starved of oxygen and may be damaged. If the damage is severe, the heart may stop working entirely, thus causing death. While this is a true account of why people have heart attacks, it is awfully narrow. Heart attacks are not merely mechanical malfunctions.

Arteries get clogged largely because people eat badly and don't exercise. Arteries are also damaged by smoking. Certainly these behaviors must be taken into account to understand why people have heart attacks. Stress is another risk factor for heart trouble. That, too, must be considered. But even after we have taken all this into account, we must ask, "Why do people eat badly, get so little exercise, harm their bodies by smoking, and feel so stressed?" To answer these questions we would have to examine the social worlds in which people live.

This wider view of heart disease—a view that takes behavior and social context into account—is "holistic." In medicine, a holistic view helps us understand more fully the causes of disease. It helps us see that fighting disease and creating health may require changes in the environment, in behavior, and in cultural habits. The idea is to try to see the whole and see how things within it are connected.

Being sociologically mindful and thinking holistically are much the same. Being sociologically mindful, we try to see the whole—that is, to see the larger contexts in which people act and cultural habits arise. To put it another way, it is a matter of looking at the bigger picture.

Consider again the postgame rampage. Why do people seek these situations that license them to get carried away? Perhaps it is because they resent the restrictions normally placed on them by parents, teachers, and bosses. People who feel such resentment may be eager to create occasions where they can run amok with impunity. "So why is it," we should also ask, "that in our society there are so many people trying to control us?"

Historical Context

One time in class a white student said, "It seems to me that black people are racists among themselves. I mean, look at how they give higher status to those who have lighter skin." Some of the black students scowled at this. After a moment, one of the black students, a very dark-skinned man, said, "What Todd said is true, in a way, but he doesn't really know what he's talking about." Before Todd could respond, I broke in and asked the black student to elaborate. He began, "Well, he doesn't understand the difference between racism and colorism, and he's also ignorant of history."

Despite its tense beginning, the discussion that followed helped us to see the differences between prejudice, racism, and colorism. The understandings we reached were these: *Prejudice*, we said, refers to believing that people in certain groups are inferior or evil. In this sense, anyone can be prejudiced. *Racism*, however, refers to the beliefs and practices that a dominant group uses to keep another group of people down. Members of an oppressed group thus could be "prejudiced against" members of the dominant group, in the sense of seeing them all as evil, but it would be wrong to call this racism, since members of the oppressed group have no power to enforce their prejudices.

What, then, of *colorism* among African Americans? Why have light-skinned people (often those with one or more European ancestors) enjoyed higher status in the black community? Part of the answer lies in the beliefs, created and spread by Europeans, that light skin is more attractive than dark skin and that light skin is a sign of superiority. This is a myth, of course. But the belief has been powerfully enforced—by the group with the power to enforce it—for centuries. So it is not surprising that members of the oppressed group would be affected by it.

Another part of the answer lies in the practice of whites giving extra privileges to Africans with light skin. Under slavery, such privileges might have included a job in the house rather than in the field. Along with a house job came better clothes, better food, and, sometimes, a chance for education, friendship, and land ownership. What happened, in other words, is that some whites gave extra resources to those Africans who, because of their lighter skins, looked more European. These resources then gave lighter-skinned Africans advantages in striving for wealth and status in their own communities. Today we see the cumulative results of these advantages.

Perhaps you can see why this has created a complex problem having to do with skin color. Many light-skinned blacks are reluctant to admit that the advantages they enjoy today derive from a kind of skin-color collaboration with whites. And so light-skinned blacks have sometimes sought to justify their advantages over dark-skinned blacks by adopting the idea that light skin is a sign of better character. It is thus true that some African Americans have embraced a racist idea as a way to justify their own privileges.

Being sociologically mindful, we must put all this in context. Colorism in the United States was not invented by Africans; it is an artifact of racism, as invented and practiced by Europeans. Colorism arose because of the conditions under which Africans, brought to North America as slaves, struggled to survive and gain their freedom. To understand why colorism arose and why it persists we must take this historical context into account. The lesson is that to understand the troubles that exist in any community, we must be mindful of how it is connected to the larger community that surrounds it.

Ordinary Insanity

Earlier I used the example of people running amok and how this might be understood in context. Perhaps this made it seem as if being mindful of context is useful mostly for explaining outrageous behavior. All behavior, however, even that which seems perfectly normal, must be understood in context. Being mindful of context can even lead us to reconsider what is outrageous and what is normal.

Suppose that instead of running amok, people carry on politely and calmly. What could be wrong with this? After all, isn't this what most of us are taught to do? Yes, and most of the time it is fine that we do. Unfortunately, we can get so used to being polite and calm that we fail to be outraged by horrific things going on around us. Nazi Germany is the most often cited twentieth-century example. Millions of people were killed in concentration camps while most Germans went about their business without protest. How can we understand this complacency?

In Germany, as in other nations, the government claimed the right to use violence to control people within its borders. The German government, like other governments, collected taxes and used this wealth to build the means to do violence (by creating police forces, armies, spying agencies, weapons, and so on). Germans relied on this government to protect them from outsiders, to keep internal order, and give them a feeling of belonging to a special group. Before and during World War II most German people thought their government was doing these jobs reasonably well—or at least not so badly as to inspire a mass revolt.

Think of the German government—its employees, the rules by which it operated, and the resources it possessed—as an *instrument* wielded by those who controlled it. When the Nazi leaders gained control of the German government, they gained control of an organization that was equipped with (or had the legitimacy to gather and employ) vast resources of people, information, money, and weapons. It would have been hard for unorganized dissenters to resist such an entity.

The German government was also highly bureaucratic. Like any such organization, it had many rules and policies and layers of management for keeping people under control. It was thus hard for people to challenge their bosses or even to find out what was going on. If you have had much experience working in large bureaucratic organizations, you know the problem.

Even when people began to see what was going on, most felt powerless and afraid to do anything. People who worked in the government and military bureaucracies—people who morally opposed the mass murder that was going on in the concentration camps—could justify their failure to protest by saying, "I'm not killing anyone. I'm not pulling the trigger. I'm just doing my job." After the war, many of the Nazi leaders who were tried for crimes against humanity defended themselves by saying, "I was only following orders." If those who actually killed could invoke this defense, imagine how much easier it was for people far from the killing to do so.

Looking back, the Nazi regime seems monstrous and insane. We wonder how anyone could have supported it, directly or indirectly. But again, consider the context. After losing World War I many Germans had feelings of injured national pride. Many were also angry about the terms under which they were forced to surrender in World War I. The German economy was faltering (in the context of a global recession in the 1930s), and many people worried about their jobs and income. So it was that many people were angry, resentful, and insecure—and confused about who was to blame.

In this context the Nazis offered appealing messages: other nations were to blame for limiting Germany's ability to recover from World War I; Jews, communists, and homosexuals were to blame for weakening Germany from the inside; and Germans were a naturally superior people who, if given a fair chance, could again build a great nation. These messages reinflated national pride and gave people easy answers to resolve their fears and anxieties.

We should also remember that once the Nazis gained control of the German government, they gained great power to shape people's thoughts and feelings. They used the government to make and control the news, to spread propaganda, and to stifle dissent. Many German people were thus at the mercy of the Nazi government when it came to knowing what was going on in their country and in the world. As in any nation-state, the Nazi government in Germany was a powerful tool for creating social reality.

If you have stayed with me through this unpleasant example, you might be wondering what is the point of all this. Is it to show that we can, by taking context into account, understand why the German people got caught up in acts of great evil? Yes, that is part of it. The more important point, however, is not about Germany in the 1930s and 1940s. It is about how we live here and now.

We still live in a world of nation-states, none of which is truly democratic and all of which have governments that can be captured by those seeking power for their own benefit. The governments of these nation-states still use violence to resist serious threats to their authority. Most of these nation-states are capitalist, which means that many people are likely to feel insecure about their jobs and income. There is also still plenty of racism to fuel scapegoating. Conditions thus remain ripe for holocausts to happen.

Perhaps you think, "All this is true, and so it is fortunate that we live in a country with a benevolent government." That is certainly a comforting illusion. Being sociologically mindful, however, we will try to look at matters in a larger context and consider how things appear to Iraqis, Vietnamese, Nicaraguans, Cubans, Chileans, Guatemalans, Afghans, and the citizens of other countries that have been invaded, bombed by, or otherwise forced to obey the wishes of those who run the U.S. government. We might also want to consider the perspectives of Native Americans, who can tell us something about the benevolence of the U.S. government.

An Antidote to Ordinary Insanity

Being sociologically mindful, we can understand why, given the propaganda power of the state, many people believe that their government is benevolent. The leaders of most governments try to foster this sort of belief because it helps them hold on to power. If we are mindful—in the sense of taking different perspectives in an attempt to get a more accurate and complete picture of how the world works—we will be less susceptible to the illusions that are supposed to keep us polite and calm while horrors go on all around us.

Sociological mindfulness can also help us to be aware of our own tendencies to resolve anger, frustration, and confusion by accepting easy answers. If we are mindful in this way, we are unlikely to be seduced by politicians and other would-be leaders who want us to blame our troubles on powerless people. Sociological mindfulness is a good antidote to this eagerness to find scapegoats. Being mindful, we are more likely to see that our troubles arise from the abuse of power by those who have it, not from the adaptations of those who don't.

Being sociologically mindful, we try to see the big picture. We try to understand how people adapt to the conditions of their lives, how they perceive their circumstances and options, and how they respond to the presence, expectations, and actions of others. All this is part of being mindful of context. We can take an even more holistic view, however, and try to understand people's behavior in the context of a culture, a community, a society, a nation-state, a global economy, and the course of history. Seeing the connections between action and context—and the next larger context, and the next, and so on—is much of what it means to be sociologically mindful.

Mindfulness itself is part of any context. A context in which people are sociologically mindful is different from one in which they are not. When being mindful, people can perceive the causes and consequences of their actions more fully. This awareness can in turn change people's behavior, which can in turn create new contexts. Where mindfulness thrives, there will be less ignorance, fear, and suffering in which evil can take root.

Dialogue

Preconditions for Ordinary Insanity?

Some readers of *TSEL* have told me that I should use more recent examples than the Nazis and World War II to discuss what I call ordinary insanity. But the point of using historical examples is to teach about being socio-logically mindful. So I use events with which I am familiar and that make for clear illustrations. I am also more concerned with general principles than with specific cases. My hope is that by illustrating these principles, even with examples that might seem old, readers will be able to apply them to analyzing what is happening today. Nonetheless, let me offer some examples more recent than World War II.

In February 2003, George W. Bush was to give a speech at a high school in a suburb of Atlanta. The motorcade route was lined with people who had come out to catch a glimpse of the president. One of these people was a forty-two-year-old mother of four, who hoped the president would see the sign she was holding. The sign read, "No War for Oil." This woman meant to express her opposition to Bush's plans to attack Iraq.

Merely for quietly holding her sign she was screamed at: *"Go to hell! Get out of the country! You don't belong here!"* Some people spit on her. Others made obscene gestures. A group of men surrounded her and chanted loudly, "Go USA!" Some of those who yelled at her were women who had brought along their children.

At the beginning of the day, the woman felt proud to be part of her community. But the abusive behavior of her neighbors changed her outlook. Later, she wrote, "I was frightened that my neighbors were going to hurt me because I dared to express my opinion. This could not be happening. Not in America, right?"

The second case happened in early March 2003, in upstate New York. A sixty-year-old man had gone to a mall and bought a T-shirt that said "Peace on Earth" on the front and "Give Peace a Chance" on the back. Like the woman in Georgia, this man was also expressing his opposition to George W. Bush's plan to attack Iraq. While sitting in the food court, wearing his new T-shirt, the man was approached by security guards and told to remove the shirt or leave the mall. The man refused to do either, and so the police came and arrested him for trespassing.

These incidents are disturbing because they are so contrary to American political values. As citizens, we have not only the right but also an obligation to speak out against the actions of government when we think those actions are wrong. It is by doing this, for more than two hundred years, that Americans have resisted domestic tyranny. Yet in these stories we see precious values being thrown out by people whose overzealous and narrow patriotism makes them unable to tolerate even mild acts of dissent.

You might think, "Well, it was surely inappropriate for people to scream at the woman who held the sign, and a clear overreaction to arrest the man for wearing a T-shirt, but these are isolated incidents and no long-term harm was done." But in fact, after September 11, 2001, these kinds of incidents were not so isolated. If you had read newspapers carefully, you would have found quite a few short, back-page stories of people being punished, in one way or another, for stating anti-war opinions. As for harm, it's important to see how shutting down dissent can create extremely dangerous conditions.

How did it happen that most German citizens, before and during World War II, went complacently about their business while their government was perpetrating horrors? It was not that people knew nothing of what was going on. There were reports and suspicions, and, before the Nazis consolidated their power, there were protests. But by quashing dissent—through violence, intimidation, arrests, and economic pressure— the Nazis got most people to shut up. The lack of visible dissent then created the impression that things were not really so bad and that most people supported the government.

It is also important to remember that dissent can be quashed without beating everyone up. All it takes are a few examples of what happens to dissenters. Perhaps there were other people who agreed with the woman who held up the "No War for Oil" sign. But would they speak up, after seeing what happened to her? Would most people want to risk getting arrested for wearing a pro-peace T-shirt? Many people, even if they disagreed with what powerful political leaders were doing, might decide to stay quiet and not call attention to themselves.

What happens then? We have seen, historically, what can happen. Conditions are created for ordinary insanity to take hold.

A skeptical reader still might say that the examples I've chosen come from unusual times, such as the aftermath of 9/11 and the U.S. invasions of Afghanistan and Iraq—a period when emotions were running high. But the same kind of bullying behavior occurred at campaign rallies during the U.S. presidential election primaries in 2015 and 2016. What we saw in these cases was no different from what we have seen in the past: verbal abuse and physical force employed to stifle dissent and enforce conformity. It is this kind of behavior, which is hardly a thing of the past, that can make people reluctant to speak out against what they see as wrong.

There is one other kind of precondition that does not take the dramatic form of people being shouted down or ejected from a campaign rally. I am referring to a precondition that is now mostly taken for granted: government surveillance of public behavior and private communication. As recently as twenty years ago—around, say, the mid-1990s—a person who predicted that Americans would accept surveillance cameras nearly everywhere and would barely object to government surveillance of private communications by ordinary citizens would have been seen as crazy. "Freedom-loving Americans would never stand for this!" it might have been said.

Today, it is the person who strenuously objects to these surveillance practices, the person who sees them as potential threats to freedom of thought and association, who is more likely to be seen as crazy or alarmist, at least in some quarters. Here again, things are not so different from the past. When those in power begin to secretly monitor what ordinary, law-abiding people say and do, people may stop saying and doing the kinds of things that distinguish the citizens of a democracy from the subjects of a political regime.

Being sociologically mindful does not mean dissenting all the time or always protesting what politicians are doing. Dissenting or protesting are actions that one decides to undertake *after* analyzing a situation. But being sociologically mindful does mean paying attention to how the expression of ideas is controlled, to the conditions that are thereby created, and to what history tells us about the dangers of suppressing dissent and enforcing conformity.

A Note on Deviance

I've occasionally been asked to add material to *TSEL* that speaks to topics covered in conventional sociology textbooks. One topic that has often been mentioned is deviance. Until now, I haven't said anything about deviance, at least not explicitly, because it has seemed to me that I had little to say that wasn't obvious. But perhaps it's worth noting the obvious, since it's possible to overlook something that's in plain view if we don't expect to see it.

Here is the main thing I have to say: what counts as "deviant"—that is, what gets defined as abnormal and immoral—depends on the perspective of a person or group. A behavior that appears deviant from one perspective might appear normal and acceptable from another. This is a fairly simple sociological point. Matters get complicated, however, when we ask, Who gets to say what counts as deviant? How are those judgments arrived at? What if there's disagreement? What are the consequences of labeling a person, a group, or a type of behavior as deviant?

Once upon a time, women who wanted to vote, to work outside the home, or to retain control of their property after getting married were considered deviant. Women who accepted political disfranchisement and control by their husbands were seen, in contrast, as "good and proper" women. Today, after decades of feminist activism, most people in Western societies think differently about women's rights. Now the person who thinks women don't deserve full human rights is seen as strange. As this example suggests, power has a lot to do with what is defined as deviant. Context matters, too. What counts as acceptable behavior in a boxing ring (punching someone in the nose) would be considered deviant in a classroom.

It's important to examine the values and processes that lead to defining people or their behavior as deviant. There are of course harmful behaviors that we might agree, as a society, to condemn under almost every circumstance. But what about civil disobedience to protest an unjust war? Is that deviant? What about relationships between gay and lesbian people? Cases like these remind us that labeling people or their behavior as "deviant" is often what a dominant group does to maintain its control over others.

Paths for Reflection

1. The bystander problem discussed at the outset of this chapter is often illustrated by cases in which it seems obvious that someone needs help and no one responds. But a version of the bystander problem occurs fairly often in everyday life. For example, some white people genuinely abhor racist language and jokes, yet they will remain silent when someone in a group uses such language or tells a racist joke. Likewise, some men dislike the sexist language that other men use to refer to women, yet they remain silent when their male friends use such language. How do you explain this tendency to remain silent in the face of hateful and hurtful remarks? What might make it easier to speak up in these kinds of situations?

2. Imagine that you have gone back in time to about 1840 so you can witness the settling of the American West. On one occasion you are having

dinner with a nice homesteading family when the conversation turns to praising the army for its fine work in "ridding the territory of heathen savages." Your hosts are delighted, it seems, with how well the government has managed to remove the Indians who once lived where you are now sitting. When you question the morality of how the native people are being treated, one of your hosts says, "How dare you question us and try to make us feel guilty! You don't understand the situation here." But what is it that you might in fact understand better than your hosts? Now come back to the present and imagine that you are hosting a time traveler from 150 years in the future. About what current events or arrangements might this person question you?

3. Money from student tuition covers only a fraction of what it costs to run a public university. The rest comes from various sources, including state revenues (i.e., the pot of money generated by taxes). So if you attend a public college or university, you receive a form of welfare. Perhaps you feel fine about this. After all, you are on your way to becoming a productive citizen, so public support for your education can be seen as a kind of investment. Of course, the people whose taxes pay for your schooling want to ensure that you are not squandering their investment, and so they would naturally insist that you attend all your classes, do all assigned readings, complete your assignments on time, make wise use of the library, and generally strive to learn as much as possible. If you do all these things, your conscience should be clear. But if you don't do all these things, how would you explain your apparent laziness to the people whose taxes pay for your education? What would you want these people to understand before they passed judgment on you?

Related Readings

Arendt, Hannah. (1963). *Eichmann in Jerusalem: A Report on the Banality of Evil.* New York: Viking.

Bandura, Albert. (1999). "Moral Disengagement in the Perpetuation of Inhumanities." *Personality and Social Psychology Review* 3:193–209.

Bellamy, Edward. (1966 [1888]). *Looking Backward.* Boston: Houghton Mifflin.

Bourgois, Phillipe. (1995). *In Search of Respect: Selling Crack in the Barrio.* New York: Cambridge University Press.

Jackall, Robert. (1988). *Moral Mazes.* New York: Oxford University Press.

Kelman, Herbert, & Hamilton, V. Lee. (1989). *Crimes of Obedience.* New Haven, CT: Yale University Press.

Lever, Janet. (1983). *Soccer Madness.* Chicago: University of Chicago Press.

MacLeod, Jay. (2009). *Ain't No Makin' It: Aspirations and Attainment in a Low-Income Neighborhood* (3rd ed.). Boulder, CO: Westview Press.

Majors, Richard, & Billson, Janet. (1992). *Cool Pose: Dilemmas of Black Manhood in America*. New York: Touchstone.

Milgram, Stanley. (1974). *Obedience to Authority*. New York: Harper & Row.

Sandstrom, Kent, Martin, Daniel, Lively, Katherine J., & Fine, Gary Alan. (2013). *Symbols, Selves, and Social Reality* (4th ed.). Los Angeles: Roxbury.

Schneier, Bruce. (2015). *Data and Goliath: The Hidden Battles to Collect Your Data and Control Your World*. New York: Norton.

Solove, Daniel. (2013). *Nothing to Hide: The False Tradeoff between Privacy and Security*. New Haven, CT: Yale University Press.

CHAPTER 7

....

Seeing Patterns

I sometimes ask my students to read a story called "A Typical Date Rape." The story describes a situation in which heavy drinking, misplaced trust, poor communication, the subtle threat of violence, and a man's refusal to take no for an answer result in rape. One time a woman read the story in class and said, "There is no such thing as a typical date rape. Each case is unique." I disagreed.

I said that the man who wrote the story had studied many cases of date rape and that the story summed up what he had learned. This explanation didn't convince the student. She insisted that each case is unique. I said, "Yes, each case may be unique in its *details*, but many cases have common features." Another student then offered this: "I've done counseling at the women's center, and I can tell you that this story is very realistic. It fits the pattern that I've seen over and over."

As it turned out, the student who insisted that each case is unique admitted that she knew of only one other case—one that didn't quite fit the pattern described in the story. Because of this she thought that there were no patterns and that it was impossible to generalize. She was mistaken.

Part of being sociologically mindful is seeing that the social world works in patterned ways. Many of the patterns are easy to see. Millions of people get up in the morning, go to work for eight hours, come home, eat, sleep, and then get up and do it again. That is one kind of pattern, which exists because many people do things together in the same way, over and again. In fact, that is what a pattern is: a regularity in the way the world works.

The story about date rape described a pattern, one that was harder to see. It required the study of many cases of date rape to bring the pattern to light. It often takes a lot of work to discover patterns in social life, because some kinds of events don't happen every day. If you were asked to describe a typical bank robbery, you would have to study quite a few cases to see what they had in common. Perhaps then you would see a pattern.

Some of the patterned ways in which the social world works are obvious; some are not. Being sociologically mindful means paying attention in a disciplined way, so that we can begin to see patterns that are not obvious. To be "disciplined" in this sense is to stick to certain rules of procedure when trying to see what is going on in the world. If we pay attention carelessly, we will still see things going on, but many patterns will remain invisible to us.

For example, it would be possible to examine many date rapes, bank robberies, or other crimes and find no patterns. This might happen because we failed to get the same kinds of facts about each case, so we might fail to see what a lot of cases have in common. A good rule of procedure for paying attention might therefore be to always get the same facts about every case. To stick to this rule—when it would be easier to ignore it—is what it means to pay attention in a disciplined way.

In Chapter 14, I will say more about rules for paying attention. Here I want to say more about why we should try to be mindful of patterns and why it is important to be *sociologically* mindful of them.

One reason to be mindful of patterns is that if we want to change the world, we must be aware of the patterns that make the world what it is. If we would like to prevent rape, for example, it is helpful to know what conditions, thoughts, and actions typically lead to rape. This awareness can help us to see which conditions, thoughts, and actions we should try to change, so as to disrupt the pattern that produces rape.

We can apply this principle—the need to grasp the pattern that produces a particular result—to anything we might like to change. To stop the spread of a disease, for example, we must know how it is spread, and to find this out we must look for a pattern. Where do cases pop up? Among which people? What do these people have in common? Have they all been to the same place, engaged in the same activity, or eaten the same food? By answering these questions we can figure out what the pattern is and how to keep the disease from spreading.

Sometimes it's important to be aware of and to disrupt patterns in our own thoughts and behaviors. Imagine a person who always agrees to help other people with their projects. Helping others makes this person feel good, but too much helping keeps her from getting her own work done. Because she doesn't get her own work done, she feels like a failure and gets depressed. Suppose this happens over and again. If the person becomes aware of the pattern, perhaps she can change. All that might be necessary is learning to say no when the requests for help become too great.

Patterns within Patterns

Sometimes larger patterns encompass smaller ones. Consider, for example, the problem of sexual harassment at work. The typical harasser is a man. In fact, almost all harassers are men, and almost all victims are women, so there is a clear pattern of men sexually harassing women. Does this mean that women never harass men? No. In a small percentage of cases women are the perpetrators.

Perhaps you think, "If women can be harassers and men the victims, that means you can't generalize about men being the villains all the time." That's true; men are not the villains *all* the time, but the pattern still exists: most perpetrators are men (and even when men are the victims, the perpetrators are still usually other men). But if women can sometimes be perpetrators, then we need to look for a larger pattern. If we study actual cases, we find that women who harass are like men in one important way: they have power over others at work.

The larger pattern thus has to do with power. If we look only at the most obvious pattern (men harassing women), we might fail to see the importance of power. But if we also look at rare cases (women harassing men), we are forced to think about what else might be going on. What we would see—the commonality that reveals a larger pattern—is that harassment (of all kinds) is most likely to occur when one person has control over another person's fate.

To see a pattern is not to know why it exists. Why do some people repeatedly trap themselves in bad situations? Why are rates of disease higher among some groups than others? Why do some people abuse their power and exploit others? Such patterns might be easy to see but hard to explain. Often we must dig deeper to find out why things happen as they do.

To see patterns in how stars work, we must study them in the ways that physicists and astronomers do. To see patterns in how organisms work, we must study them in the ways that biologists do. To make sense of the social world—to see and explain the patterns that make the world what it is—we must study how people do things together, the meanings and arrangements they create, the ideas they embrace, and the cultural habits they form. Only by paying attention to these things can we see the patterns that matter in people's lives.

There is more to this than looking for typical cases. To identify a typical case of something is to discern one kind of pattern. Other kinds of patterns can be seen if we pay attention to the social world in different ways. Being sociologically mindful, we may discover that the world is patterned in many ways.

Patterns of Difference

One way to describe how the social world is patterned is to say, "The world is divided into groups of people, and often the people in these groups share characteristics that make them different from people in other groups." This is no great insight. We learn early in life that there are different kinds of people in the world. What we don't learn, usually, is how to be sociologically mindful of the differences between groups.

Again, it might not be easy to see these patterns of difference. Do people in the group called "women" live longer than people in the group called "men"? Perhaps you have seen or known many old men but few, if any, old women. You might thus believe that men live longer than women. Actually, on average, they do not. Women, on average, outlive men (in the United States) by about five years. You would see this pattern, however, only by paying attention in a systematic way.

We should bear in mind what is meant by "on average." It does *not* mean that all women outlive all men or that there aren't some old men who outlive most women. To say that women outlive men by about five years, on average, just means that more women than men live to an older age. We might not see this if we looked at just a few cases. But by looking at all cases (or at representative samples), the pattern becomes apparent.

Being sociologically mindful, we will ask, "How do groups in our society differ in important ways?" Some groups have more money, more education, better health, more prestige, and longer lives than others—on average. By looking at these average differences we can see patterns that reveal how the social world works. Or perhaps it is better to say that looking at such patterns can give us a snapshot of the social world. We would also want to know how these group differences come about.

We should be mindful, too, that group differences are not mere abstractions. They are indexes to how the lives of people in one group differ from the lives of people in another. If, for example, white families have much higher income, on average, than Hispanic and black families, this tells us, or should lead us to suspect, that people growing up in these groups might have different kinds of experiences.

Group averages don't tell us about individuals. Even if white families have more money, on average, than black and Hispanic families, it is still true that many whites are poor while some blacks and Hispanics are rich. In each group there is a range of incomes and wealth, so those at the top of one group can be ahead of those at the bottom or middle of the other group. Still, the average difference remains, and this pattern tells us about the status and power of various groups, even if it doesn't tell us about the experiences of every person in each group.

Interpreting Group Differences

It is important to be mindful of how we interpret group differences. A lack of sociological mindfulness can lead to interpretations that reinforce inequality. For example, on average, men are physically stronger than women. This is a clear pattern, but its meaning is often distorted.

To see the distortion, we should remember, first, that the difference is just an average difference. Not every man is stronger than every woman. Some women are stronger than some men, and the strongest women may be stronger than most men. We should also remember that the average difference is a result not only of biology but also of culture. If men are encouraged to develop their strength and women are not, that will lead to a group difference. If we are mindful of these matters, the "strength gap" between women and men does not seem terribly significant.

Yet this gap is often interpreted like so: "On average, men are stronger than women; therefore, men are stronger than women." That interpretation is misleading because it turns a group average into a claim about every member of the group. It is not true that "men are stronger than women," as if all men were stronger than all women.

Why would anyone make such a mistake in reasoning? Perhaps because of the value attached to bodily strength in our culture. Strength is usually seen as a desirable trait, especially for men. In addition, men have often cited strength as a reason for their domination of women. It is thus tempting, especially for men of average size and strength—men who could perhaps be handled like children by the strongest women—to turn an average difference into a claim about a universal difference between women and men.

The problem is not that men can't think straight about these matters. Once again there is a larger pattern here. Members of dominant groups often make the same kind of mistake. For example, whites, on average, have higher IQ scores than blacks. Although many blacks have far higher IQ scores than many whites, the average difference between the two groups is often seen by whites as meaning that whites are smarter than blacks. To whites, especially those whose IQ scores are merely average, that is a comforting, although illogical, conclusion.

(Having raised the issue, I should explain that the small black–white difference in IQ scores—a difference that persists even when schooling and social class are taken into account—has nothing to do with innate capacity. The difference results from two things. One is that many questions on IQ tests subtly favor people who are steeped in middle-class Euro-American culture, and this puts black students at a disadvantage. The other reason for the difference is that anxiety aroused by the meaning of IQ tests can lead black students to do less than their best. If you were told that your score on a test was going to be used as a measure of your human worth, or the worth of your people, your performance would no doubt be impaired by anxiety. It is also necessary to be mindful of context. In a society free from racism, these problems of bias and test anxiety would not arise.)

To be sociologically mindful when considering differences between groups, we should ask, "Is there more variation *within* these groups than *between* them?" If the people within a group are more different from each other—with regard to some characteristic—than from people in another group, then the difference between the groups is probably not meaningful.

Suppose, for example, that we wanted to know whether the women or the men in the town of Greasy Lake are kinder. Some people might guess, based on hearsay, that the women are kinder than the men. But if we wanted to know for sure, and if we wanted to know how big the difference was, we would have to measure kindness. Perhaps we could ask people how many acts of kindness they performed in the past year (presuming we could agree on what counts as an act of kindness). Anyhow, let's say that we get all the women and men in town to take the "kindness test" so that we can calculate a Kindness Quotient (KQ) for everyone.

It should be easy now to tell who is kinder, because all we have to do is calculate the average KQ score for each group. Suppose we find that the average score for men is higher than that for women. It might thus seem that we have our answer: men are kinder than women. Suppose, however, that KQ scores within the categories "women" and "men" vary greatly. In other words, in each category there is a wide range of scores, telling us that, when it comes to kindness, women can be very different from other women, and men can be very different from other men. Yet, because of the high scores of some men (who perhaps overrate their kindness) and the low scores of some women (who perhaps underrate theirs), it turns out that men as a group have a slightly higher average. Where does this leave us?

Being sociologically mindful, these results should tell us that we have been on a wild goose chase. If there is so much difference *within* the groups we are trying to compare, and relatively little difference *between* them, we should realize that the categories we began with—women and men—probably have nothing to do with whether people are kind. (We need not reach such conclusions by eyeballing the KQ scores; there are statistical means to tell if the differences are significant.)

The Kindness Quotient example might seem silly, but it is not so different from what psychologists who have studied "gender differences in personality" have done for many years. Ironically, the overall conclusion of many such studies is that, when it comes to personality, women and men are more alike than different. Sociological mindfulness would thus suggest looking for more meaningful groupings, if one must look for group differences at all.

A final point is that documenting a group difference is not the same as explaining it. To explain a group difference, it is necessary to look at the human action that underlies it. This is true of all patterns in the social world. Whatever kind of pattern we might be looking at, we should ask who does what to whom, where, when, and how, such that the pattern comes about. If we take this further step and try to unpack the process (see Chapter 13) that produces a pattern, we will be less likely to misinterpret it.

Trends and Tendencies

Some patterns are visible only over time. We can see them when we watch how the world changes. A change that is sustained over time—for example, the continuing increase in the human population—is a trend. To say that most new jobs created in the United States since the mid-1980s have been service (rather than industrial) jobs is to cite another trend. Part of being sociologically mindful is paying attention to such changes and wondering where they might lead.

As with other kinds of patterns, there can be trends within trends. For example, since 1800 the U.S. population has never declined or remained the same; it has always grown. That is the overall pattern. There have been times, however, when it has grown faster than others—for instance, in each decade following a decade in which a major war ended (e.g.,

1920–1930, 1870–1890, 1950–1960). We could thus say that there is a pattern within a pattern: overall growth, with periods of more rapid growth after wars. Again, to make sense of the whole, it is important to look for patterns within patterns.

Tendencies are patterns of probability. For example, chances are that people born into working-class families will end up in working-class jobs themselves. Of course, this is only a tendency. Some children from working-class or poor families will become doctors, lawyers, and professors. It is even possible that children of parents who are professionals will become factory workers, truck drivers, or trash collectors. Even so, the usual pattern—the strongest tendency—is for people to end up in about the same social class as their parents.

To see tendencies we must watch closely, over time, and track what happens and how often. Smokers, for instance, are fifteen to thirty times more likely to get lung cancer than non-smokers, depending on other risk factors. By mid-life, men get about a 45–70 percent greater payoff (in terms of earnings) from their education than women do, depending on the degree attained. These kinds of tendencies, like the tendency for women to outlive men, can be found by looking at group differences.

Trends and tendencies can remain invisible if we do not look at what happens in enough cases over a long enough period of time. Suppose you were the first person from a working-class family to go to college, and suppose that most of your friends in college are from similar backgrounds. It might thus seem wrong to say that children from working-class families tend to stay in the working class—after all, you and your friends are proof that class mobility is possible. Yes, but beating the odds doesn't mean that there are no odds.

To see the real tendencies we would have to look at representative samples of children from working-class families, over a long period of time, to see what kinds of jobs they ended up in. Only by looking at the big picture would the true tendency become apparent. Being sociologically mindful, we would want to avoid the mistake of overgeneralizing from personal experience and wait until we had information about many cases before saying what the pattern really is.

The point of trying to see trends and tendencies is to get a better sense of how the world works—although, again, observing a trend or tendency is not the same as explaining it. Doing that requires study of who is doing what to whom, where, how, and why. Seeing the trend or tendency is a step toward figuring these things out. Once we have identified the trend or tendency, we can begin trying to discern the human actions that produce it.

If we are not aware of the trend or tendency, we might not realize that there is any action for which to look.

By identifying trends and tendencies we can also get an idea of where we are going. What if corporations continue to outsource production and put people in the United States out of work? What if there are fewer and fewer secure jobs for people? What if the gap between the rich and the poor continues to widen? What if our inner cities continue to decay? What if the earth's population continues to grow at its current rate? What if more and more people feel they have no control over their lives? Where will these trends lead? What new problems will arise?

Sociological mindfulness does not answer these questions, though it does help us see why they are important to ask, and it may help us find better answers. Being sociologically mindful, we will see connections, we will see the social world being made by human action, and we will see how people's behavior is shaped by context. If we are mindful in these ways, we can arrive at a fuller understanding of the patterns in which we are caught up and that we might like to change.

Things That Go Together

Seeing patterns is often a matter of seeing what kinds of things tend to go together or happen together. One pattern in nature is for flight and feathers to go together. Any creature (other than an insect) that flies is more likely to have feathers than fins or fur. Perhaps that doesn't seem like a useful pattern to know about. Here, then, is another: any slithering legless creature with a triangular head is likely to be equipped with fangs and venom. Knowing about this pattern might save your life someday.

Creating knowledge about the world is largely a matter of discerning patterns. When we learn what tends to go with what, or what kinds of events tend to happen together, we begin to know what's going on. If we know the patterns by which the world operates, the world becomes a more predictable and controllable place. If we know the patterns, we can do better at avoiding or solving problems. If we know how things tend to happen, we can perhaps intervene and make them happen some other way.

Being sociologically mindful, however, we should recognize the difference between patterns in nature and patterns in the social world. Patterns in nature (e.g., the connection between flight and feathers) are not human inventions. Our ability to see and describe these patterns is socially constructed, but the patterns themselves are simply there. Patterns in the social world are the results of beliefs and cultural habits—our invented ways of doing things together. As such, these patterns are change-able. If people thought and acted differently, the patterns would change.

For example, you probably know that income tends to increase along with education. Just as feathers tend to go with flight, money tends to go with degrees and credentials. This pattern, however, is not a law of nature. We could change our economy to pay people for working hard—no matter what kind of work they do—rather than paying them for getting degrees. Or we could pay people based on how much money they need to care for themselves and their families. There are many possible arrangements, which is to say we could create different patterns.

Relationships among Variables

Some people will say that thinking sociologically is about chopping the social world into "variables" and then seeing how the variables are related. We could, for instance, measure income (dollars per year) and education (years of schooling) and see if they rise together or are related in some other way. Perhaps, after a certain point, more education produces no more income. If that is the pattern, it might be worth knowing about, especially if one is hoping that a Ph.D. will lead to a big salary.

We could also look for patterns using the Kindness Quotient. Perhaps education tends to increase kindness, so that college graduates have higher KQs, on average, than high school dropouts. On the other hand, income might tend to decrease kindness. This would mean that the effect of educa-tion is canceled out because education also tends to increase income. If so, this would explain why people who have gone to college are no kinder than anyone else. All this is silly, of course. It is just a way to illustrate how some people look for patterns in the social world.

Being mindful of patterns in this way is not always silly. It is worth knowing, for example, if people in certain racial, ethnic, or gender groups are more likely to be unemployed, paid low wages, or mistreated in some way. Looking at differences in group averages is one way to discern such patterns. Looking at what goes with what, under what conditions, is an-other way to get at patterns. Seeing these patterns, if they are indeed there, is essential to understanding how the social world works. But it is not enough.

To know that one variable goes with another is a starting point. Once we see a pattern, we must try to see how it is produced. Why, for example, does income tend to increase as skin color gets lighter? That is a troubling pattern that ought to be explained. To explain it, we would have to look closely at who does what to whom, how, and under what conditions, such that people with darker skins are paid less, on average. If we are sociologically mindful, we will pay attention to the people and actions that produce the patterns we see.

Patterns and Individual Lives

A satellite camera can show us that clouds and storms are patterned in ways that we can't see from the ground. Being sociologically mindful is like taking a satellite view of society. It means trying to see the patterns that are not evident as we muddle through from one situation to the next. Sociological mindfulness requires gaining altitude, so to speak, so that we can see the patterns of human action that swirl around us and in which we are caught up.

It is not easy to take this view. Usually we focus on our everyday problems. This is understandable, because these problems seem most pressing to us. We might also think that we have about as much chance of changing the social world as of changing the weather. So why bother with the big picture?

Being sociologically mindful, however, we will see that many of our daily struggles grow out of the larger patterns of human action in which we are caught up. If it is hard to achieve dignity, security, and peace in our lives, it is largely because we lack control over our workplaces, communities, and governments. If we are not mindful of how these patterned features of social life operate to diminish our control, we will never see how to change the conditions that keep generating many of the problems we face in everyday life.

One thing that is important to try to see when we look at patterns in social life is where we fit into them. Sometimes we are much like the typical case; sometimes we are right at the average; sometimes our lives play out according to the usual tendencies; sometimes we are at the center of the pattern. Other times we might be at odds with the pattern.

Perhaps our lives run against the grain. If so, we should try to understand why. For example, I said earlier that children tend to end up in about the same social class as their parents. But suppose that's not true for you. Suppose you have experienced "upward mobility"—that is, you have (or are on your way to getting) a more prestigious and better-paying job than either of your parents. This seems to break the pattern. How can you make sense of this?

You might think, "My life is different, because there is no usual tendency; every individual is unique." This would be incorrect. If most people born into any given social class end up in the same social class, that is hardly evidence of uniqueness. We can truthfully say that the *usual* tendency is for there to be little class mobility. So if, say, 10 percent do achieve class mobility, that is just another interesting piece of the pattern. Perhaps you are part of the 10 percent.

What is important, in any case, is to be sociologically mindful about how your life fits or doesn't fit the usual pattern. If it fits, ask how and why this is so. What do you have in common with other people whose lives have unfolded like yours? What kinds of circumstances do you share with them? What sorts of problems and opportunities? Being sociologically mindful, you will try to see how common contexts have created similar lives for you and others, whether you are in the 90 percent or the 10 percent. You can thus make better sense of the overall pattern by seeing how it connects to your life. By doing so, you can also make better sense of your own life.

Sociological mindfulness does not imply that people's lives can be understood simply by knowing the categories they fall into. Being a white male born into a middle-class family does not mean that your experiences will be the same as those of all white males born into middle-class families. Nor does it mean that you will have no experiences in common with people in other categories. Even so, by virtue of being in certain racial, ethnic, gender, and class categories you are likely to have a lot of experiences in common with others in the same categories. You are also likely to get caught up in similar patterns.

Trying to determine who or what is a typical case, examining differences between groups, and looking for trends and tendencies and for what goes with what are ways to see more about how the social world works. If we pay attention carefully, we will see large patterns and many smaller ones. Being sociologically mindful about our own lives, we will also try to see where we fit into these patterns. We may thus discover that many of our "personal" habits of thought and behavior are adaptations to the larger patterns of social life that carry us along, although we need not resign ourselves to being carried along. Being sociologically mindful of patterns in social life makes it possible to change them.

Dialogue

The Language of Social Structure

A comment I have heard from some teachers is that *TSEL* "focuses on the micro level" and does not say enough about social structure. I do not think this is correct, though I understand why it might seem so. It has to do with misunderstanding what social structure is and how it is related to the goings-on of everyday life. Perhaps I can clear this up.

I have already said that much of everyday life is a matter of routine. Customs and habits can change, of course. But in the short run they tend to be fairly stable. And so we see people doing things together, day in and day out, in customary and habitual ways. We see, in other words, stable patterns of action and interaction. Many sociologists use the term "social structure" to refer to these patterns.

We can also talk about how a society is organized. We might look, for example, at how the economy is organized, how education is organized, how health care is organized, how government is organized, how the police and courts are organized, how family life is organized, and so on. In each case, we would look at who does what with whom, how they do it, and what is accomplished. Sociologists might also look at how these different realms of activity are linked. To study these matters is to study social structure.

Here is yet another way of putting it. If we say that one society is based on hunting and gathering and is ruled by tribal elders, another is based on settled agriculture and is ruled by warrior aristocrats, and another is based on industrial production and is ruled by property owners, we are speaking of each society having a different social structure. Such large-scale arrangements are what some sociologists call the "macro" features of a society.

In sociology, the term *micro* (contrasted with *macro*) does not refer to tiny things that are hard to see. This term usually refers to what goes on between people in concrete situations. To study face-to-face interaction is thought of, by many sociologists, as studying the micro aspect of social life. If you studied, for example, precisely how lobbyists talk to elected officials, this would be to study something micro. If you studied how international trade policies affect domestic labor markets and thus in turn affect class formation, this would be to study something macro.

If you recall the discussion of reification in Chapter 2, you might see a problem with focusing solely on what is considered macro. It is fine to say that society operates like a kind of system, such that a change in one thing (trade policies) can lead to changes in other things (labor markets, social classes). We can even say that such dynamics are beyond the full awareness or control of any single group, so that society often seems to have a mind of its own. Yet we must be cautious about making people disappear.

We should not forget that what happens in the social world happens because people create and act on certain meanings, identify themselves and others in certain ways, and define situations in certain ways. All of this is accomplished through interaction, in person or at a distance (e.g., as I am now interacting with you, or via mass media, such as television). Likewise, it is fine to talk about social structure as long as we remember that what we are calling "structure" is constituted by action—people doing things together in orderly and stable ways.

Yet even while I stress the importance of being mindful of how social life is created and sustained through interaction, this does not imply ignoring big things like capitalism, corporate power, the federal government, the education system, social classes, nationhood, or even world systems. We should of course be mindful about these "structural" matters—again provided that we do not lose sight of their interactional foundations.

Perhaps this is more than you wanted to know about sociology's jargon. But if you are reading *TSEL* for a sociology course, then you will probably run into this jargon, and it will help to know what it means. You will also be better equipped to make sense of what people mean when they use a different sociological language. If you encounter terms like *social structure* or, worse, *macrostructural phenomena*, pause to consider what they mean. Often, when the meaning is unpacked, you will arrive back at interaction, which will remain to be analyzed.

A Note on Theory

When I teach courses on social theory and want to talk about what a theory is, I like to ask, "Is evolution a fact or a theory?" This is a good discussion question because most people can be counted on to say that it's a theory. I then explain why that answer is wrong.

It's true that most people, including most scientists, biology teachers, and science writers, refer to the "theory of evolution." But this phrase is misleading, because a lot of people take the word "theory" to mean guess or hunch. Referring to the *theory* of evolution thus creates the impression in many people's minds that scientists are just guessing that evolution occurred. They're not.

The proposition that all life forms, including humans, evolved (or, in Charles Darwin's phrase, "descended with modification") from prior life forms is as solid a fact as can be found in science. Evidence from many disciplines—mainly physics, chemistry, biology, genetics, geology, and paleontology—documents the occurrence of evolution. In view of this evidence, evolution is no more in doubt among scientists than is the proposition that the earth revolves around the sun.

So, properly speaking, we might say, "Evolution is a fact that scientists have used the theory of natural selection to explain." Natural selection was Darwin's favored theory. Since his day, scientists have learned that sexual selection, genetic drift, mutation, and environmental change also drive evolution. There are indeed arguments about which process is most important, about how these processes affect each other, and about how quickly they can produce change.

Theories, then, are ideas devised to make sense of facts or, in fancier terms, "to explain patterns in the data." A theory that explains the most facts, that makes no assumptions that are implausible in light of what else we know, that is logically coherent, and that makes correct predictions is usually said to be a better theory than one that doesn't meet these criteria. Because theories can also shape our perceptions of what the facts *are*, it's good to be able to try out different theoretical perspectives. We might eventually decide to reject a theory, but first we should test it to see if it can help us identify and explain patterns that we might otherwise overlook.

Paths for Reflection

1. If you look at a globe or a map of the world, you will notice that the contours of the continents match each other like pieces of a puzzle. It looks as if the continents, if you could move them around, would fit together into one giant landmass. This matching of land contours was obvious for a long time, but most scientists took it as an illusion arising out of mere coincidence. What had to happen before geologists could see this "illusion" as a meaningful pattern? (It might help to Google *plate tectonics*.) In the case of the natural world, new ideas can help us see patterns that exist apart from human action. How might a new idea actually create or change a pattern in the social world?

2. Two students are talking about how people in similar kinds of jobs tend to have similar personality traits. They agree that such a pattern exists. But one says that this is because jobs shape people's personalities, while the other says people's personalities determine the jobs they end up in. Suppose they ask you to help them figure out who is correct. What kind of data would be needed to identify the true pattern? Suppose it turned out that, everything else being equal, jobs shape people more than people shape their jobs. How would you make sense of this pattern?

3. A number of studies have shown that elementary school teachers often treat girls and boys differently in the classroom. Most teachers deny doing this, claiming that they give girls and boys the same kind and

amount of attention. In some cases, even after observers reported results showing that the teachers gave boys more attention, some teachers still refused to believe they were doing it. Only when watching themselves on videotape did they acknowledge the patterns in their behavior. How would you explain the teachers' refusal to see these patterns? What kinds of patterns in your behavior are likely to be hardest to see, and why?

Related Readings

Ball, Philip. (2016). *Patterns in Nature: Why the Natural World Looks the Way It Does.* Chicago: University of Chicago Press.

Becker, Howard S. (1998). *Tricks of the Trade.* Chicago: University of Chicago Press.

Epstein, Cynthia Fuchs. (1988). *Deceptive Distinctions: Sex, Gender, and the Social Order.* New Haven, CT: Yale University Press.

Gould, Stephen J. (1981). *The Mismeasure of Man.* New York: Norton.

Inzlicht, Michael, & Schmader, Toni. (2011). *Stereotype Threat.* New York: Oxford University Press.

Kohn, Melvin L., & Schooler, Carmi. (1983). *Work and Personality.* Norwood, NJ: Ablex.

Laszlo, Ervin. (1972). *The Systems View of the World.* New York: Braziller.

Nisbett, Richard E., & Ross, Lee. (1980). *Human Inference.* Englewood Cliffs, NJ: Prentice Hall.

Pagels, Heinz. (1988). *The Dreams of Reason.* New York: Bantam.

Sadker, Myra, & Sadker, David. (1994). *Failing at Fairness: How Our Schools Cheat Girls.* New York: Touchstone/Simon & Schuster.

Zerubavel, Eviatar. (1997). *Social Mindscapes.* Cambridge, MA: Harvard University Press.

CHAPTER 8

....

Contingency and Cause

What caused you to read this book? That might seem like an easy question, but, in fact, it is so hard that you could never answer it fully. To do so you would have to say how you became able and willing to read this book. You would also have to say how reading, writing, and book publishing came to exist, how this particular book came to be, how you and I came to be, and how you and this book fell together. All that is more than you could explain.

In everyday life we don't have to give an account of the universe to explain why we read a book. Most people are satisfied if we say, "It looked interesting," or "It was assigned." Even so, if language and books, you and I, and the circumstances that brought this book into your hands had not come into existence, this moment would not be happening. Everything that led to your act of reading these words is part of what caused it. No one could ever identify all these causes, each of which has causes of its own.

Here is another question: what causes colds? You might say, "People catch what we call a 'cold' when their mucous membranes become infected with a rhinovirus." That answer is right, as far as it goes. The real situation, however, is more complicated.

For one thing, rhinoviruses don't always cause trouble. The immune system normally keeps them in check unless it is weakened for some reason. So we must think about what causes the immune system to weaken. We must also think about how the environment allows rhinoviruses to survive long enough to be transmitted and about what kind of behavior transmits them. A good explanation of why people catch colds would thus have to go beyond "bug gets into body, body comes down with cold."

Part of being sociologically mindful is recognizing that all explanations are incomplete. In trying to say what causes an event, a behavior, or a trend, we always face the impossibility of saying how all the enabling conditions came about. So we have no choice but to take most of these conditions for granted and settle for incomplete explanations of why things happen as they do. Such explanations are still useful, of course. You don't need to know how an engine works to know that if you turn the key it will (usually) cause the car to start.

In trying to make sense of the social world, we often try to say what causes things to happen as they do. We don't usually care if our explanations are incomplete, as long as they make the world more predictable and controllable. Sometimes our explanations seem so good that we think we've found the One True Cause of an event. But this is an illusion. Events are the result not of a single cause but of a web of causes. Circumstances must come together in just the right way, at just the right time, to make things happen as they do. All events, in other words, are *contingent*, meaning that they are the result of a unique mix of circumstances and actions.

Perhaps the example of the 1991 Persian Gulf War can make this idea of contingency more concrete. Looking back, can we say what caused the Gulf War? Did it have one true cause? If you read about the war, you will find that each of these has been suggested as its primary cause:

- George Bush, then president of the United States, ordered the use of military force against Iraq because he wanted to raise his standing in the polls, distract attention from the nation's economic problems, make his place in history, and prove he was a man.
- The profits of U.S. oil corporations were threatened by Iraq's takeover of Kuwait, and so George Bush, acting on behalf of those corporations, used violence to put Saddam Hussein, the leader of Iraq, back in his place and restore U.S. control of the Middle East.
- Capitalists in developed countries profit by exploiting less developed countries for their labor and raw materials, and so any attempts by these countries to get free from capitalist control cannot be tolerated; the United States thus crushed Iraq to show leaders of other less-developed countries what would happen if they got out of line.
- The Gulf War was fought to help justify the U.S. government's continuing huge expenditures on the military by showing that, even

if the Soviet Union was no longer a serious threat, a strong military is still necessary to put down ruffians like Saddam Hussein.

Is one of these the true cause of the first Gulf War? Each is plausible, and they are not incompatible; they could all be true. Perhaps (if you have other knowledge about this episode in U.S. history) you can think of other causes. What is important to see is that each of these explanations leaves much unsaid. Being sociologically mindful, we should pause to consider what is left out.

Nothing is said, for instance, about why the U.S. economy depends on imported oil, why people in the United States feel entitled to have access to the natural resources of other countries, why or how Saddam Hussein happened to have a well-equipped army at his disposal, why U.S. soldiers were willing to follow orders to kill people in another country, or why most U.S. citizens were willing to accept this violence being done by their government.

The Gulf War was *contingent on* these conditions. If conditions had been different, the war could not have happened. We should thus be wary of any claims that the war had only one cause. The same principle applies to all events, large and small. Being sociologically mindful, we will avoid rushing to identify a single cause and instead try to see how events emerge out of a combination of circumstances and actions.

We can still try to determine whether certain actions or conditions—like a virus getting into the body, an idea getting into minds, or weapons getting into the hands of soldiers—are necessary to make something happen. Even so, we must see that what ultimately happens depends on many other circumstances, some stable and some rapidly changing, coming together in just the right way. If we are mindful of how this swirl of contingencies can sometimes give rise to terrible events, we will pay attention to how things are shaping up at any given time.

Stability and Change

Perhaps I make it seem that social life is random and chaotic, as if every event is unique and surprising. Clearly, this isn't true. Most of the time social life is orderly and predictable. You might think that this orderliness refutes the idea that events and actions always arise out of a swirl of contingencies. There is really no contradiction, however; the social world is both changing and stable at the same time.

Because human lives are short, we often mistake temporary stability for permanence. You might think this book, for example, will last a long time. Yet even now it is crumbling to dust, as are all the mountains and buildings of the world. The sun and earth might seem truly permanent; but in another 4 billion years the sun will burn out, collapse, and then explode to obliterate the earth before collapsing again. So even the planet on which we live is temporary.

Consider too that it takes work to keep the world orderly. If the sun didn't pump energy into the earth's atmosphere, all the plants and animals we know—including ourselves—would soon vanish. To keep the social world humming along from day to day we have to put energy into forming and transmitting cultural habits. If we didn't do so, order would break down. The order we see in the world is thus not simply how things are or the result of inertia. Order and stability are the results of action.

So when circumstances shape up in just the right way to produce surprising change, it is always against the background of conditions that are relatively stable. In the case of the first Gulf War, the background was an oil-hungry global economy dominated by a few powerful capitalist nations. Even though the war was brief, these background conditions existed before the war and still exist today. Being sociologically mindful, we remember not to take such conditions for granted, seeing them as part of the web of causes and the swirl of contingencies out of which emerges all that is predictable or surprising.

Being sociologically mindful means recognizing not only that our explanations are always incomplete, but also trying to see *how* they are selective and incomplete. Why do we choose to identify certain conditions as causes, while taking other conditions for granted? The answer lies in examining our preferences for seeing some things as extraordinary, while not seeing other things at all.

Reasons, Conditions, and the Possibility of Choice

If you throw a piece of chalk out the window and it falls to the ground, it would be reasonable to say that gravity caused it to fall. To understand why this happened, you might read a physics book. You would not ask the chalk to explain why it fell. However, if you threw yourself out of a window and fell to the ground, we would want to know why. Most people would not accept "gravity" for an answer, if you could answer at all.

Our actions are not caused by natural forces—the way that gravity causes chalk to fall. Does it make sense to say that heat causes people to go to the beach? Even though a lot of people might go to the beach when it gets hot, to say that the weather caused them to go would be silly. People can choose other ways to cool off. Or they can choose to do nothing at all. Chalk can't make choices, so it is fair to apply the language of causes to chalk and other inanimate objects. We should be wary, however, of applying this language to humans.

One time in class a student said, "I read in a textbook for another class that race causes criminal defendants to get longer sentences." He meant that black people who are convicted of crimes tend to get longer jail and prison sentences than whites who are convicted of similar crimes. He was right about the pattern; black people do tend to get longer sentences, on average, for the same crimes, all else being equal. But it was misleading, I said, to say that this pattern was caused by race.

Being sociologically mindful, we would try to understand this pattern by looking at who is doing what to whom. Being sentenced to jail or prison is not something that just happens, like rain falling on one's head. Judges make decisions about these matters. So then we must ask, Why do judges give longer sentences to black people? Does race *cause* them to do it? Not really—no more than heat causes people to go to the beach.

As we all do, judges make decisions about people's character, and one sign of character on which judges rely, perhaps unconsciously, is skin color. In our kind of racist society, African features are often taken as signs of bad character. Judges, most of whom are white, may thus decide that blacks need or deserve harsher punishment than whites. But it is not a defendant's race that causes a judge to see things this way. The problem, rather, is a body of racist beliefs and biases that affect how judges think and choose to act.

We should not attribute the harsher sentences merely to ideas in judges' minds. Here, too, there is a web of causality. To explain the pattern of harsher sentencing we would have to know, for example, why judges feel pressure to appear tough; how images of black people have been shaped by the media; and why so many white people, not only judges, persist in seeing skin color as a sign of character. We should also keep in mind that, unlike gravity, all of these "social causes" are changeable.

Enabling Conditions

Another time, during a discussion about pornography, a student said, "I've read the chapter in the book and I can't tell if the author is saying that pornography causes sexual violence or not. Please just tell me if it does." This student wanted a yes-or-no answer and probably thought I was waffling when I refused to give one.

You can probably see why a statement such as "Pornography causes sexual violence" is wrong. Pornography is not a natural force that causes people to behave in any particular way. But if you are mindful of connections and context and the web of causality, you can probably also see why it is wrong to say, "Pornography has nothing to do with sexual violence." Pornography indeed has something to do with sexual violence by men against women, but the connection is not simply cause and effect.

Sexual violence involves one person hurting another. For one person to inflict harm on another, the person doing the harm must disregard the feelings of the person being harmed. It is as if the injurer treats the other as an object—a thing with no feelings worthy of respect. How do some people's feelings come to be seen as unworthy of respect? This can happen only because some people create and spread the idea that other people's feelings don't matter.

Through words and pictures, pornography conveys ideas about women, ideas that can affect men's thinking about women. One idea conveyed by much pornography is that women are always ready and willing, despite outward appearances, to satisfy men's sexual desires. Another idea is that women are desirable because of their looks and their willingness to serve men sexually. A woman's thoughts and feelings, in other words, are less important than the shape of her breasts or her interest in having sex with men.

The ready availability of pornographic films and images (you could probably find them in a nearby grocery store or certainly on the Internet) also conveys a message: it is okay to portray women as sex objects. If pornographic representations of women are everywhere and there is little protest about this, then it can begin to seem natural and perfectly acceptable to view women as sex objects.

Do these ideas and their pervasiveness cause sexual violence? No, that is too simple a way to put it. Most men do not look at pornography and then feel compelled to commit sexual violence, even if they are aroused by the images. But this is not proof that pornography and sexual violence are unrelated. Being mindful about cause and contingency, we can see pornography and its ready availability as enabling conditions.

In our culture, young men are taught to believe that manhood is signified by having sex with women. So one way that men compete with each other—to see who is more of a man—is by trying to score sexual conquests. In this competition a man's goal is to get a woman to comply with his sexual wishes. Her feelings are worth considering only if they impede a man's sexual advances. A woman's feelings are thus not respected but are seen as problems for a man to overcome.

The larger context in which this competition for manhood status goes on ensures that most men will lose, because winning depends not only on sexual prowess but also on wealth and power, of which most men have little. As you might imagine, or as you might know from your own experience, these conditions can make many men feel angry and insecure. Now add pornography, which reinforces the ideas that women are sexual objects and that men know women's sexual desires better than women do. Under these conditions, sexual coercion, in violent and subtle forms, is likely to occur. And often it does.

Being sociologically mindful about the "causes" of sexual violence, we arrive back at the idea of contingency. We have seen sexual violence as emerging from a conjunction of enabling conditions. So while we cannot say "Pornography causes sexual violence," we can say that it helps create the conditions that enable and promote sexual violence. In this sense, pornography is one of a multitude of causes, a strand in the web.

If we are mindful about cause in this way, we can also see why abolishing pornography would not end sexual violence. One reason is that the ideas that promote sexual violence are not found only in pornography. And most of the other enabling conditions would not be changed by a ban on pornography. Then again, as some people argue, abolishing pornography might reduce sexual violence by making the ideas it conveys less readily available and by making it clear that those ideas are harmful and should be rejected.

Reason and Choice

Raising the possibility of banning pornography brings us back to the matter of choice. Suppose that many people came to see pornography as a contributing cause of sexual violence. Suppose that many people came to see that using women's bodies to sell beer and cars and sporting events was also part of the problem. What then? Some people might say, "That's just how things are; there's nothing we can do about it." Others might say, "If these things cause problems, even if they are not the only causes, why accept them? If we have good reasons to get rid of them, let's do so."

To arrive at a sound opinion about whether we should abolish pornography or advertising that exploits women's bodies would require considering more issues than I have raised here. In any case, it would be incorrect to say, "There is nothing we can do; this is just how the world is; we must live with all the bad effects of pornography and sexist advertising." Being sociologically mindful, we see that enabling conditions can be changed. We can decide to do things differently and thus encourage different results.

Applying the language of cause to human behavior can lead us to forget that people act on ideas and meanings and that people can rethink their ideas and meanings and choose to act differently. Of course, if people never question the ideas and meanings on which they act, then they will keep acting in the same old ways. If people believe that skin color is a sign of character, then it might seem as if race causes discrimination. Being sociologically mindful, however, we see that humans create the ideas and conditions that sustain these patterns of behavior, patterns that mindfulness gives us the power to change.

Rules as Constructed Causes

If a teacher grades on a curve, giving A's to only the top 10 percent of the students in a class, does this grading scheme *cause* students in the top 10 percent of the class to get A's? You might say no, because the scheme is not a natural force; it is merely a chosen way of doing things. But the rule that says "Only the top 10 percent get A's" has a kind of causal force because it always leads to certain results. No matter how hard students try or how well the teacher teaches, only 10 percent will get A's. There is no way around this as long as the 10-percent rule is followed.

The rules that guide a way of doing things together are like the rules of a game. As long as the rules are followed, certain results are inevitable. In tennis, for example, the rules ensure that no match ends in a tie; the rules of tennis always produce a winner and a loser. What's more, you can't win by jumping the net and tickling your opponent. That is not allowed.

Rules also produce unintended consequences. For instance, the rules of competitive sports ensure not only that there will be winners, but also that most people will be losers and will suffer some feelings of anxiety and dejection. No one necessarily intends for this to happen, yet the logic of competitive sports makes it inevitable.

Part of being sociologically mindful is looking at the rules that govern social arrangements and asking what sorts of results those rules are bound to produce, regardless of people's intentions. We can do this with games, organizations, economies, and governments—with any patterned way of doing things together. All will operate according to some discernible rules and will, if the rules are followed, produce certain inevitable results. Capitalism is a good example.

A Life-and-Death Game

The most basic legal rule of capitalism is that a few people are allowed to control great wealth and property. If capitalists think they can make more money by shutting down a factory and putting thousands of people out of work, they have the legal right to do so. If capitalists think they can make more money in the long run by letting their property sit idle, they can let it sit, even if people are starving and could use the property to support themselves. The rule, in brief, is that property rights take priority over human needs.

Capitalism's other basic rule is this: to make the most profit, get as much work out of workers as possible, for the lowest possible wage. Paying workers less means that products can be sold for less, while still making a profit. A firm that pays its workers more will make less profit unless it can sell its products at a higher price. But raising prices usually means losing customers, who can pay less elsewhere. So a capitalist who doesn't drive workers hard and keep wages low is likely to go out of business. This isn't a matter of people being nice or not; it's just what capitalists must do to survive.

What happens when an economy operates by these rules? For one thing, there will always be inequality in wealth, since capitalists control the means to create vast wealth for themselves, whereas workers have only their time and energy to sell for a wage. Inequality will also tend to grow, although workers, if they are organized, can resist this. It is also likely that a great many people will be allowed to go without work, or with too little work to make a decent living, so that capitalists can control workers by threatening to replace them with more desperate people.

One time when I was talking about how capitalism works, a student (a business major) folded his arms across his chest and leaned back in his chair. "Are you saying that capitalism causes poverty?" he asked, with a mix of anger and skepticism in his voice. Before I could answer, he sat straight up and added, "It seems to me that capitalism *creates* jobs." This was a useful challenge.

Yes, capitalists create jobs, I said, but only if doing so will yield profits. If they did so for any other reason, they would not survive as capitalists. I said that capitalists will destroy any number of decent-paying jobs if they can replace them with low-paying jobs, because capitalists make more money when they can reduce the total amount they pay for labor. In fact, I said, capitalists create jobs only when necessary, try to pay as little as possible when they do, and try to get rid of jobs if they can, often by means of automation.

Much of what I said seemed to be familiar to this student from his business courses. But he was still unhappy with my way of putting things. He said, "Of course, businessmen try to make a profit, but that doesn't necessarily cause poverty." He was right. I said that even though capitalists had incentive to push wages down to the poverty level, that didn't mean they could always do it. Workers sometimes resist successfully; and sometimes workers with special skills can command high wages.

To get back to his point about poverty, I asked him, "So why is it that people will take such lousy jobs?" He said, "For one thing, people need to work, and then there are always people who don't have enough education to get anything better or enough self-esteem to try." I said that his first point—about people needing to work—was important. If people have no other way to survive, then we should not be surprised if they take whatever jobs they can get.

His point about education led me to propose a thought experiment. "Suppose," I said, "that everyone had a Ph.D. and high self-esteem. What then? Would everyone get a good job?" While he puzzled this out, another student said, "I don't think everybody could have a good job, because someone would still have to clean floors and pick up garbage and dig ditches. And even if people with Ph.D.'s were willing to do that, there probably still wouldn't be enough jobs for everybody. Look at how much unemployment there is now. There just aren't enough jobs to go around." The business major admitted that this was true.

"So, then," I asked, "why don't we use the government to create jobs for everyone, so that everyone who wants to work can have a decent job?" This time the business major answered, "Businessmen wouldn't like that." I said he was right, and that business*women* wouldn't like it, either. But why? Don't employers often criticize welfare and say that everyone should work? If so, why would they object to using the government to create jobs? He answered, "Well, I think it's like you said. If everybody knew they could get a decent job, they'd be a lot fussier and less willing to work at a crappy job for low pay. That would probably mean that employers would have to pay people more to keep them, and that would hurt profits." I was pleased that he was seeing these connections.

We still had not answered the question about poverty. "So does this mean that poverty is an inevitable result of how capitalism works?" I asked. No one spoke, so I rephrased the question. "If a capitalist economy can produce as much wealth as ours does, why does anyone have to be poor?" After a few moments a student said, "I don't think anyone would *have* to be poor; it's just a matter of how the wealth is distributed, and those who have it aren't going to give it up, at least not without a fight." Now we were getting somewhere.

"Where would the fight take place?" I asked. Another student said, "If you're talking about using the government to create jobs, then I suppose it would be a political fight." I asked who would win. We agreed that capitalists—those who benefited from conditions that forced people into lousy jobs—would probably win because they had more resources and more control over government. "Would they *necessarily* win?" I asked. The business major said, "Not necessarily. If workers in all industries got together, they could win. But it would take a huge fight."

We were running out of time, so I tried to sum things up. Capitalism tends to push working people toward poverty, I said, because profits depend on keeping wages low and even putting people out of work if machines can do the work more cheaply. Poverty also benefits capitalists because it means that many people will be desperate for jobs at any wage. Capitalists are thus in no hurry to end poverty. So while capitalism doesn't inevitably cause poverty, it does create incentives for capitalists to act in ways that make poverty a likely result, especially if workers are too disorganized to fight back.

The point of telling this is not to show that capitalism is all bad, but that certain bad results—inequality, lousy jobs, unemployment, poverty— stem from the way that capitalism works. If we think of capitalism as a kind of game, one that is played for high stakes and for keeps, we see that its rules make some bad results inevitable and others extremely likely. Once people are locked into the game, these results are bound to come about unless people change or break the rules.

Avoiding Reductionism

The rules that underlie social arrangements are seldom spelled out like the Ten Commandments. They are more like a hidden logic that has to be discovered. But once we see what the rules are, we can consider their consequences. It is like saying, "If we do things together in this way, if we follow these rules, where will it lead? What sorts of results will we create for ourselves?" These are just the first questions, of course. Being sociologically mindful, we would also ask who makes the rules and who benefits from them.

Being mindful about rules as causes can also help us avoid trying to explain social life in psychological ways, a mistake called "reductionism." For example, if someone said that football was violent because football players have personalities that make them prone to violence, that would be reductionist. Football is violent because of the rules of the game. It can be more or less violent, depending on how hard it is played, but the basic rules of football require people to slam into each other.

A lack of sociological mindfulness leads many people to fall into reductionist thinking. For example, many people believe that poverty is caused by laziness. But if millions of people are poor even though they work hard at jobs that don't pay decent wages, then it is wrong to attribute the problem to a character flaw. If we are sociologically mindful, we will pay attention to the rules of the game in which people are caught. In this case we should be able to see that the problem is not lazy or greedy individuals, but rules that cause people to treat each other as tools for profit-making rather than as human beings.

Chance, Pattern, and Paths

To say that people are "caught in the rules of a game" might make it seem as if the paths of people's lives are set by these rules. Not exactly. Even in sports, the rules say only how a game should be played; they do not say what will happen in the game or how it will turn out. There can always be surprises. No matter how many spoken and unspoken rules there might be, social life remains a swirl of contingencies out of which can emerge events that no one expects.

We see this when we watch people's lives unfold. No matter how much we know about a person's background, we can still be wrong when we guess how that person's life will turn out. But this doesn't mean that it's all a matter of chance. In people's lives, as in social life more generally, there is both chance and pattern. Being sociologically mindful, we will try to see how chance and pattern are linked. Perhaps the best way to show this is with a story that has two endings, either of which could be true. Here is the story.

*   *   *

Moira needed an elective. A friend told her to take Professor Valkyrie, but Moira had no interest in philosophy. "Besides," Moira said, "I can barely make sense of what's going on in English 212. I'd be way over my head in philosophy." Her friend said, "Yeah, I expected philosophy to be either totally boring or impossible to understand—you know, like Plato and stuff. But Valkyrie's great. She really makes you think. You ought to try her." When it came time to register, the astronomy class that Moira wanted was full. The only class that fit her schedule was Introduction to Philosophy, taught by Professor Valkyrie.

Moira's friend was right. Professor Valkyrie was good. She could explain complex ideas in a way that made them understandable. She also tied philosophy back to problems in everyday life. Moira liked this and found that it was helping her make sense of a lot of things. Moira worked hard in the course and impressed Professor Valkyrie. At the end of the semester Valkyrie wrote on Moira's final paper, "You've come a long way. Your writing and thinking are first-rate. If you ever need a letter of recommendation, let me know."

A few weeks later, after the spring semester had ended, Professor Valkyrie was going to lunch when she ran into a professor from another department. They decided to try the Penny University, a new café near campus. The food, as it turned out, was okay, but the service was slow and the cappuccino wasn't hot enough. It was as if no one had taught the people behind the counter how to do their jobs.

As they walked back to campus, the other professor said to Valkyrie, "The service at that place reminds me that my research assistant has got to go. He's screwed up too many times. I need someone more dependable, but I don't know where I'm going to find anyone during the summer." Professor Valkyrie said she knew a student who was sharp and might still need a job. When they got back to campus, they looked up Moira's phone number.

The other professor called Moira, who said she was willing to quit at GrabnGo if the research assistant job worked out. They arranged for Moira to come in the next morning at nine o'clock for an interview. Moira was excited about the prospect of better pay and more interesting work, but she was nervous, too. Even though she'd done well in Professor Valkyrie's course, Moira wasn't sure she was smart enough to do research.

Moira wore what she thought of as sensible clothes—nice, but not too fancy. She didn't want to give the impression that she cared more about clothes than about books and ideas. And even though she'd had to clean up her roommate's dishes before she could eat breakfast, Moira left in plenty of time to be on campus by eight thirty. She certainly didn't want to be late for a job interview.

About three blocks from her apartment, Moira was starting to make a right turn when a bird flew into her windshield. There was a splash of blue feathers and Moira jerked the steering wheel slightly, enough to cause the right rear tire to bounce over the curb. She stopped the car and stared at the spot on the windshield where the bird had hit. Moira felt sad, as if she had just intervened in the bird's life, only to destroy it. A car honked and Moira realized she was blocking traffic. "It wasn't my fault," she thought, taking a deep breath, "these things just happen. I'd better get going or I'll be late."

Moira had gone only another block when she heard a flap-flap-flap sound coming from the back of the car. The tire that had hit the curb was flat. "Shit!" Moira hissed to the inside of the car, checking her watch and pounding the steering wheel with her fist. She found a spot to pull over and quickly got to work changing the tire. As Moira jacked up the car, she kept seeing the bird hit the windshield. Now it made her angry, as if the bird had intervened in her life, knocking her off course.

Changing the tire left Moira dirty and sweaty. She knew she would be late for the interview and would be a mess when she got there. Moira used her cell phone to call the professor and tell her what had happened. The professor said, "I see. Well, look, I've got another person I'm talking to about this job and I need to hire someone today. So I'll call you if I still need someone tomorrow." That was the last Moira heard from her. Later, when Professor Valkyrie asked the other professor what had happened with Moira, she said, "We arranged an interview but she didn't show. She called and gave me a flat-tire story. And frankly, I'd had enough of those sorts of excuses from the guy I fired. So I found somebody else."

Moira was disappointed about not even getting a shot at the job. She could tell that the professor didn't believe her about the flat tire. For a moment she fantasized about rolling the damaged tire into the professor's office and saying. "Here's the tire I told you about. I wrote my phone number on it in case you ever want to call me about another job." But all Moira could do was to go back to work at GrabnGo and try to save money for school.

Later that summer the assistant manager left and Moira was asked if she wanted the job. She wasn't sure. Moira had hoped to get her degree and a professional job of some kind. But with the exception of Professor Valkyrie's course, she hadn't exactly been taking college by storm, and she was tired of being broke. So she decided to take a year off from school and give the job a try. Moira figured that if she hated it, she could always quit and go back to school in the spring.

Moira found that she liked running the store. It was a challenge, at first, to learn how to do inventory, order stock, schedule maintenance, and keep track of payroll. Doing all this gave Moira a sense of competence. The hardest part of the job was not the job at all, but the loneliness she felt. She missed her friends from college.

That fall Moira started dating a guy who delivered beer to the store. At first she didn't want to get serious, but one thing led to another, and by January they were living together. After some adjustment, the arrangement seemed to suit them fine. A few months later, Moira and her partner were vacationing in Virginia. One morning, while feeling very much in love, they decided to get married—and they did, that afternoon.

Soon after they got back from the trip, Moira was offered the job of manager at a GrabnGo store in another part of town. By now Moira had found a new circle of friends and was thinking less and less about going back to school. "Why bother?" she thought, since she could make what seemed like good money as a GrabnGo manager. Her new husband had never liked the college idea, either.

Moira ran a good store and hoped to become a regional manager for the company. But three times she was passed over for promotions. Twice the jobs went to men who were a few years older and had degrees. Moira didn't see why a degree was necessary, but she didn't think it was unfair if someone with a degree edged her out—if everything else was equal. A year later, a slightly younger man who had been with the company less time than she had, and who didn't have a degree, was promoted to regional manager. Moira began to wonder what was going on.

After four years as a store manager, Moira was bored. She had learned all there was to know about running a GrabnGo store. So when she found out she was pregnant, it wasn't that hard to decide to quit and stay home to raise the child. Moira thought she would have one more child after that, and then, after both were grown, maybe go back to college.

That is one ending to the story. Here is another.

Moira was locking the front door behind her when she felt a flash of panic. Had she turned off the stove? She opened the door and went back in to check. Of course it was off. She had never forgotten to turn off the stove. But whenever she felt nervous about something, she imagined leaving it on and being blamed for burning the house down. "Maybe I should stick to cold cereal in the morning," Moira thought, as she spun around and headed to her interview.

About three blocks from her apartment, as Moira was turning a corner, a bluebird darted in front of her windshield. It came so close that she could see it was carrying a piece of straw in its beak. Then she remembered one of her grandmother's old sayings, "If the first bird you see in the morning is blue, you'll have good luck that day." Moira smiled and relaxed a bit as that thought crossed her mind. "Thanks, Grandma," she said out loud, feeling sure she hadn't seen any other birds that morning.

Moira found a parking spot near the professor's building. She sat on a bench outside the building for a few minutes, then went in and climbed the stairs to the third floor. Moira was still ten minutes early and was reading cartoons on office doors when a tall, dark-skinned woman with braided hair came down the hall. She was carrying a leather shoulder bag and wearing jeans and a gold vest over a white T-shirt. Her round wire-rimmed glasses matched the vest. "You must be Moira," the woman said. "I'm Professor Sesheta. Come in and have a seat. Would you like some coffee?"

The interview went well. Moira liked the professor, who was not what Moira had expected. When Moira asked what the job entailed, the professor pointed to a table in the corner of her office. It was piled two feet high with manuscripts and old newspapers. "The first task would be to go through that mess and create a bibliographic database," the professor said. "It isn't hard, once you get the hang of it, but you have to be careful and precise."

Moira admitted that, other than writing papers for classes, she had no experience doing this sort of thing. After talking for about an hour, the professor surprised Moira again when she asked, "When can you start?"

Moira gave her notice at GrabnGo and started working for the professor the next week. In a way, the work was easy. All Moira had to do was to put the title, author, and source of each manuscript or newspaper story into a computer program. Once Moira learned how to use the computer, the work went fast. But there were times when information was missing and Moira had to track it down in the library. She liked doing this sort of detective work.

It took about a month to get through the stack of manuscripts and newspapers in the professor's office. Then there were more manuscripts to go through in a special part of the library, a room in the basement where few people ever went. Moira liked taking the laptop down there and doing her work. It was quiet and meditative, and time passed quickly. Moira would also sometimes pause to read part of a manuscript. She seemed to be learning a lot without really trying.

Moira also talked with the professor about her research. The professor explained what her project was about and how she had gotten interested in it. Moira would sometimes ask about things she read in the manuscripts. These were the talks Moira enjoyed most, even though she didn't quite grasp everything the professor said. What was most satisfying, Moira felt, was that when she asked the professor about the meaning of something she'd read, the professor would give a careful answer that tied everything together. Moira wished her classes during the semester were like this.

Summer was over too soon, although Moira felt that a lot had changed for her in that brief time. School felt different somehow. Before, Moira had seen her classes as dreary ordeals to be endured on her way to a job and a real grown-up life. Now she felt that there was something to be gotten out of every class and that it was up to her to go after it and not let a dull professor or textbook get in the way. It was both exciting and frustrating to realize that the world was a more interesting and complicated place than she would have time to fully explore.

A few weeks into the fall semester, Moira ran into Professor Valkyrie. "Did you have a good summer?" Valkyrie asked.

"It was great," Moira said. "I worked for Professor Sesheta, mostly doing archiving and bibliographic work. The money was good, and I learned a lot."

"So does this mean you're not going to major in philosophy?" Valkyrie asked, half-teasingly. Moira laughed.

"Well, I had been majoring in 'undecided,' but now I'm leaning toward history. When I register for the spring I'll probably declare a history major with a philosophy minor. I want to come by and talk to you about that," Moira said.

"Come by any Tuesday or Thursday afternoon," Valkyrie said. "I have office hours from three to four." As it turned out, Moira decided to major in both history and political science. It took her an extra year to finish the double major, but she wasn't in a hurry. She knew that she'd never again be so free to pursue her interests. Moira was also absorbed in work she was doing for a student group that helped the university's janitorial staff fight for higher wages. When Moira had learned that the university paid its full-time cleanup people a wage that kept them below the poverty level, she was outraged. She decided that before she left school she'd try to change that situation.

By the start of her fifth year Moira knew she wanted to go to law school. Some of her professors suggested graduate school, but Moira didn't want to play academic games while there was so much that needed to be changed in the world. Her experience with the housekeepers had opened her eyes to other situations where powerless people were exploited. Moira felt she could do more to fight these injustices as a lawyer than as a professor. After three years of law school Moira got a job with a firm that represented unions, consumer groups, and activist organizations. Moira made partner after she won a big sex-discrimination suit against GrabnGo Corporation.

*   *   *

The two endings to this story show how people are caught up in a swirl of contingencies in which small events—like a bird hitting a windshield—can cause their lives to turn out differently. We can also see from these stories that it is not the small event alone that causes things to turn out as they do; it is a whole set of circumstances that come together just so. Even a small change in circumstances can bump a life onto a path that leads to a very different place.

Perhaps this makes it seem as if it is pointless to be sociologically mindful about individual lives, since each life unfolds as the result of a unique series of random events. If so, why bother to think analytically about individual lives? What sense can we hope to make of randomness? Lives are not really random, however, even if the swirl of contingencies makes their outcome unpredictable.

Moira's life was not random. It was part of a pattern. To see this, consider that there are millions of Moiras: young women who try to get ahead by going to college, but who must face conflicting demands from people in their lives, demands that arise because of cultural ideas about work, gender, marriage, and so on. The circumstances these women face are similar in many ways, and these circumstances make some results more likely than others. Even though the swirl of contingencies can produce surprises—like Moira becoming a lawyer—we are *surprised* only because there is a departure from what *usually* happens.

You can see this with Moira's story if you rewrite it. What if Moira's father had been a surgeon and her mother a university president? Would she have been working at GrabnGo trying to scrape together money for school? Not likely. Would she have seen a beer delivery man as partner material? Probably not. Or what if Moira had been male? Perhaps he would have been promoted to regional manager and had a long career with GrabnGo Corporation. Any of these changes might have gotten Moira caught up in a different pattern.

Imagine flicking the tip of a twig into a stream. It is possible that a fish will mistake the twig for an insect and will swallow it. It is possible that an eagle will snatch the fish out of the water and eat it, twig and all. It is possible that the twig, a bit worse for the wear, will end up on the forest floor miles above the spot where you threw it into the stream. All this *could* happen. But what is most *likely* is that the twig will float downstream for a while, become waterlogged, sink, get stuck under a deadfall or against a bank, and decay. That is what happens to most twigs, because of how the natural world works.

Moira's life, like everyone's life, fell into a swirling stream of time and events. Yet the swirling, for all the surprises it might produce, is not random but patterned, as we can see if we are sociologically mindful. We can think of these patterns—and where we step into them—as what cause us to be pushed and pulled, like twigs in a stream, more strongly toward some places than others. We can think of the swirling, the ever-changing mix of circumstances, as what sometimes pops us out of one pattern into another, or toward unlikely places.

Dialogue

Freedom, Constraint, and Unforeseen Contingencies

Thinking about cause and contingency raises the question of how much control we have over our lives. Certainly we make choices, and these choices affect how our lives turn out. Yet it seems that much is beyond our control. As children, we are shaped by a social environment, and then, to get along as adults, we must adapt and react to the circumstances we find ourselves in. The old saying that people make history, *but not under conditions of their own choosing*, is thus quite true.

It is worth thinking a bit more, however, about exactly what it is that limits our actions. I have already said (see the Dialogue in Chapter 5) that people cannot change themselves into whatever they want to be, at any time. But what is it that keeps us from doing whatever we take a notion to do?

One obvious answer is *other people.* To get through the day, we have to be able to coordinate our action with others. If we behave strangely, or in some way that is very different from what others expect, others will not cooperate with us. They either won't know how to deal with us or they will think we are dangerous or crazy. In any case, we can't go too far outside the bounds of expected conduct, or else we will lose the cooperation of others that is essential for getting along in the world.

This doesn't mean that you couldn't do something very strange. You could make up your own private language, cover your body with grease and chicken feathers, and then stand on a street corner preaching against the evils of social media addiction. You *could* do that. Nothing would physically stop you. But such action might have the effect of making it hard for you to function normally in the world because of how others would react to your display of weirdness.

The example above serves to remind us that we have more freedom of choice than we often admit. When someone says, "I *had* to do X; I had no choice," this isn't quite true. What it really means is, "I chose to do X because the consequences of not doing X were more than I could bear." If someone sticks a gun in your ribs and demands your money, you still have a choice about how to respond.

So, presuming that we care about getting along in the world, other people constitute the main constraint on our behavior. We are also limited by the ideas we use to make sense of the world. Think of it this way: we have great freedom to decide how to behave, but *we can't make choices that we don't know we have*. If you have been taught to believe that your options are C, D, and E, then it might never occur to you to consider A and B or F and G. If those options are literally unthinkable because of how you have been taught to think, then your action is effectively constrained.

We are also constrained by the physical world. No matter how hard I flap my arms, I can't fly. Nor can I hammer nails with a feather. Nor can I ignore for very long my body's needs for food, water, clothing, and shelter. The nature of the physical world, including our bodies, thus imposes certain demands and sets limits on what we can do (I'll say more about this in Chapter 12).

One time when I was talking about the things that constrain our behavior, a student asked about drug addiction. She wondered if it was fair to say that people who are addicted to drugs could just behave differently if they wanted to. "Isn't it a disease that they can't control?" she asked.

To answer this question, we should first note that people begin using drugs (alcohol, nicotine, caffeine, or whatever) for various reasons. For some it's a way to cope with stress. For others it's a matter of fun and sociability. Whatever the reason, we can say that initially a person chooses to use a drug or not. We should, however, acknowledge two other things. First, many people face stressful circumstances that they are not responsible for creating. And, second, people learn from their culture about the acceptable ways of coping with stress and of having fun.

But the real concern behind the student's question was about whether disease causes addiction, which in turn causes loss of control. It seems unlikely that any organic disease can cause a person to choose to smoke cigarettes, drink coffee, or snort cocaine. It is possible, however, for some people's bodies (for biochemical reasons) to react to certain drugs in ways that make the drug's effect more pleasurable. In this case, they might quickly develop a strong craving for the drug. But does this necessarily imply loss of control?

On the one hand, no, because people still choose how to respond to their cravings and desires. They can resist, distract themselves, or give in. This presumes, however, that people are in their right minds and can weigh the consequences of their actions. Some drugs can so disrupt the normal functioning of the brain that a person is unable to think straight. And so, on the other hand, it's also true that overuse of some substances can impede rational thought to the point where control is lost.

It might seem as if I have gone off on a tangent here. But I am still making a point about cause and contingency. The point is this: our actions today are, in part, the causes of the conditions we must cope with in the future.

To go back to the drug example, choosing to take a drug can create a condition in which a person later needs that drug just to feel normal. Almost no one foresees this. Yet once a physiological craving takes hold, it is a reality that an addict must deal with. A smoker, for example, might say, "My addiction to nicotine keeps me from quitting." It would be more accurate to say, however, that a choice at one time (smoking) led to conditions under which other choices (quitting) have unpleasant consequences (anxiety, irritability).

We are always acting in ways that give rise to unforeseen consequences. In seeking to satisfy our needs and desires today, we help to create conditions that we will have to deal with tomorrow. We are, in other words, creating a set of contingencies that will channel our future actions in directions we cannot fully anticipate. The choices we make today will also change us, so that when tomorrow comes, we will face it as different people.

Being sociologically mindful, we can apply this principle to larger situations. Think of our petroleum-based society. When fossil fuels were first exploited, no one foresaw the extent to which everyday life and an entire world economy would come to depend on the energy they contain. Oil, we might say, has made us who and what we are today. We can go further and say that without oil, most of the social arrangements we have come to take for granted would not exist.

Yet we now know that petroleum is a finite resource that will eventually run out. What then? What contingencies will we face and what choices will we make? And how will we make those choices? We might do it in the manner of a person who accepts the inevitability of change and wisely seeks a healthy path into the future. Or we might do it in the manner of an addict who denies the need for change and then grasps at straws as things come crashing down. How we respond will depend on the degree of sociological mindfulness with which we are able to assess our current situation, where we are heading, and the kind of people we have become.

A Note on Luck

When it's hard to tell what caused things to happen in the way they did, we often invoke the notion of luck. If we like what happened, we say it was a case of good luck. If we don't like what happened, we say it was bad luck. Sociologists don't usually say much about luck, because the term implies that human destiny is shaped by mysterious forces, and most sociologists prefer to think that, in principle, there is a discernible explanation for everything that happens.

Yet in everyday life people do talk a lot about luck. They also use the idea of luck to think about why things happen and why their lives turn out as they do. So perhaps luck is a matter that is worth trying to be sociologically mindful about.

To make any particular thing happen in social life requires a complex conjunction of circumstances. Landing a job, for example, requires that a great many circumstances come together in the right way at the right time. If one circumstance is different, the job might go to someone else. Because we can't see what all these circumstances are, because their conjunction might seem to be a fluke, and because many of them are beyond our control, it makes sense that we would invoke "luck" to explain what we can't otherwise account for.

Of course, our own readiness to take advantage of improbable opportunities is a relevant circumstance. And we do have some control over this readiness. As a famous golfer once said, "The more I practice, the luckier I get" (the line is variously attributed to Arnold Palmer, Gary Player, Sam Snead, and Ben Hogan). Many people like to apply this quip to real life, as a way to say that success is more a matter of hard work than of luck.

But in games and sports the environment is impartial—meaning that the rules and challenges are the same for everyone. Real life is different in that not everyone gets an equal chance to get into the game, so to speak. Nor does everyone have an equal chance to learn the game, to be expertly coached, or to practice. Some people may even find themselves facing tougher rules than do others. All of which is to say that in real life what we call "luck" is not quite random but is distributed in patterned ways, for reasons that aren't always easy to see.

Paths for Reflection

1. When I was a child, my father worked as an electrician for a railroad. He was eventually promoted to a managerial job, which brought a big increase in status and pay, along with demands for a lot of travel. Moving up in the company also meant moving the family to a new city every year. My parents found that they did not want that kind of life, and so my father quit the railroad and went back to work as an electrician. This decision, made

when I was seven years old, dramatically altered my life. If you can, ask your parents if they ever had to make a similar choice. How did that choice alter the course of your life? How might your life have been different if your parents had chosen otherwise?

2. There is an old saying that artists do not choose a form of art, but rather a form of art chooses them. This means that as people explore ways of doing creative work, they eventually find a way to which they are, for reasons hard to fathom, powerfully drawn. We can take this idea beyond the realm of art and observe that many people find a hobby, a sport, a craft, a topic of study, or a kind of work that seems naturally to compel their devotion. When this happens, people often strive with great intensity to acquire knowledge and skill. What social conditions enable people to have this kind of experience? What difference does it make if a person never has the experience of being chosen by a form of activity?

3. Not all social phenomena have been equally well studied, in the sense of trying to find their underlying causes. Perhaps such things as juggling and hog calling have escaped scientific attention because they are arguably trivial. But some blind spots are curious indeed. For example, a lot of research has tried to find out what causes homosexuality, but not much has tried to find out what causes heterosexuality, which seems to be more common. Likewise, a lot of research has tried to find out why a small percentage of poor people manage to get ahead, but not much has been done to find out what causes inequality and exploitation in the first place. If social scientists in the United States are free to study whatever they want, how do you explain the relatively little effort made to find out what causes such central features of our society? What might be the consequences of this kind of selective science?

Related Readings

Becker, Howard S. (1994). "'Foi por acaso': Conceptualizing Coincidence." *Sociological Quarterly* 35:183–194.

Bloor, David. (1976). *Knowledge and Social Imagery*. London: Routledge & Kegan Paul.

Brown, Robert. (1963). *Explanation in Social Science*. Chicago: Aldine.

Davidson, Donald. (1963). "Actions, Reasons and Causes." *Journal of Philosophy* 60:685–700.

Frank, Robert H. (2016). *Success and Luck: Good Fortune and the Myth of Meritocracy*. Princeton, NJ: Princeton University Press.

Inman, Mason. (2016). *The Oracle of Oil: A Maverick Geologist's Quest for a Sustainable Future*. New York: Norton.

Quine, W. V., & Ullian, J. S. (1978). *The Web of Belief.* New York: McGraw–Hill.
Toulmin, Stephen E. (1972). *Human Understanding.* Princeton, NJ: Princeton
    University Press.
von Wright, Georg Henrik. (1971). *Explanation and Understanding.* Ithaca, NY:
    Cornell University Press.

CHAPTER 9

....

Images, Representations, and Accounts

The old saying "Do not judge a book by its cover" reminds us that appearances can be deceiving. What seems true at first glance can turn out to be quite wrong. Yet we judge books, people, and other things by their covers all the time. We look to see what we can see—the design of a book jacket, the clothes a person wears, the rust on a car's bumper—and make inferences about the qualities underneath. Why do we do this if we know it is so risky and can lead us astray?

One reason we rely on appearances is that we need to know what to expect from people and things. When we meet an unfamiliar person, we might wonder if s/he is friendly or dangerous, trustworthy or devious. We might wonder if s/he can give us help or will try to get something from us. Until we get to know a person we can't be sure about these matters. But still we need to have an idea of what a person is like, so we must make judgments based on the signs of character we can detect.

Another reason we rely on appearances is that we deal with many people whom we will never get to know well. Many of our encounters with others are brief, and many people we see only once. Yet we still must determine how others are likely to act toward us—and thus how we should act toward them. To get along, we must learn to "read" others quickly. We do make mistakes, of course. We are most likely to misjudge a person's character when a stereotype interferes with a careful reading of the person as an individual.

Being sociologically mindful does not mean that we overcome the need to make judgments about others based on limited information. If we all lived in small villages, where everyone got to know everyone else well over many years, then things would be different. But in a society like ours, we are forced to rely on what we can see and interpret quickly. Being sociologically mindful means being aware that we are doing this, being aware of *how* we are doing it, and being aware that all around us appearances are being crafted to influence our thoughts and feelings.

The social world is full of strategically crafted images and representations. To say that they are "strategically crafted" means that they are made with the aim of creating a particular impression. Consider the images you craft for yourself. On a job interview, for example, you must craft an image of yourself as capable and enthusiastic—all the while appearing natural, so that you don't come off as phony. On a first date you will probably try to craft an image of yourself so that the other person will see the most attractive side of who you are. It works both ways, of course; others are crafting images for you, too.

Perhaps this makes social life seem like a game of deception. You might think, "So, then, being sociologically mindful means seeing that everyone is a fraud, since everyone is trying to con everyone else with these bogus images." That is not really what sociological mindfulness leads us to see. Not everyone is a fraud, nor are all images crafted to mislead others. The point is that whether we seek to mislead or to reveal our truest selves, we must still craft images.

Suppose you want to express your love for another person. How can you do this? You must put your feelings into actions that the other person will interpret as signs of love. This is all you can do, since the other person can't look inside your skull to check for a feeling labeled "love." The other person must make an inference about your feelings, based on what you say and do. This means that you must craft an image that the other person will see as revealing your true feelings. Whether we are faking or being as honest as we can be, there is no getting around our reliance on images.

To use a workplace example again: it is good to be competent when you are seeking to be hired and promoted, but it is even more important to *appear* competent, because decisions about your future will be based on what powerful others perceive you to be. If you are competent and fail to create the impression of competence in others' minds, you will not do well. Then again, a person who puts more effort into creating an image of competence than into developing real competence may also fail when a crucial test arises.

The images we create are tremendously consequential. Our lives can depend on them. Others decide how to treat us, and we decide how to treat them, based on appearances. When we do this, we are not thinking, "I will rely on appearances to judge this person." What we do, more or less by habit, is to look for signs of people's inner qualities. The signs we rely on are those we have learned to see and interpret.

A curious result of this reliance on images is that we *create each other* in interaction. For example, you have probably been in situations where you felt as if you said and did everything right—and where you thus created an image of yourself as witty, charming, and good-natured. In that situation, that is what you were; from your performance, others could infer that you were indeed a witty, charming, and good-natured person.

You have probably also been in situations where you felt as if you did everything wrong and thus probably led others to think you were a clod. Why did this happen? You might say, "I had a bad day." That might be true, but if we are sociologically mindful, we will see that there is more to it, that having a good day or a bad day has a lot to do with what happens between people: others can bring out the best or the worst in us.

If others show interest in what we say, if they respect our opinions, if they laugh at our jokes, then we will probably perform better—that is, speak more smoothly and confidently, with more wit and charm—than if they look away when we speak, remain silent at our jokes, or dismiss our opinions. By affecting our performances, others thus help make us who we are in a situation. If their behavior elicits a fine performance on our part, they will have evidence from which to infer that we have good qualities. If they treat us in a way that makes us foul up, then they will have a bad performance from which to infer that we are inept.

Again, it goes both ways; we affect others' performances, too. This is not just a matter of treating others in ways that let them show the best of who they are. Sometimes it is a matter of accepting others' claims to being a little better than they are. A friend might boast a bit, exaggerating some quality or feat. Do we let the boast pass without comment, or do we challenge it? Whichever we do, our action will affect the image the friend is trying to create. Others can likewise support or challenge the claims we make about ourselves.

These images on which others rely to make inferences about our character are thus social creations. We can't make images by ourselves. And the exact images—and therefore the "virtual selves" that others impute to us—depend on what we can pull off with various audiences. But there are even more profound ways in which this creation of images and virtual selves depends on social life.

Resources for Creating Images

Consider what it takes to create a favorable image of one's self. We must be able to present the signs—in the forms of speech, behavior, and material objects (e.g., clothing)—that others can use to make inferences about us. All these resources come from social life. We must learn how to speak and act in ways that others will interpret as signs of competence, morality, or other good qualities. We must also acquire certain resources (skills, money) that will allow us to obtain other signifying resources, such as a good job, nice clothes, a car and a home, and so on. In other words, all the signs that we can muster to create images, impressions, and creditable selves are products of social life, as is the ability to use these signs in an impressive way.

Perhaps you are thinking, "Sure, signs come from social life, and so does the ability to use them. So what?" The answer is this: in a society where there is a great deal of inequality, the resources and skills necessary to signify a creditable self will be unequally distributed. This means that not everyone can create a creditable self, at least with some audiences. It also means that some people will be able to create impressions of goodness by virtue of their power, rather than by the power of their virtue.

Being sociologically mindful, we will pay attention to who is able to access and wield what kinds of signs, who learns how to use them properly, and who gets a chance to use them with certain audiences. We will also ask, Who gets to say what will be taken as an important sign of character? This is part of being mindful about why, in U.S. society, a male body, light skin, an Anglo-Saxon surname, heterosexual inclinations, and wealth are interpreted as signs of a worthy self.

We should try to be mindful, then, that images matter because they affect how we treat others and how they treat us; that images are not the result of personalities but of how people define things, how people treat each other, and how much inequality exists between groups in a society; and that people in dominant groups can use their advantages to create images of their own competence and morality, while denying people in less powerful groups the resources to create images of equal value. Part of being sociologically mindful is paying attention to how such images are created, how they affect people's chances for good lives, and how they help to maintain (or to change) the way the social world works.

Representations

A student once told me that "The Sixties" was a time of rampant drug use, wild sex, permissiveness, anti-Americanism, and widespread social disorder. His point was that nothing good had come out of the 1960s and that it was best to put that foolish and destructive era behind us. I asked him when he was born. "Nineteen-seventy-five," he said. How could he know so much about the 1960s? "Various sources," he said. When I pressed him to be more specific, he admitted that he had not read any books about the 1960s but had gained his knowledge "from TV and stuff."

There is nothing wrong with learning about distant times, places, and people from television, but we should be mindful that television offers us knowledge in the form of representations that are usually designed more to entertain than to inform. This means that someone, or some group of people, has selected for us a part of the picture—a subset of all that could be known about something else—and presented it to us as if it were the whole picture. What we thus get is a crafted, partial re-presentation of a reality to which we might have no direct access.

The student who told me about the 1960s had not checked out the representations he had been given. If he had, he might have learned that during the 1960s most college students did not protest or riot, take drugs, or participate in orgies, and although many repressive aspects of U.S. society— racism, sexism, imperialism, militarism—were challenged through polite and impolite protest, there was mostly business as usual, not "widespread social disorder." He might also have learned that many of the gains in civil rights that he took for granted were made during the 1960s.

Of course, even if this student read books about the 1960s and talked to people who lived through that time, he would still be relying on representations. Not having been there, and having no way to go back and see for himself, he had no choice but to rely on representations created by others. Unfortunately, the student relied on representations that were clichés or stereotypes and did not question how or why they were created.

Images and representations are similar but not quite the same. An image is created by a "signifying performance" that we can witness directly. A representation is an image of a time, a place, a kind of people, a thing, or an event that is not readily available for witnessing. To talk about what the 1960s were like, or what the Chinese are like, or what the dark side of the moon is like, or what a quark is like, or what happened last week at a party is to create a representation. The representation brings the distant or unobservable reality into the here and now.

The Necessity and Danger of Representations

Like images, representations are indispensable. If we are going to talk about distant realities at all, we must create representations of them. Also like images, representations are created with help or hindrance from others. Sometimes others affirm our representations ("Yeah, that's how it happened"); sometimes they offer competing versions of their own ("Let me tell you what *really* happened"), in which case we might have to do some revising. The representations we finally agree upon are usually the result of negotiation.

Being sociologically mindful, we see not only that representations are indispensable but also that what we take reality to be depends on the particular representations we create and agree upon. Failing to be mindful, we may fail to see that representations are indeed representations and we may mistake them for an unmediated view of reality. If we are not mindful of representations as re-presentations, we may also fail to see how they are often distorted to serve the interests of their creators.

A student once told me about a TV program that purported to show real cops in action. I said that he should not take the program too seriously, because its representations of police work were probably fabricated to make them more entertaining. The student insisted that the program showed events exactly as they happened. I could not convince him otherwise until I found an article, written by a person who had helped produce the program, explaining how the apparently real crime scenes were contrived. The student then realized that he had been fooled, but no doubt millions of people believed that the program was an unfiltered, accurate portrayal of distant realities.

Being sociologically mindful, we should be suspicious of representations—like the cop show—that claim *not* to be constructed. We should be suspicious because someone is trying to convince us what a distant reality is like while hiding the fact that they are choosing how to represent that reality to us. If we are mindful, we will always see representations as constructed, and then we'll ask who is doing the constructing, how, for whom, and why. Sometimes the answers will be obvious, sometimes not. In any case, if we ask the questions, we are less likely to be taken in.

It is important to be wary of representations precisely because we are so dependent on them. Consider all the matters that are represented to us: historical events and eras; events in other countries; the state of our own economy; the character of the leaders and people in other countries; the actions of corporations and of governments; the various worlds of scientific research. In some cases, we may have direct access to what is being represented. When we don't, which is most of the time, we would be wise to examine representations from several sources and, again, to consider how they are constructed, with what interests in mind.

Misrepresentation by Stereotype and Habit

Being sociologically mindful of how representations are constructed does not mean presuming that all representations are designed to fool us. Some *are* designed to fool us, of course. If a mining corporation, for example, is represented (by its public-relations firm) as a champion of environmental preservation, the fakery is easy to see. But it can also happen that misleading representations are created as a matter of cultural habit, by people with no intent to deceive.

Suppose you heard a thirty-second news story (a typical length for radio or television) about a six-year-old boy who was charged by school administrators with sexual harassment for kissing a classmate on the cheek. You might think, "This has gone too far! A legitimate concern about sexual harassment has turned into hysteria. It's crazy to charge a six-year-old with sexual harassment!" Your reaction would be understandable. Many people would react the same way. But it might be wise to pause and ask if there could be more to the story.

It might turn out that knowing more of the story would make a difference. Suppose you knew that the boy had been bothering several of his classmates for a long time; that the boy had resisted gentler efforts to discipline him; that the school administrators had been sued previously for failing to take action against a slightly older boy who engaged in the same kind of misbehavior; and that the administrators were reluctant to invoke the sexual harassment charge but felt they had no choice, since the boy's parents refused to cooperate in disciplining him. If you knew all this, you might feel differently about the situation.

The point of this example is not just that more information can lead to a more intelligent response to a situation, but also that complex situations are often represented in stereotypical ways. In this example, a story that was too complex to fit into thirty seconds was reduced to a cliché: "Over-zealous administrators go to absurd lengths to be politically correct." This sort of reporting is common, though not because of a conspiracy to deny the seriousness of sexual harassment. It happens because stereotypes are helpful for quickly creating easy-to-grasp representations of complex distant realities.

Much the same kind of stereotyping had affected my student's view of "The Sixties." He had no doubt been exposed to many representations of the 1960s as a time of irresponsible youthful rebellion. This stereotypical representation, because it was so frequently used, came to seem like the version of reality upon which everyone agreed. Not knowing any better and having no good reason to be suspicious, he accepted it.

All representations are incomplete and simplified. There is no avoiding that. What we can avoid, if we are sociologically mindful, is being caught in the illusion that representations are direct views to distant realities. What we see, in other words, is the *constructedness* of representations. Again, this does not mean dismissing all representations as fantasies contrived to mislead us. It means paying attention to how representations are constructed, by whom, to serve what purposes.

In some cases it might be clear why some person or group would like us to accept a particular representation. We might see, for example, that if we accept one group's representation of history, then this will make them seem like victims of injustice who are deserving of our sympathy and support. To recognize that people have an interest in portraying history in a particular way does not necessarily make their representation of history incorrect; it simply alerts us to look for bias and to seek more information.

Perhaps most simply, to be sociologically mindful about representations is to ask, What else is there to know about these people or events? How is the version I am being offered shaped, consciously or unconsciously, by the values and interests of its source? Has this representation been constructed through careful investigation, or is it just hearsay? Who might represent things differently? Why? If such questions habitually come to mind, we are less likely to be taken in by stereotypes or duped by malicious fabricators.

Giving and Receiving Accounts

Suppose that you are going to miss a deadline. To avoid being penalized, you can ask for an extension. To get the extension, you must give an acceptable account for why your work is late. For example, you might say, "My work is late because I am lazy, irresponsible, and don't care if my behavior hurts anyone else. But if you'll give me an extension, I'll get the work done when I feel like it." That is one possible account. The person who hears it might at least give you credit for honesty.

Here is another possible account: "I'm sorry my work is late. I really tried to get it done, but my father got laid off this week, and my mother got sick right after she came home from my aunt's funeral, and I've had to put in extra hours at the store because of the holiday season. So things are a real mess right now, and I got a little behind. But if you could give me some extra time, I think I can get the work done in a day or so." Unless the person who hears this is coldhearted or thinks you are a liar, you will probably get the extension.

As long as we do what others expect us to, we do not usually have to give accounts. It is only when our behavior is unexpected or violates a rule that we have to account for it, perhaps with a justification or an excuse. Like images, accounts matter. The right account can make the difference between getting an extension on a deadline or getting fired, between being acquitted or being found guilty, between saving a relationship or losing it. To keep social life working smoothly and to avoid trouble for ourselves, we must know how to give proper accounts.

Perhaps you are thinking, "This giving of accounts wouldn't be such a big deal if people just told the truth all the time. The truth is always the best account." That is a noble sentiment, perhaps, but in real life things are more complicated, since the truth can be told more or less completely and in different ways.

Suppose that a friend tells you about a problem s/he is having, in hopes that you will listen and show understanding. Instead, you brush off the problem as trivial and thus hurt your friend's feelings. Perhaps later s/he calls you to account for your behavior. What can you say? The truth might be that you like this friend very much but are tired of all the obsessing about problems that seem small to you. So you might say, "I wasn't listening closely because I was tired of your whining about penny-ante troubles while there are people starving in the world." That account might end the friendship. If you didn't want that to happen, you could try this: "I do care about how you feel. It's just hard for me sometimes to understand why certain things affect you so strongly. And when I don't understand why you feel the way you do, I get impatient and drift off while you're talking. I'm sorry."

As this example suggests, it is not the truth that determines how an audience will react to an account. What matters is the account itself—how it is shaped, the reality it implies, and the feelings it evokes. As with images, there is no way around this reliance on accounts, since the truth, whatever it might be and no matter how much we might want to tell it, is tellable only through accounts. There is no getting at it directly.

If you showed up at work wearing only a robe made from pages out of this book, you would surely be called to account for your attire. If you said, "I am dressed like this because it's a hot day and this is a cool book," you would probably be seen as crazy, sent home, or fired. Some accounts just don't fly, and, again, it's not truth that makes the difference. An account works when it is plausible and reasonable to the audience hearing it. Members of a fan club might think it perfectly fine to wear pages from a book written by the club's hero.

Behind and Underneath Accounts

If we pay attention to how accounts are fashioned, we can see what it is that people take for granted. For example, if you ask someone, "Why did you get so drunk last night?" and that person says, "Because I lost my job and was feeling awful," you might be inclined to accept this account. You might say, "I understand." Now consider what is taken for granted here: jobs are important, losing a job is a big deal, bad feelings should be escaped, and drinking is an effective way to escape them. If you did not take these matters for granted, the other person's account for getting drunk would make no sense.

Accounts work because the givers and receivers of accounts share assumptions. Every account, if viewed mindfully, can thus be a way to see deeper into the shared beliefs that hold a community together. To see these beliefs, we must ask, Why does this account work? What assumptions must be accepted for this account to seem plausible and reasonable? To practice this kind of mindfulness we do not have to go looking for accounts to study. We can begin by paying more attention to our own.

There might be many people—teachers, bosses, politicians, corporate executives, administrators, bureaucrats—from whom you would like to demand accounts. Perhaps you think that some such people should be forced to explain what they are doing and why. And if they can't give acceptable accounts, then they should be fired, defrocked, booted out of office, put in jail, or punished in some other way. The problem, however, is that your demands for accounts (you could write angry letters to the editor of the local paper) would probably be ignored. Who are you, after all, to demand an account from Chancellor Phogmann, Senator Lootscam, or the president of BioDynaTek?

Obviously, there is a connection between power and accountability. In fact, a good index of a person's power is how free that person is to ignore others' demands for accounts. Having power also means being able to force others to account for their actions, under threat of punishment if they don't comply. Being mindful of who feels obligated to give accounts to whom, of who can force others to give accounts, and of who can ignore demands for giving accounts is thus a way to see the inequality that exists in a group, organization, community, or nation.

Tools for Making Reality

Social reality is constructed in part by formulating and giving accounts. In giving accounts, people say what they think is real—or what they want others to believe is real. And when accounts are accepted, it is as if an agreement has been made: "Okay, we accept this account as a description of what is the case; we will proceed from here." Perhaps, then, you can see why it is important to be mindful of how accounts are formulated, given, and judged. It is because in this process a social reality is being created that we may all be stuck with for a while.

Perhaps it seems that images and accounts are one thing and reality is another. There is a sense in which this is true. An image can be false, in that it can be crafted to produce incorrect inferences about the character of a person or a group. An account can be false, too, in the sense that it does not faithfully correspond to how things actually are or were—as might be found out through an impartial and careful investigation. On the other hand, we have no choice but to rely on images and accounts in determining what is real. A false image can be replaced only by another image, just as a false account can be challenged only by another account.

Being sociologically mindful, we see that there is no getting around our reliance on images, representations, and accounts because it is only by fashioning images, representations, and accounts that we can create shared beliefs about what is real and true. We see, in other words, that our ideas about what is real and true depend on a process from which we cannot escape—a process of creating and acting on appearances. With this awareness, we can become better analysts of who creates what kinds of appearances, for what purposes, and with what results for whom.

Significant Absences

Suppose you have just met a person whom you find attractive and would like to impress. You've heard that this person values honesty, so when this person asks, "What do you do?" instead of talking about your job you say, "I pick my nose when no one is looking. I clip my toenails in the sink. I toss dirty socks on the floor around my hamper. And sometimes I go for months without changing the sheets on my bed." In this case, your honesty would probably backfire. The other person might say, "Hmmm, well, yes, that's interesting. I'd like to talk more, but right now I have to rotate my tires. Good-bye."

What did you do wrong? You were just trying to craft an image of yourself as an honest person in the eyes of someone you thought would appreciate it. And it's not as if you admitted to being a serial killer or a tobacco company executive. So what's the problem?

This silly example makes two serious points. One is that violating cultural rules about what is appropriate to tell about yourself, on what occasions, can lead others to see you as inept. To put it another way, following the usual rules about how to present ourselves to others is part of crafting an image of ourselves as sane, normal, and safe to be around. Another point is that appearances are crafted by leaving certain things out of the picture. When crafting images of ourselves, we must know what to tell and what not to tell, or else we are likely to spoil the image.

You have no doubt learned that when meeting others it is usually best to lead off with positive information about yourself, so as to make a good first impression. Then, once you have convinced others that you are a decent person, you can gradually reveal your flaws. If you put all the bad news up front, you will probably have a hard time salvaging a creditable image of yourself later. To create a good impression you must know what to leave out.

The absence of information is important when it comes to creating representations. For example, the history of the United States can be represented like this: "Once upon a time, brave European explorers discovered a vast, untamed land, which was later settled by colonists seeking freedom from rule by kings and popes. Eventually these colonists fought a war to break their ties to a corrupt English king. After thus freeing themselves, the colonists built a new republic, founded on principles of liberty and democracy. The republic grew and, over the next two hundred years, expanded to reach the far sea, turning an undeveloped land into the richest, most productive, freest nation on earth."

That is an impressive, even inspiring, representation, much like what is taught in grade-school civics courses. It is, however, a representation that achieves a positive effect by leaving out important things. Specifically, it does not mention that the "vast, untamed land" was already populated by indigenous peoples, most of whom were killed to make way for European settlers; it does not mention the enslavement of Africans or the fact that "liberty and democracy" were originally intended only for white men who owned land; and it does not mention the expansion of the United States by the violent theft of land from Mexico. Putting these matters back in the picture makes for quite a different representation.

Organized Exclusion and Invention

Representations of groups of people are also shaped by absences. For example, if books or films that tell about great scientists, philosophers, writers, and politicians never mention Africans or women, it will thus appear that women and Africans are not capable of achievement in these fields. A careful study of U.S. history shows, however, that Africans and women have done outstanding work as scientists, philosophers, writers, politicians, and so on. But if their work is overlooked in official accounts of who has done great things, then an unjust, inaccurate, and harmful representation is created. In this way, representations of groups—like images of selves and representations of nations—are created by leaving things out of the picture.

Perhaps you have noticed that there is a difference between how images of selves are created in everyday life and how representations of nations and groups are created. When you create an image of yourself, you do so in collaboration with a small group of others, usually in face-to-face interaction. Even if people affect your image by talking behind your back, it is still likely to be done informally, by a small number of people. Rarely in everyday life is there an organized effort, involving more than a few people, to destroy or uphold the image of an individual person.

In contrast, creating representations of types of people and of nations requires cooperation on a large scale. For example, it requires the cooperation of many people—writers, publishers, teachers, school boards, and parents—to create and uphold the sanitized representation of the United States described earlier. It also takes cooperation on a large scale to create representations of black males as violent and criminal; of feminists as angry man-haters; of working-class men as rednecks; of women as better suited to nurturing than to governing; of political leaders as competent; and so on. Representations like these—ones that come to us through television, films, newspapers, books, churches, and schools—are institutional products.

Being mindful of representations as institutional products suggests that we need to know who controls institutions and who benefits from the representations they create. This is not to say that we will always find a top boss or committee telling others to distort reality. More likely we will find a group of people who are comforted by, or derive other benefits from, creating particular representations of history, politics, other people, and so on. We might also find that many people who take part in creating representations act on habit and do not think to question the assumptions underlying their work.

Seeing how representations are created institutionally can also help us understand why some representations are so widespread and hard to change. It is not because people stupidly insist on believing what is false, but because they are constantly fed misleading representations that are passed off as true. If these representations come from institutional sources—the mass media, schools, government—they can be hard to escape and hard to refute; they also seem to have a great deal of authority. If a teacher says, "You must read this book to learn," we are more likely to fear being bored than being misled.

Challenging Representations

To change well-established, institutionally created representations requires an organized effort. Rarely is it enough to speak out alone and say, "That is untrue! Here is how things really are. . . ." Of course, speaking what we see as the truth is worth doing, because even if it turns out that we are wrong, more will be learned if we speak up than if we don't. But if we are convinced that an institutionally created representation is wrong, then we must work with others to change it, perhaps by creating a newspaper, a school, an anti-defamation league, or a think tank. The absence of challenge, like the absence of information, is part of what allows false representations to stand.

Being sociologically mindful about images, accounts, and representations means seeing them as constructed. It also means suspecting, as a matter of habit, that something has been left out, that what we are seeing contains significant absences. If we are offered no view of the dark side of what is represented to us, we should suspect that such a side exists and keep an eye open for it. The purpose of such wariness is not to debunk everything that seems too good to be true but to be able to see all things more fully and honestly—and as more complex than first appearances might suggest.

If we are sociologically mindful, we will look for alternative images, accounts, and representations and try to create our own picture of things— of people, places, events, history, groups, and so on—rather than accepting the pictures that are handed to us. Only by doing this can we find out if there are alternative versions of reality and if those versions have been suppressed. Being mindful in this way, we may also discover the significant absences in official accounts of reality. We will see, too, how appearances are linked to power. At the same time, by being sociologically mindful of how appearances are constructed, by and for whom, we will develop our own power to see more deeply into how the social world works.

Dialogue

Seeking Alternative Representations

I am often asked how we can be less dependent on the representations fed to us by the mainstream media (the television networks, radio stations, newsmagazines, and newspapers that are owned by large corporations). The question usually comes from someone who has begun to wonder if we are being told the truth about what is happening outside the United States. If we can't travel to distant lands to see for ourselves, what can we do?

Once upon a time, I would have said, "Go to the library." I would still say that, of course. The library is where you can find many alternative representations and much of the information that is left out of reports that come through the mainstream media. I learned the importance of this during my second semester of graduate school (the spring of 1980). Here is what happened.

For a class project, I decided to study how people interpreted the messages encoded in political cartoons. Because I needed a lot of cartoons that dealt with a similar issue, I chose ones that concerned Iran. This might seem like an odd choice, but at that time Iran was much in the news. During the Islamic Revolution of 1979, a group of Iranian students had taken sixty-two Americans hostage at the U.S. embassy in Tehran. Every day, as the "hostage crisis" dragged on, Iran was in the news.

During this time, many political cartoons commented on the situation in Iran. In the cartoons and in much other media coverage of what was going on there, Iranians were portrayed as religious fanatics who were driven by an irrational hatred of the United States. I didn't know any better.

In fact, I knew little about Iran in general, so I did some background reading. I learned that in 1951 the elected prime minister of Iran's parliament was Mohammed Mossadegh, who was widely popular among the Iranian people. He was liked because he promised to use the wealth generated by Iran's oil wells to improve his country's public services. To do this, Mossadegh took control of the oil away from the U.S. and British companies that had dominated Iran in colonial times. Mossadegh's behavior was not acceptable to the United States, and so the CIA engineered a coup and put Mohammed Reza Pahlavi, the dictator who was known as the shah of Iran, in charge. The shah immediately reverted control of Iran's oil back to the U.S. and European oil corporations.

I also learned that the shah had maintained his power through the use of a secret police force that killed and tortured dissidents and that the U.S. Army and, again, the CIA, provided training and economic support for his efforts. After twenty-five years of repressive rule, the shah was hated and was finally overthrown when a resistance movement developed around the leadership of the Islamic fundamentalist Ayatollah Khomeini.

It didn't take a lot of work to gather this information. I read half a dozen articles in foreign policy journals and alternative newspapers. There was some disagreement about how popular Mossadegh had been and about how brutal the shah had been. But there was no dispute about the U.S. role in ousting an elected leader and installing a dictator, primarily for the benefit of U.S. and European oil companies. (If you want, you can look this up for yourself.)

To learn all this made me feel angry and deceived. Why had none of this information been provided by the mainstream media? It took me only a few hours to dig it up. Surely the television and newspaper reporters could have found it, too.

For almost two years—before, during, and after the Islamic revolution—the mainstream media ignored the history of the shah's regime and its unsavory origins. Without this history and context, Iranians looked like religious zealots whose grievances were not worth hearing. And so, like most people who relied on the mainstream media for reports of foreign events, I had no real understanding of events in Iran, the U.S. role in those events, or why Iranians were angry at the United States. It seemed to me that if Americans knew the full story, they would have had a different perception of the Iranian people and perhaps, too, of the U.S. government.

This experience of learning about Iran taught me several lessons. One was to be skeptical of mainstream media reports of events in foreign countries, especially if the United States is involved in any way. Another was that current events could not be understood without studying history. A third lesson was to seek alternative representations of matters that I could not directly check out for myself. A library is still a great place to learn these lessons, but things are even easier today.

In 1980, when I did my project on political cartoons, there was no Internet. Today much of the same information I found in the library can be accessed online in a few minutes. So it is easier than ever to find alternative representations, by which I mean ones that provide history, context, and critical analysis. I would also encourage you not to rely solely on the Web but to use the library to track down scholarly books. If you are a student in a college or university, you might also ask a local professor (presumably someone with relevant expertise) to direct you to reliable sources. You will still have to judge the quality of whatever sources you find, but having found them, you will at least be aware that there are other points of view to consider.

A Note on Passive Voice

Here is a mini-story told in an odd way:

> Once upon a time, a country was invaded. Many bombs were dropped, and thousands of people were killed. The invasion went badly, because mistakes were made. Lies were told to justify the invasion and to cover up the mistakes. Because many people were angry about the mess that had been created, efforts were made to distract their attention by starting another war elsewhere.

In this story, events appear to just happen; the people who did the invading, bombing, killing, lying, and distracting are absent. That's what the passive voice does: it leaves out the people whose actions cause things to happen. A story told this way makes it hard to tell who should be held accountable for doing anything wrong.

The active voice, in contrast, identifies the source of action. If we say, for example, "George cut down the cherry tree," we know exactly who (George) did what (cut down a tree). If we use the passive voice and say, "The cherry tree was cut down," we are left to wonder who is responsible for damaging the tree.

In everyday speech we often use the passive voice when we're unsure who did something. So we might say, for example, "The classroom floor was waxed over the weekend" or "A new grading policy was approved." There's nothing necessarily wrong with talking this way; we don't always have to say exactly who did something to be able to talk sensibly about what happened.

When we need to hold people accountable for breaking the law or for intentionally causing harm to others, the passive voice can be a problem. Understandably, the guilty usually prefer the passive voice because it obscures their responsibility. This is why people in positions of power—people whose decisions really do make things happen—are likely to say, when they are called to account, "mistakes were made."

We should be wary of representations of events that obscure the source of action. What happens in the social world happens because of how people choose to do things together. If we keep this principle in mind, we will be less likely to be hoodwinked by stories told in the passive voice.

Paths for Reflection

1. Think of a living person whose life interests you. Imagine that you are going to make a biographical film about this person. It will be a short film, only about thirty minutes. To gather information, you interview the person about whom the film is being made. You also interview the person's family members, friends, lovers, teachers, coworkers, employers, and so on. You even film a day in the life of your subject. Then you edit this mass of material down to thirty minutes. When the film is shown, your subject says, "This is horrible! You've misrepresented me and my life!" But everyone else who sees the film thinks it does a wonderful job of capturing the essence of your subject's character and life. How would you explain this discrepancy in views about your film? If someone were going to make a biographical film about you, what would you worry about, and why?

2. It is a truism to say that society provides us with resources—language, clothes and other meaningful objects, styles of bodily movement—that we use to create images of ourselves and impress others. But we ought to think about where those resources come from and what consequences arise when people use them. For example, a lot of young people will choose a brand of clothing, a brand of beer, or a brand of cigarette as a way to say, "Notice that as a user of this brand, it's clear that I am a special kind of cool, smart, playful, daring, and desirable individual." There is, however, a contradiction here, since using a mass-marketed product that is available for purchase by millions of people is hardly a sign of one's special qualities as an individual. So how are people seduced into using such products to create images of themselves? Who benefits and who pays when they do? Are there alternatives?

3. By reading a good daily newspaper you can learn a lot about what is going on in the world (far more than you can learn from television). Still, newspapers report only a fraction of what goes on locally, nationally, and internationally; more happens than can possibly be covered and reported. Newspaper people therefore must decide what to report and what to ignore. These decisions, made by newspaper owners, publishers, and editors, determine how social reality is represented to readers. See if you can get an editor or reporter to give you an account of how these decisions are made. Then consider how this decision-making process is likely to yield certain kinds of representations and not others. How also might a newspaper's need to make a profit (through selling advertising space) influence decisions about what to report and how to report it?

Related Readings

Blum, William. (2014). *Killing Hope: U.S. Military and CIA Interventions since World War II* (updated ed.). London: Zed Books.

Brissett, Dennis, & Edgley, Charles, Eds. (1990). *Life as Theater* (2nd ed.). New York: Aldine.

Farr, Robert M., & Moscovici, Serge. (1984). *Social Representations.* London: Cambridge University Press.

Goffman, Erving. (1959). *The Presentation of Self in Everyday Life.* Garden City, NY: Doubleday.

Schwalbe, Michael, & Shay, Heather. (2014). "Dramaturgy and Dominance." Pp. 155–180 in Jane McLeod, Ed Lawler, & Michael Schwalbe, Eds., *Handbook of the Social Psychology of Inequality.* New York: Springer.

Scott, Marvin, & Lyman, Stanford. (1968). "Accounts." *American Sociological Review* 33:46–62.

Tavris, Carol, & Aronson, Elliot. (2007). *Mistakes Were Made.* New York: Houghton Mifflin Harcourt.

Zinn, Howard. (2015). *A People's History of the United States* (reissue edition). New York: Harper Perennial.

CHAPTER 10

....

Understanding Power in Social Life

One time I told my class about an angry professor who wanted to take over the university. His plan was to march into the chancellor's office, tell him to pack up and move along, and declare himself in charge. My students laughed. I said, "Is this funny? Don't you think his plan would work?" No one thought it would work. Most thought the professor would end up in jail or in a psychiatric hospital. I said that that wasn't necessarily true.

"What if the professor *explains* to the chancellor why it would be wise for him to step aside? Wouldn't that make for a smooth transition?" I asked. One student said that this wouldn't work either, because the chancellor would call the campus cops to haul the professor away. I said that the professor could just explain to the cops why they ought to support him and not the old chancellor.

Another student said it still wouldn't work. She said that even if the professor convinced every cop on campus to accept him as the new chancellor, no one else would. "Who else matters?" I asked. "If the cops support the professor, isn't that enough?" One student said that to be accepted as chancellor, the professor would need the support of state legislators, the governor, other professors, and staff. She also said that if he didn't follow the proper procedure for getting the chancellor's job, he'd never get the support of these people.

I said that the professor just needed to write a pamphlet explaining how the old chancellor had botched the job and should be replaced. Then, if everyone read the pamphlet, they would understand why it was time for change and why they should support the professor when he took over. Some students shook their heads; some squirmed in their chairs. I heard at least one sigh. There was a lot of doubt in the room.

The student who was fond of procedure said, "This whole thing is crazy. If people could take over by doing what you're talking about doing, there would be chaos. There would be no legitimate authority, and there'd be constant fighting." Another student said, "The plan isn't crazy at all—but it is scary, because it could work. I mean, how does anyone get legitimate authority in the first place? It probably always comes out of a fight."

I said that legitimate authority could be created in various ways, but that *power* on a large scale always depends on shared belief and people working together. Neither presidents nor revolutionaries have power in a vacuum; they always need the support of others, if only a few disciples at first. What's more, getting the support of others requires resources created by a human community: language, ideas, money, media, weapons, and food. Being sociologically mindful, we can see, then, that power arises out of social life, not out of charismatic personalities.

It isn't necessary to be a boss in an organization to have power. To be able to make something happen somewhere is to have power, no matter how little it might be. Still, this power depends on social life, since this is where our skills, knowledge, motivation, and even bodies come from. Even though we don't need to be bosses to make things happen, we still ultimately depend on others for whatever power we have.

Ideas and Illusions

An old saying has it that "power comes from the barrel of a gun." This is true in the sense that guns can be used to coerce people, since most people would rather obey just about any order than be shot. And when groups are fighting, the side with the most guns usually wins. So guns can indeed be used to make things happen. Here is another old saying: "Give me a child for the first five years, and s/he will be mine for life." This second saying contradicts the first, because it says that what a person can be made to do depends on what s/he is taught. So which is more powerful, ideas or guns?

Suppose you had lots of guns and you got an itch to overthrow a government. Do you have enough guns to do the job? No number is enough unless you can find people willing to use them. Unless you can convince followers to use the guns to shoot other people, your revolution will go no further. You might as well sell your guns for scrap.

Suppose you are the ruler of Upper Slobovia. Suppose that your awful policies have sparked a movement to oust you from office. One day 50,000 people march on the capital, so you call in the police, the army, and the palace guard to protect you. As the protesters storm the palace, you give the order to shoot to kill. What happens? Nothing—because the police, soldiers, and guards think the protesters are right and you are corrupt. The protesters succeed because their ideas have made your guns useless.

Power is plain to see when guns are used to coerce people. It is not so easy to see, however, when ideas are used to shape people's thoughts and desires. If a rebel leader says, "Let me tell you why the government is corrupt and why the Shining Militia should be in charge," that is an obvious attempt to use ideas to gain power. A direct approach like this would of course put you on guard, lest you be persuaded to support an outrageous movement. Suppose, however, that ideas are used more subtly and on those least able to defend themselves.

Think of children in schools. If you were the leader of a country (or a member of a group that benefited from what the leaders were doing) and you wanted to preserve the social arrangements you had created, you might develop a plan like this:

- Every morning in every class in every school, students will face the flag, join hands, and recite the Pledge of Unity, collectively raising their hands over their heads when they come to the lines "My heart for my land/When I hear my land's call/God's blessings will be upon us/My country above all."
- Students at the elementary level will be required to study the history of our nation, from the time when the first settlers began pushing back the savage frontier up to the present. The objective will be to help students appreciate the great progress in civilization that has resulted from the heroic efforts of our nation's founders and later leaders.
- Students at the secondary level will be required to take at least one course in comparative government. The objective will be to help students see that our system of government offers the best possible balance between freedom and equality. Other systems will be examined to see how they fall short of this ideal.
- Students at the secondary level will be required to take at least one course in comparative economy. The objective will be to help students see that our economic system provides everyone with an

equal chance to succeed and that differences in wealth result from natural differences in talent.

- Although schools will not be required to comply with this plan, special funds will be available to schools and school districts that do. Funds can be used for construction, teacher salaries, travel, equipment, and hiring of staff. Funds will be distributed in the form of block grants to approved schools and districts, with expenditures controlled by local administrators.

This is just one way you could try to instill ideas that will encourage people to accept things as they are, including the fact that you are in charge. If you can instill these ideas in school, when people are very young, they may never think of thinking differently. This is a more efficient and durable way to control people than holding guns on them.

Instilling Needs

Another possibility (and for this you don't need to control a government) is to use ideas to instill needs in people—needs that only you, or your product, can satisfy. If you can create a situation like this, people will want to give you things—money, adoration, or obedience—so as to get from you what they desire. Here is an example of how this could happen.

Imagine you are the chief executive officer of BioDynaTek. Profits are falling, and you need to revive them by increasing sales. So you've told your research lab to come up with a hot new product. After several years of work, one of the lab teams invents a way to build eyeglasses that look ordinary but can project a small computer-like screen, visible only to the wearer, on which can be displayed information from memory chips hidden in the earpieces. Users of the glasses can thus have all kinds of information available at the tips of their eyeballs.

Your engineers and accountants calculate that your Virtual Memory Vision (VMV) glasses can be sold at about the same price as a smartphone—not cheap but still affordable for a lot of middle-class folks. Your marketing people think that VMV glasses could sell big and revive BioDynaTek's sagging profits, so you decide to manufacture and sell the glasses yourself for a few years to establish the market and then license the technology to other companies.

There is, however, one problem: no one feels a need for VMV glasses. What you must do, therefore, is create a need for your product. Your advertising people are paid to do exactly this sort of thing. So you turn the problem over to them, and soon they come up with several ways to pitch VMV glasses. They suggest television ads like these:

- A man arrives home after a day at the office. Child or partner sees he is empty-handed and says, "You forgot, *again*?" Cut to man leaving work and checking VMV calendar display; man sees reminder to buy birthday gift; man arrives home and delivers gift to delighted partner or child. Message: VMV glasses can prevent the embarrassment and hurt feelings that come from forgetting important dates, such as birthdays and anniversaries. Catch phrase: "VMV. Because love means never having to say 'I forgot.'"

- A professional type (physician, lawyer, stockbroker) is asked a question in a tense meeting and fumbles for an answer. Cut to irritated/anxious look on face of boss/client. Second professional type—wearing VMV glasses—speaks up and crisply delivers the right answer. Cut to approving nod and smile from boss/client. Message: VMV glasses are the solution to the otherwise impossible task of keeping up with current knowledge in any business or professional field. Catch phrase: "VMV. When it's important to know. Now."

- A couple stands on a busy big-city street corner, apparently looking for something. One leafs through a tattered address book and says, "I thought it was right here, but I guess we missed it. We'd better head back." The other, wearing VMV glasses (and more fashionably dressed), tilts head down and says, "Hold on, let me check. I see. It's just moved around the block. C'mon, we've got plenty of time." Message: Smart, successful, sophisticated people use VMV glasses to manage modern life and still have time for fun. Catch phrase: "VMV. For people who refuse to let life get away from them."

These ads don't try to argue people into buying your product. Instead, they arouse people's insecurities about appearing insensitive, incompetent, or uncool—and then suggest that these insecurities can be relieved by a product they had never heard of before. If these ads work, BioDynaTek will make millions from the sale of VMV glasses.

(Some readers will know that in 2014 Google sold a product, Google Glass, which is much like the fictional VMV glasses described above. Priced at $1500, the product sold poorly and was taken off the market, pending further development. It seems that Google did not convince many people that they needed Google glasses to enrich their lives. Smartphone manufacturers, in contrast, have succeeded wildly in this regard.)

The point here is not about how to sell high-tech gadgets, but about how ideas can be used to get others to do what you want. One way is to get others to feel a need for what you have to give. Even more power can come from getting people to think that only you can give them what they want. Instilling such ideas makes others dependent on you, in which case you can demand from them what you want. If the need is strong enough, people will meet very high demands.

Using ideas to instill feelings of need and dependency is not just an advertising ploy. It is common and does not require the resources of a corporation. Being sociologically mindful, we can see that power is created in this way in many places. We can also see that there is great potential for harm in this way of creating power.

For example, suppose that one person in a relationship feels insecure about his or her looks or intelligence. If the other person wants to control the relationship, s/he can exploit this insecurity by saying, "Yes, you are flawed—so badly that no one else would want you. I, however, am willing to overlook your problems and be with you anyway. For this you should feel lucky and grateful and be willing to meet my needs, or else I will dump you and leave you to the miserable fate you deserve." Such messages are usually conveyed more subtly. The effect is to make a person feel dependent, which is likely to make the person more controllable.

Sometimes this happens between teachers and students. Perhaps a teacher feels threatened by a student's growing knowledge and confidence. To put the student back in place, the teacher might say, "You think you're so smart? Ha! Compared to me you are still an ignoramus. And remember, I'll be writing your letters of recommendation, so don't get uppity." The teacher is trying to reassert control by reminding the student that s/he still depends on the teacher for many things. It is this dependence, plus the student's desire for what the teacher can give, that cements the teacher's power over the student.

Impeding Critical Thought

Other ideas help to sustain power by making change seem impossible or foolish. For example, while it is easy to show that an economy driven by greed is harmful to humans and to the earth, when this point is made in regard to capitalism, many people will say, "Capitalism may not be perfect, but the only alternative is communism, which no one wants because it would take away all our property and freedoms." I have heard this often in the classroom.

What many people seem to believe is that there is no good alternative to capitalism and that much of what we enjoy about life in our society would be lost if major change were attempted. These ideas make it hard to think seriously about what could be done to make better lives possible for more people. By impeding critical thought and conversation, these ideas help to maintain the current system and the privileges of those who enjoy power within it.

The idea that if things change they will only get worse is much older than capitalism. Whenever people have tried to hold on to power the same idea has cropped up. The ideas that current arrangements, whatever they might be, are the best possible and that everything good in life depends on sticking to these arrangements are used to make people fear change and feel that it is wise and mature to accept society as it is.

But people are not always so easily discouraged. In many instances people have felt that some arrangement was too unjust or painful to bear, so they began to struggle for change. The civil rights and women's movements in the United States are two examples; the overthrow of the apartheid regime in South Africa is another. We could make a long list of similar examples. In each case we would find people who refused to accept the idea that change was impossible or foolish.

The powerful do often succeed, however, in using ideas to hold on to power. Perhaps it will help to show how else this might be done. Many of the ideas used to hold on to power are well worn by now, although they are still effective if an audience does not think critically. The leaders of a government that is being challenged by revolutionaries might use any or all of the following ideas to defend themselves:

- You who are threatening our great society are engaged in a futile effort. You do not have the resources, the leadership, the vision, or the popular support to win control. Our forces are superior in every way. What's more, God is on our side, and He has told us not to relinquish our responsibilities to govern. So it is clear that you cannot prevail. It would be best now if you ceased your wasteful struggle and returned quietly to your everyday lives.

- You who are demanding change are reckless and foolish. You are not competent to run this complex society of ours. In fact, you should be grateful that we who are of superior spirit and intellect are willing to do it. If you think there is something wrong with how things are being done, let us know, and we will look into your complaints. If we determine that they are valid, we will take appropriate action. You must trust us to look after the best interests of all.

- You who are causing disruption are being misled. Your leaders do not really care about your needs or well-being. They simply want you to take risks for their benefit. If you follow them, they will sacrifice you to satisfy their own lust for power. Our purpose, unlike theirs, is to serve you by keeping our society operating peacefully and productively. So please turn away from your corrupt leaders before it is too late. Let us all try to feel like good neighbors again.

As you can see, political speech writers and advertising copywriters have much in common. When they are paid to do it, both know how to use ideas to generate doubt, undermine feelings of strength and hope, and cloud people's thinking. They have mastered the art of using ideas as resources to make things happen or to keep them from happening.

Because this sort of manipulation is so common, you might think, "I won't believe any of the crap I'm told. It's all lies. I will doubt *everything*." This is a posture of radical skepticism, and I suppose it is better, or less dangerous, than believing everything you are told. It is impossible, however, to doubt everything. We always have to make sense of the world from some point of view, and this means taking certain ideas for granted (if we really doubted everything, we couldn't function at all). Rather than trying to doubt everything, it is perhaps better to be skeptical in a disciplined way.

It is clear that ideas are often used to create, acquire, and hold on to power, and we should be wary of this. Being sociologically mindful can help, because we will think to ask, Where did this idea come from? Who would like me to believe it? Who will benefit and who will be hurt if a lot of people believe it and act on it? Remembering to ask these questions makes us less vulnerable to manipulation. Of course, sociological mindfulness does not ensure that we will find true answers. It is merely a way of seeing that makes us less likely to be taken in by what is false and harmful.

Controlling Information

If I asked how many candidates ran for president in the 2016 U.S. presidential election, would you say two? That's the usual answer. Some people will remember the primaries, add those candidates, and guess a dozen. The correct answer is more than five hundred.

Most people are surprised to learn this. Perhaps you think, "Yes, that is more than I expected, but those aren't all serious candidates. A lot of them probably file the papers and pay the fee just to say that they ran for president." You would be right; many of the five hundred ran as write-in independents in only one state, and for most of them it was a lark. Yet many more than two or two dozen candidates can offer intelligent policy statements on a range of issues. About fifty candidates are at least this serious.

Perhaps one or more of these alternative candidates has ideas and plans that would appeal to you. Unfortunately, you will probably never know if this is the case, because information about these people and their ideas is filtered out by the very organizations that are supposed to bring it to you. If we consider how and why this happens, we can gain some understanding of how power often rests on the control of information.

One reason that alternative candidates are ignored is that media people see them as having no chance to win. Media people are right. Restrictive election rules and the high cost of television advertising make it hard for alternative candidates to compete. But what truly dooms them is a lack of coverage. In this way, a self-fulfilling prophecy is created. Alternative candidates are not covered because they are seen as having no chance to win, and they have no chance to win if they are not covered.

Some candidates' ideas also get filtered out because they are considered unrealistic. For example, a candidate who wanted to cut military spending by three-fourths and use the money to build schools, mass transit, and affordable housing and to provide free education and medical care to everyone would not be taken seriously by the media. Why? Because corporations and the very rich would resist such changes so fiercely that any candidate who proposed them would find it nearly impossible to win. Journalists who covered a candidate who held ideas like these would be accused of wasting time on a crank.

Perhaps you can see the problem here. If the media will cover only "serious candidates" and only those candidates whose policies do not threaten corporate power are considered serious, then voters will not hear the ideas of candidates who propose more fundamental changes in how the economy works. That information is filtered out. Alternative candidates can *say* what they want, but without coverage, few people will hear. To most voters it thus seems like everybody pretty much agrees that nothing basic needs changing and that no one has any good ideas about how to change things anyway.

People-Filtering and Self-Censorship

You might think, "Ah, he has exposed a dastardly conspiracy! No doubt the media bosses meet with the bosses of other corporations to plan all this out. To protect their own capitalist backsides, the media bosses agree to ignore radical candidates and to fire any reporters who show anti-corporate sympathies. No wonder it is so hard to change things or even to get new ideas into the system." Actually, that is not what I am saying. Being sociologically mindful, we can see why such a crude conspiracy is unnecessary.

We should see, first of all, that people who work for media corporations— as janitors, secretaries, reporters, editors, producers, or executives—are products of a culture in which capitalism and extreme inequality are taken for granted. And so it takes no special coercion to get media people to accept capitalism as normal. In fact, that's how they're likely to think when they show up looking for work.

Media people also learn that being too critical of government or corporations will get them labeled "extreme" or, worse, "biased." It is better for their careers, reporters learn, to stay within the bounds of conventional political opinion. To give serious attention to an alternative candidate, or to make an issue of a candidate's embrace of capitalism, would be seen as strange and would probably be suicidal for a journalist's career. A boss might wonder, "Doesn't this person know what the real story is? Maybe this person is in the wrong business."

And so no conspiracy is necessary for information to get filtered in a way that favors those in power. All that is required is a little people-filtering: hiring and rewarding those who accept dominant assumptions about what is right and true and weeding out those who think differently. The result is an organization in which everyone seems to agree about what's worth covering and what's too far out to deserve attention. Even though this is not the result of a conspiracy, we can see that it is not an accident, either. Certain resources (primarily money) are being used to create agreement about what is normal and what is far out.

All this is not to say that media people never report stories about corporate crime or political corruption. Of course they do. Such stories are usually interpreted, however, as examples of misbehavior by individuals or by individual firms. They are not seen as evidence that the system itself and the rules by which it operates are flawed. You will probably never see this kind of story on a major American television network news program: "Tonight, the first in a six-part series on what's wrong with capitalism and why socialism is the sensible alternative."

Powerful people and organizations do sometimes act in heavy-handed ways to control the flow of information to the public. News stories are sometimes squashed at high levels if they might be too damaging to political leaders or corporations. Threats of lawsuits and withdrawal of advertising dollars can also be used to influence decisions about which stories to report and how to report them. More often, however, the flow of information is controlled by self-censorship—that is, by reporters and editors doing what they know is acceptable and likely to be rewarded and shying away from what they know will get them in trouble.

In some times and places the flow of information is controlled by coercion—"You will be shot if you print that story." But coercion takes a lot of energy and tends to breed suspicion and resistance, so it is not a smart strategy in the long run. It is more effective to control information by shaping thinking about what is good and right and true and by offering rewards: "If you focus on what's important and interesting [in our judgment], you will get a raise and a promotion." In this way people can be conditioned to want to do what suits the interests of more powerful others.

If writers who criticize the government are killed, or if their books are burned in the streets, everyone will know that an effort is being made to control information. It is much harder to see information being controlled by shaping ideas about what can be taken for granted and about what is interesting and important. It is also hard to know when alternative points of view are being ignored or when conformist work is being rewarded inside organizations.

Information as a Resource for Power and Resistance

It is probably clear by now that acquiring and holding on to power depend in large part on the control of information. Or perhaps it is more accurate to say that power depends on shaping the content of information and controlling its flow to certain audiences. In this way consciousness can be managed so that people are usually compliant, rather than unruly.

A general principle here is that information is a resource that can be used to make things happen—which is to say that information can be a source of power. If you knew, for instance, that BioDynaTek stock was going to triple in value this year (because the company will soon announce the invention of VMV glasses), you could use that information to get rich. You could buy stock now and sell it later for a big gain.

Or suppose you knew of a job opening and knew exactly what a person should say in an interview to impress the boss and win the job. That would be valuable information to someone seeking a job. If you knew such a person, you could trade your information for a favor or create an obligation to be repaid later. You could make some things happen and others not.

Even in intimate relationships people might seek power by controlling information. For example, if one person refuses to say how s/he feels, this keeps the other person guessing. It is as if one person is saying, "I will not tell you how I feel because then you will know what my vulnerabilities are, and perhaps you will someday use that information against me." Or it is possible that one person wants to appear emotionally tough and thus willing to walk out at any time. This too is a way to maintain power, because it can make the other person feel weak and dependent and perhaps a bit foolish for caring so much.

Being mindful of how information is linked to power, we can see that a great deal depends on context and the nature of our relationships to others. Nothing is a resource in a vacuum—not information or money or guns or anything. Power is the capacity to make things happen, but exactly what can be made to happen always depends on the context in which the resources we possess are or are not usable.

We can again use simple questions to remain mindful of how the information we receive is filtered and shaped. For instance, we can ask, What assumptions are shared by everyone whose ideas are presented on this program (or in this publication)? What issues are never discussed? What image of the government, the nation, or the economy is created by the information presented here? What would be a truly alternative, not just slightly different, point of view? Being sociologically mindful, we must *seek* answers, too, rather than letting others feed us whatever information they like.

A way to see how information is filtered and shaped—and to see what we're missing when we rely on one source—is to consult a variety of sources and to see how they compare. It also helps to remember that all stories have more than two sides. Being sociologically mindful, we will try to grasp as many sides as we can. When people are able to do this and when they are willing to think critically, exploiters and fakers of all kinds lose their power.

Making Rules and Agendas

Tear off a corner of this page, a piece about half as big as a pencil eraser. Now pop it in your mouth and chew it up. How does it taste? Would you say it is (a) wonderful, (b) delicious, (c) delightful, (d) fantastic, or (e) superb? Perhaps you are thinking, "These are stupid choices! The paper tastes like nothing. If anything, it's kind of icky." Too bad. You must choose one of the categories above or your choice will not be counted.

You are probably familiar with this kind of forced-choice situation. In school you were probably allowed to choose among a whole array of boring courses, and within each course you might have been allowed to choose to write a paper, do a book report, or take an exam. Or perhaps you once had a job in which you could decide whether to use a mop, a brush, or a sponge to scrub a floor.

Here is another example. Suppose you live in a country in which people choose their government representatives by voting. But suppose that it is so expensive to run for office that only those candidates whose ideas appeal to the rich can attract the money needed to mount an effective campaign. And suppose, to hark back to the earlier example, that only the candidates who can attract huge amounts of money are covered by the media. What then? The actual range of choices is likely to be narrow. Only those candidates whose ideas and plans are acceptable to the rich and powerful will appear on the ballot. Now you are back to the choice to use a mop, a brush, or a sponge to do the same job.

Perhaps it seems as if these aren't real choices. It might seem that someone else, someone more powerful, usually decides ahead of time what we can choose from. If this is how it seems, you are probably seeing things clearly. Most of our choices are constrained in some way. Being sociologically mindful, we can see how our choices are often constrained in ways that allow others to hold on to power.

To show how this can happen, it will help to turn things upside down. Although it makes me a bit nervous to do this, I am going to turn you into a Power Monger for a few pages. Hold still for a moment while I work the transformation. *Sociotransequitur Bebop Kaboozle!* Now, if you are not too woozy, please keep reading. I will later turn you back into a decent human being.

Now you are rich and powerful and want to stay that way. You could try to use the resources you control to force people to obey you, but the more force you use, the more anger and resistance you will provoke. A better strategy would be to allow people some room to make choices, because this will give them a satisfying feeling of control and will make them less angry and rebellious. The trick is to make sure that whatever people choose is acceptable to you.

How do you do this? Your best bet is to try to create rules and agendas to steer people toward doing what you want. Once these rules and agendas are accepted as legitimate, your power will be largely invisible and quite secure. At least for a time.

First of all, do *not* make a rule like this: "I will decide what the options are, and then you will pick one of these." That would not hide your power at all. People would just feel manipulated and resentful.

Here is a better rule: "A range of options consistent with organizational goals will be formulated by a committee of appointed executive officers, line managers, and staff." Rules like this are often used to control people in large organizations. What such a rule really means is this: *The bosses, who have already decided what the organization's goals are, will pick people who agree with these goals and have them come up with the same set of choices that the bosses would come up with if they were doing the job themselves.* As a smart Power Monger, you would know that this is a better way to get things to turn out to your liking.

Here is another case. Suppose that the ruling group to which you belong is challenged for control of the government by various small groups that want to create a more egalitarian society. Your group could use its control of the government to suppress these groups, but if you didn't want all the trouble this would cause, you could create an arrangement in which the less powerful groups felt that they had a chance to win control, when in fact this would be nearly impossible.

For example, you might devise an election system in which whoever gets over 50 percent of the votes wins and whoever gets less than 50 percent is out of luck. If you could convince people to accept this arrangement, your control of the government would be almost guaranteed, since no minority group by itself could muster enough votes for its candidate to win. Besides, your group would also have vast resources to promote its candidates. So even when you won election after election, it would look as though your success was the result of people's free choices.

Another principle to observe is that when making rules, laws, and other policies, make them appear neutral and impersonal, so that people will not blame you if they feel angry at being controlled. For you as a Power Monger it is ideal if people experience the rules as "just there" to be dealt with and not as tools that serve your interests. Then, instead of thinking about how, why, and for whom a rule has been made, people will think only of their choice to obey it or not.

Of course, ideas are still needed to make all this work. Someone must believe in the rules and be willing to enforce them for you. Once there are rules, however, it is usually easy to find enforcers, since telling others what to do is a way to have a small piece of power in a system where big power belongs to those on top. And there are always others who are eager to enforce rules because they fear that without rules the world will fall apart. It would certainly be in your interests, as the rule maker, to cultivate such fear.

Despite your best efforts as a Power Monger, some people still might see what's going on and say, "Wait a minute, there's no way for us to win under these rules! How can our needs be addressed and our ideas put into practice if the winner takes all and we get no representation in government? We think it's time to change to a system of proportional representation so that every group gets some say-so. That would give us something more like real democracy."

Many Power Mongers would react harshly to a proposal to do away with the system that ensures their power. But let us suppose that you are smart enough to know that violence breeds no end of violence and that, despite your greed and lust for power, you are not a monster. So you prefer a softer strategy.

You could try to discredit the challengers by spreading word that they are crazy, evil, or foreign spies. This might work if the challengers are few and unpopular, though such discrediting might be hard if there are others who don't like the existing system and think that the challengers have a good point. You could try to refute the challengers' claims, perhaps in a debate. But if you do this, you will give the challengers publicity and a chance to look like heroes, thus helping them attract support.

What you need is a way to neutralize the challengers' claims that the system is unfair, without arousing too much critical thinking about exactly that matter. Ideally, you would do this in a way that leaves people thinking that the system is even fairer than they imagined. So you and your staff come up with this response: "In a free society such as ours, it is important to periodically reexamine our institutions to make sure that they are working to provide fair representation for everyone. Therefore, we are forming a new twenty-member, nonpartisan study commission to review our election procedures, identify any problems, and propose ways to fine-tune our system to make it more effective for achieving our cherished democratic ideals."

Such a statement makes it seem that the system is responsive to criticism and open to change. It makes you seem like a wise and benevolent leader, eager to serve the people. These appearances will help defuse any anger stirred up by the challengers. Now go ahead and rig the game in your favor. Just load the study commission with people who think that a winner-take-all system is the best way to go. It also would be smart to appoint one person who believes in proportional representation, just to polish the impression of openness.

Most important, you must make sure that the commission understands that its job is to fine-tune the existing system, not overhaul it. Thus it is crucial that the chairperson be on your side. Then if anyone proposes radical changes, the chairperson will say, "That proposal is beyond the scope of what we have been asked to do. Now, let us get down to the task at hand, as it has been given to us. We have a deadline to meet."

Power Mongers must be good at setting agendas. The trick is to arrange the situation so that serious challenges to business as usual are excluded from consideration right from the start. At the same time, it is clever to allow a lot of discussion about matters that do not bring the fairness of the existing system into question. If people can be kept busy dealing with an agenda full of safe matters, they will probably not even miss what has been left off.

Autonomy and Freedom

I apologize for turning you into a Power Monger for these past few pages. No doubt it was unpleasant for you. Take a deep breath now, sit still, and I will return you to your normal state. *Sociotransequitur Rebop Kaboozle!* There, it's done. You are a decent human being again.

So what does it mean to be sociologically mindful of power? It means paying attention to how resources are used, by whom, to make things happen or to keep them from happening. It means paying attention to how ideas are used, by whom, to shape thoughts and feelings and create comforting or distracting illusions. It means watching to see how information is filtered and shaped, by whom, in ways that create dependencies or keep others from acting effectively. It also means looking critically at rules and agendas to try to see who makes them, how they are made, and whose interests they serve.

Being sociologically mindful of what power is and how it works, we see it as rooted in social life—that is, in shared beliefs, in cooperation, and in the ways people do things together on an everyday basis. This way of seeing reminds us that power does not spring from individuals. If it did, power would be hard to resist without violence. But since power depends on shared belief and cooperation, we can always resist power by challenging the beliefs and withholding the cooperation on which it depends. It is thus also possible to create power with others by developing new beliefs and ways of cooperating.

Being sociologically mindful, we will also be aware of the dangers that arise whenever power is created. The danger, of course, is that some people, perhaps even those who begin with the best of intentions, will be tempted to use power to make things happen that are to their benefit only. Yet, if many people are paying attention and they know how to detect and resist the destructive or selfish use of power, then the danger is greatly reduced.

The point of being sociologically mindful of power is not merely to see how it works or to resist it individually. It is, rather, to see how the search for and exercise of power *over others* denies many people the freedom to create good lives. Perhaps you think, "If I can see how and when someone is trying to control me, I can evade these efforts and thus carve out a little sphere of freedom for myself." Yes, that is possible. Many people try to do exactly this.

We should be mindful, however, of the difference between freedom and autonomy. To be left alone is to have autonomy. And as long as we do what we're told or pose no threat to those in power, we can have a lot of autonomy. If you do as you're told and make no challenging demands, your boss will be happy to leave you alone. So will most government leaders. After all, it saves energy if you are willing to police yourself. But this is hardly freedom.

To have freedom is to be able to formulate options, not just to choose from the ones we're given. To have freedom, in this sense, we must work with others to create new ways of doing things together and thus new possibilities for living good lives. Those who benefit from arrangements of inequality will not like this. Only by being sociologically mindful can we see how to resist their power to forestall change and how to create among ourselves the power to bring new arrangements into being.

Dialogue

Power and Legitimacy

One student said that I was right about people wanting a small piece of power. "That's how cops are," she said. "They get drunk on a little bit of power." To illustrate her point, she told a story about a protest at which police officers had forced her and several hundred other people into a pen that was designated as a "free speech zone." She said that cops were bullies who enjoyed having license to abuse others. I agreed that some cops could be bullies, but said that we needed to understand police behavior in a more sociologically mindful way.

Let us begin with this observation: political and economic elites could not retain their power and privileges without the help of police (and, internationally, soldiers). Otherwise, when the majority of people became disgusted or outraged at the behavior of elites, they would rise up and throw them out of office, or possibly out of windows. But most police officers do not see themselves as helping elites hold on to power. They see themselves as preserving social order by enforcing the law.

So the first thing to recognize is that police officers, like other bureau-cratic functionaries, usually believe in the legitimacy of the system that employs them. Here again we see the importance of ideas. Whoever is doing the policing, of whatever kind, must accept the legitimacy of those giving the orders and the legitimacy of the orders themselves. If this legitimacy breaks down, then policing breaks down and elites become vulnerable.

However, it is not as if police officers get up in the morning and think, "Today I will clobber anyone who threatens the status quo." More likely, they get up in the morning and think about getting through another day of work. No doubt they also worry about paying their bills, getting along with family members, planning their vacations, and saving money for retirement. The usual stuff. In a way, however, being absorbed in the usual stuff is part of the problem.

Imagine that you have been a police officer for ten years. Let's say that you earn a decent salary and have acquired status and respect because of how well you do your job. Being a police officer also allows you to support yourself and your family; it provides you with a circle of friends; and it allows you to uphold your self-image as a useful member of society. These are the "side bets" riding on your job. You might also realize, in the back of your mind, that good jobs are hard to find. And then one day you are assigned to crowd control duty.

So what will you do? Your job, of course, as you are ordered to do it. That's what most people would do. What you probably will *not* do, at least under normal circumstances, is question the legitimacy of your boss or the orders you're given. Nor will you probably give much thought to the beliefs of the people you are told to control.

And so, most of the time, those who wield a little power, and thus ultimately protect the very powerful, are just doing their jobs, without much concern for the larger implications of their work. If they are thinking about anything beyond the job at hand, it is probably those side bets I listed above. In a way, those side bets are incentives not to think too hard about the larger implications of doing the job at hand.

I have said that power is the ability to make things happen by eliciting the cooperation of others. If so, you can see how people can be controlled through a system that encourages them to stake lots of side bets on their jobs. Yes, you can always refuse to do what your boss tells you to do. But if this is likely to result in the loss of many other things that you value, then you probably won't do it.

You can perhaps also see how bureaucracy amplifies the power of a few. One boss with sub-bosses with sub-bosses of their own (and so on) can direct vast numbers of people. Under such an arrangement, if people are taught to think only in terms of doing their jobs and getting through the day—instead of being mindful about the larger consequences that may result—then even the most horrific projects can be undertaken. The efforts of millions of people can be orchestrated to unwittingly fulfill one leader's mad vision.

I have been asked, too, how it is that the power of a system breaks down. This is an important question, but perhaps it should be rephrased. I would ask, How does the *legitimacy* of a system break down? By "system" I mean the established ways of doing things together by means of which a society functions. By "legitimacy" I mean the widely shared belief that a system is right and good and ought to be preserved.

Rephrasing the question makes it easier to find answers. If a system is supposed to keep society functioning by meeting people's needs, then it might begin to lose legitimacy if it fails to meet those needs. People might then begin to think, "The old ways of doing things aren't working. We need some change around here!" If only a few people think this way, then a system is not really threatened. If many people begin to think this way, then a system might be delegitimated.

People might also begin to question the morality of a system. That is, they might begin to question whether the system is really right and good. "Yes, this economic system meets many of our needs," people might think, "but it also causes terrible harms, so perhaps it is not so good." Again, if only a few see things this way, a system will probably not be delegitimated. But if a great many people question the moral rightness of a system, then its legitimacy may break down.

Historically, it seems that the *workability* of a system—how well it meets most people's material needs—determines its fate more so than its morality. Usually when people have been well fed, housed, and amused (or distracted), they have tolerated systems that yield awful consequences for others. This is why people "in the middle," people who are comfortable but not powerful, are often shocked when a system is challenged by people whose needs are not being met. Folks in the middle often wonder, even as a system is falling apart, why anyone is complaining at all.

It's clear why those who enjoy power and privilege within a system strive to preserve its legitimacy. They will continue to benefit if people continue to believe that the system makes sense, works well, and is right and good. But you can also see why a lot of other people—those in the safe, comfortable middle—might also wish very strongly to believe in the legitimacy of the same system.

But suppose that the questioning becomes loud, persistent, and persuasive. Suppose that people begin to think that the system isn't working as well as it should and that it really does produce a lot of bad consequences. And, beyond this, suppose that people begin to question the competence and morality of those in charge. Now it is not only an abstract "system" that comes into question, but the flesh-and-blood people who run it. Under these conditions—when both the workability of a system and those in charge of it are seriously challenged—legitimacy is likely to collapse.

Political and economic systems that are still workable often survive periods of terrible leadership. Sometimes this occurs because powerful people behind the scenes take steps to remove current leaders, thereby creating the impression that problems have been fixed. Groups of elites tend to support each other, but they will not do so at the cost of destroying the system from which they all benefit. Then again, if a great many people get hurt as elites fight for power among themselves, this too can have a delegitimating effect. The non-elites who get chewed up in these struggles might begin to think, "Down with all of you!"

To return to the example of the police (and to the "Upper Slobovia" example earlier in the chapter): if enough people question the legitimacy of a system and its bosses, then the power of those bosses will evaporate. That power depends on cooperation, which in turn depends on shared belief, which in turn can be changed by new ideas. So, again, power is at the mercy of critical thought. This is not to say that delegitimating a system or its bosses is the point of being sociologically mindful about power. The point is to recognize that bosses make history *their way* only if others let them and that ordinary people can choose to make history differently.

A Note on Nonviolence

Resistance to oppression can take many forms. People might engage in small acts of sabotage or rule breaking. Or they might express contempt for a dominant person or group by making jokes or using disrespectful body language. Other times, when oppression becomes intolerable, people might organize and resist violently. This can mean destroying material resources or, at the extreme, destroying those who do the oppressing.

In thinking about what kinds of resistance might be most effective, it's important to be mindful of the nature of power itself. If power depends on the ability (of a dominant person or group) to elicit the cooperation of others, then power can be neutralized by undermining that cooperation.

In this chapter I suggested that this can sometimes be done through critical education that challenges the legitimacy of corrupt leaders.

Bearing in mind the importance of cooperation and, implicitly, noncooperation, we can see at least two problems with violent resistance. One is that it compels members of a dominant group to cooperate all the more tightly among themselves, for the sake of their own survival. Another is that violent resistance can often make a dominant group appear—in the eyes of people who stay on the sidelines of a conflict—more legitimate as the group tries to "restore order."

This is one reason why historical leaders such as Mohandas Gandhi and Martin Luther King Jr. practiced and urged nonviolent resistance. When dominant groups responded violently to peaceful protests, the moral legitimacy of those groups was eroded. This helped people on the sidelines decide who deserved their support. Eventually, more people were cooperating to fight for, rather than against, equality and freedom.

Oppressive social arrangements and policies can always be resisted by withholding cooperation. People can refuse to obey unjust laws, they can refuse to work, they can refuse to buy, and they can even peacefully disrupt "business as usual." Such nonviolent actions require courage, because they can provoke harsh responses from those in power. The harshness of the response is often a sign that the powerful know just how tenuous their power really is.

Paths for Reflection

1. Perhaps you have had your fill of lectures and tests and would be glad to quit school now if you could leave with your degree in hand. Very well, then, write a memo to the registrar (the person who keeps track of students' academic records) saying this: "Upon consideration of what I have learned while at [school name], and in light of what little would be gained from further time at [school name], I have decided to opt for early graduation. I therefore request that my degree be granted at the end of the current semester and that an official transcript be issued verifying completion of the degree. Thank you for your cooperation." Do you doubt that this would work? Why? Suppose you had a million dollars in your pocket to spread around. How might that increase your chances of getting an early degree?

2. Managers and administrators are generally seen as having legitimate authority to hire and fire people, set wages and salaries, give promotions, decide how work will be organized, and tell workers what to do.

If this is the case, then no individual worker has much power in the face of management. Workers pretty much have to take or leave what the bosses dish out. Then again, maybe not. Imagine a situation in which you were treated unfairly by an employer. If you complained individually, you would be in a weak position to demand any change. But suppose that many of your coworkers shared your feelings and wanted to see changes made. What could you do to tip the balance of power in your favor? How might the same strategy be used by students in a university?

3. Tameka and Brinne are undergraduates at a major university. Tameka is black; Brinne is white. Both are from solidly middle-class families. Both are conventionally attractive, smart, and self-confident. They get good grades, have lots of friends, and feel as if they can accomplish anything they set their minds to. In short, they both feel very much empowered. But if we understand what power is and where it comes from, we can see that there is a difference between feeling empowered and having real power. Why is it that many young women like Tameka and Brinne might fail to see this difference? What are the consequences of this "false consciousness" about power?

Related Readings

Bartky, Sandra. (1990). *Femininity and Domination*. New York: Routledge.

Chenoweth, Erica, & Stephan, Maria J. (2011). *Why Civil Resistance Works: The Strategic Logic of Nonviolent Conflict*. New York: Columbia University Press.

Domhoff, G. William. (2014). *Who Rules America?* (7th ed.). New York: McGraw-Hill.

Herman, Edward, & Chomsky, Noam. (2002). *Manufacturing Consent: The Political Economy of the Mass Media*. New York: Pantheon.

Lukes, Steven. (2005). *Power: A Radical View* (2nd ed.). London: Macmillan.

Mills, C. Wright. (1960). *The Power Elite*. New York: Oxford University Press.

Parenti, Michael. (1978). *Power and the Powerless*. New York: St. Martin's Press.

Sharp, Gene. (1993/2012). *From Dictatorship to Democracy*. New York: New Press.

....

CHAPTER 11

Differences and Inequalities

One time, during a discussion of inequality, I said that people with more money and education tend to have different values and tastes than people with less money and education. This was a minor point that I didn't expect to cause any trouble. But a young woman came to me after class with a worried look. "Don't you think it's good to celebrate diversity?" she asked, surprising me with the question. "Well, I suppose, maybe. Diversity in what?" I said. "Like in tastes and values," she said. "You know, like you said go along with social class." It seemed that she had taken my point to be that the values and tastes of the rich were better than those of the poor. I said that that was not at all what I meant.

As we talked, I realized why this student had misunderstood me. She wanted to see social class differences as similar to ethnic differences. If people talked and dressed and ate and carried on differently because they had different levels of income and education, this was, she believed, an interesting and desirable condition. I said that things were more complicated and that we had better come back to this at the start of the next class.

During the next class we talked about the kinds of differences that exist between people. We talked about how some differences make society more interesting—for example, different styles in clothing, food, music, literature, dance, art, and language. We talked about how other differences, such as in religious beliefs, political values, or sexual preferences, can be threatening and disruptive, especially if people are intolerant and lack compassion. Then we came back to social class, and again some students wanted to see it as just another interesting kind of difference.

I said that social class was not simply a matter of difference but of harmful inequality. Why, I asked, would we want to celebrate the fact that some people work at hard, dirty, dangerous jobs for low pay while others have vastly more wealth (often through nothing more than inheritance) than they need or could ever use? Was this something to celebrate or was it a flaw in how our society worked? Certainly it was a different *kind* of difference, not like the happy differences between lefse, tortillas, rice pancakes, and crêpes.

After we talked about this for a while, one student asked, "Are you saying that nothing good comes from social class differences? Isn't it good that we have a system in which some people can be free to think and to create?" These were hard questions that moved the conversation ahead by forcing us to consider things in a larger context.

Yes, I said, money could buy a fine education and give a person time to do creative work. And, yes, it was good that at least some people enjoyed these possibilities. But did these possibilities *require* inequality? Surely we could educate everyone and allow time for creative work, l said, without vast inequalities in income and wealth. I also said it was important to consider the human potentials that were wasted because of economic exploitation and inequality. Perhaps with more equality, I said, we could have a richer society for everyone, because more people would have time to think, create, and care for each other.

One student pointed out that poverty and oppression had given rise to a lot of creative adaptations—ways to survive and to enjoy life—on the part of African, poor, and working-class people. He cited jazz, blues, gospel, and country music as examples. Another student replied that these were inadvertent results that came at a high cost. I agreed: just because some people can produce great art under horrible conditions doesn't mean we ought to tolerate such conditions. I said that even under the best conditions, human life would not lack for the tension and conflict that spark creative work.

I hoped that this discussion would help students to see differences and inequalities in a sociologically mindful way. The point was that some kinds of differences are good because they give us all a chance to enjoy more kinds of food, clothing, music, and so on, but that other kinds of differences—in wealth and income, for example—are destructive. If some people can't afford to eat nutritious meals, clothe themselves against the cold, get a good education, or take time for creative work, then not only do they suffer, but the whole society suffers, because the talents and energies of some of its members are lost.

How, then, can we be sociologically mindful of the difference between differences and inequalities? We must ask, In what ways does this difference matter? Does the difference allow one group to benefit at the expense of another? Does it give one group power over another? Does it mean that members of one group get less respect than another? In short, we must ask, Does this difference cause harm? If a difference leads to exploitation, unfair advantage, domination, or some other kind of harm, then it is more than a difference. It is a form of inequality and not worth celebrating.

Forms of Inequality

An inequality exists when a difference between people or between groups benefits one person or one group relative to another. That seems clear enough. But it is still a slippery idea, since it doesn't say what counts as a benefit. Perhaps, then, it would help to be more concrete about the forms that inequality can take in the United States. In what ways can individuals and groups be unequal, and how do these inequalities matter? Here are some possibilities:

- To start with the obvious, some people have more wealth (stocks, bonds, property) and income (salaries, wages, interest) than others. Money is a universal resource because it can be used to acquire all kinds of things that make life more comfortable, enjoyable, and stimulating. Money doesn't guarantee happiness, of course, but it is very useful for acquiring the things and experiences that foster happiness.
- Some people have more and better education than others. Education can help people make sense of the world, solve problems, avoid mistakes, articulate their ideas, appreciate history, and enjoy art, literature, music, and other cultural products. It can also be used to make connections and to get jobs.
- Some people have more prestigious jobs than others. A judge, for example, has a more prestigious job than a secretary; an engineer has a more prestigious job than a janitor. Having a prestigious job can in turn help to elicit respect from others. In U.S. culture, a person's status in a community often depends largely on the prestige of his or her job.
- Some people have more political power than others. Perhaps this comes from having money or from connections. In any case, having

political power means being able to get people in government to take your problems seriously and look after your interests.

- Some people have better health than others. This isn't necessarily a natural result of physiology. It also results from better access to quality health care, from having less-dangerous jobs, and from living in cleaner environments.

- Some people enjoy more safety than others. They do not have to worry about injuries on the job, being hit by stray bullets in their neighborhoods, or being unable to afford new tires and brakes for their cars.

- Some people have more access to art, films, theater, concerts, and other cultural events than others. Not everyone wants to go to the opera or to browse in art galleries. Even so, many people who might enjoy such activities never get a chance to take them in.

- Some people can afford to travel widely, while others cannot. Seeing other countries, meeting different kinds of people, and experiencing other cultures can be enjoyable and stimulating. Many people cannot afford these experiences.

- Some people can afford luxurious homes, some can afford decent homes, some can afford small homes, some can barely afford to rent, and others cannot afford housing at all. Not having a quiet, safe, private space in which to relax can make it hard to recover from the stresses of everyday life.

- Some people can afford to eat the most delicious, artfully prepared food, while others must make do with whatever they can scrape together. Even simple health food (organically grown fruits and vegetables, for example) can be more expensive than the heavily processed food sold in discount grocery stores. Eating well and eating healthily are thus out of reach for some people.

- Some people can afford well-made, durable, and stylish clothes. Others must buy clothes of lesser quality, clothes that are also a sign of having less money. Some people can thus feel exposed by the clothes they wear, while others can use clothes to flaunt their wealth.

- Some people have better and more powerful tools than others—not just hand tools or power tools, but all kinds of tools for making things happen. A printing press is a tool; so is a computer; so is an aircraft carrier.

- Some people have more information than others. Information is a resource that can help people make good plans, avoid being manipulated, and get what they want. To lack information is to be at the mercy of a world that seems to operate in a mysterious way.

- Some people have better networks than others. By "networks" I mean connections to supportive friends, helpful mentors, knowledgeable teachers, and acquaintances who can help make further connections. A better network isn't necessarily a bigger one, but one in which there are more people who already possess, and are willing to share, useful resources, such as money, tools, information, and so on.

- Some people have more skill and more control over their work than others. To have skill is to possess a resource that can be traded for a decent wage or salary. It is also to have a kind of power to make things happen. Having control over one's work is also more satisfying than being closely supervised and always told what to do and how to do it.

These are not the only forms that inequality takes in U.S. society. Perhaps you can think of others. In each case the inequality means that some people have advantages over others—more specifically, they have better chances to live good lives. Part of being sociologically mindful is seeing these differences and recognizing how they matter.

Perhaps you can also see that advantages tend to accumulate. For example, people with a great deal of wealth and income can turn these resources into other things: comfort, safety, security, pleasure, political power, excitement, information, networks, and so on. These things, in turn, might add to a person's ability to accumulate more wealth. Similarly, the lack of a key resource—education, for example—can make it hard to get more of other resources.

We should also be mindful that these inequalities are social, not personal. They are social because they result from how society is organized and where people fit into that pattern of organization. For example, one can be born into poverty only in a society that allows poverty to exist. Likewise, one can feel lucky to have a clean, safe, high-paying job only in a society where many people are forced to take dirty, unsafe, low-paying jobs.

To say that society is rife with inequalities is not to say that everyone who is disadvantaged lives in constant misery. Hardship is not pleasant, of course; nor is injustice. Yet many people who do not have much money or formal education, do not travel, do not have luxurious homes or go to fancy restaurants are happy. This is not terribly surprising. Human beings are resourceful and can adapt to all kinds of conditions. Once basic needs for food, clothing, shelter, and companionship are met, humans are adept at creating ways to comfort themselves and wring happiness out of simple things.

In light of this, some people might say, "You see? These folks are happy with simple things. They don't need much. They don't even know what they're missing, so there's really no need to get upset about our wealth. It is a source of happiness for us and yet takes nothing away from our inferiors. In fact, they should be grateful that we keep them busy with productive work. Now why disrupt a system that works so well?"

Statements like this have been used in many times and places (e.g., in the U.S. South during slavery times) to justify the misery suffered by working people. The premise of this justification is that some human beings are not worth as much as others. If that premise is accepted, then it becomes only logical to use the time, bodies, and energy of the supposedly inferior people to create happiness for those who are supposedly better. This sort of thinking helps perpetuate inequality by allowing some people to believe that they are entitled to live well at the expense of others.

Invisible Resources

There is a bumper sticker that says, "Dress for Success—Wear a White Penis." This wry slogan reminds us not only that white males have, on average, better chances of success in a society run by white males but also that people in other groups can't shed their disadvantages as easily as changing clothes. If the bumper sticker makes us laugh, it is because we know that as a piece of advice it is absurd; if you are not born with a white penis, it is almost impossible to put one on, at least in any convincing way.

Being sociologically mindful, we can see another point: differences between bodies are not mere differences if one kind of body can elicit more respect than another. For example, in a society where things male and masculine are more highly valued than things female and feminine, a male body is a more valuable resource than a female body. If you dwell in a male body, you are more likely to be listened to, taken seriously, and seen as a potential leader. You can always end up proving yourself to be a fool, but at the start you will be given the benefit of the doubt because of your body.

Similarly, in a society where European features, especially light skin, straight hair, and a sleek nose, are more highly valued—or seen as "beautiful"—then possessing a body with these features is a plus. With these features, you may be seen as having more innate goodness and intelligence and thus be treated better. And if those who are already in power see you as looking like they do, they may be more inclined to admit you to their circles, thus giving you access to further resources.

The heading of this section suggests that skin tone and body type are somehow "invisible" resources. How can this be? Don't these resources have to be visible to produce results? The answer has to do with who sees what. It often happens that those who possess features that are more highly valued do not see the advantages these features provide. It is as if a person were blind to a badge s/he wears every day.

White people, for example, often fail to see that merely having light skin means they will be treated better in many situations than people with dark skin and African features. Being "treated better" means being listened to, appreciated as an individual, presumed competent or trustworthy, and recognized as entitled to dignity and respect. You might think, "What's so special about this? This is how it should be for everyone." You are right, of course, but this is not how things are for everyone. That, too, can be hard to see.

Having a male body can work the same way. All else being equal, a person in a male body is more likely to be presumed credible and capable. It is as if the male body were a sign that said, "Be assured that I know what I'm talking about and can back up my talk with action." And yet, as with whites and skin color, males seldom see that their bodies bring them unearned advantages *relative to women*. The full value of a male body as a resource thus remains invisible to those who possess it.

Bodies can also possess other kinds of resources that are invisible until used. For example, strength, coordination, and muscle control are bodily resources. So is resistance to heat, cold, and disease. We could also include acute hearing, sight, smell, taste, and touch. All of these capacities reside in the body, as a result of natural endowments and training, and we might not know that a person possesses these resources until they are displayed.

Are such bodily resources differences or inequalities? Both. A difference in strength, for example, is, by definition, an inequality because it means that one person is stronger than another. What matters, however, is whether strength can be used to produce other kinds of inequalities. If people could legally enslave others who were weaker, then strength would be quite an asset. Likewise, if people were paid according to how much heavy lifting they could do, strength could be turned into inequality in wealth. So we must be mindful that what counts as a resource depends on the situation.

Visible Origins of Invisible Resources

Where do invisible resources come from? Even strength, which at first seems like a genetic matter, is affected by culture and experience (see Chapter 12). Without proper nutrition and exercise, people who are destined to grow tall and wide do not necessarily become very strong. And even small people can develop their strength to the point where it exceeds that of others who are twice as big. Much can happen, by choice or by accident, to shape our bodies in certain ways and not others.

Other kinds of resources that reside in the body depend even more on experience and training. No matter what our potential might be, we always depend on others to teach us how to do things, to give us problems to solve, and to help us correct our mistakes. Differences in skill and problem-solving ability (what some people call "intelligence") thus arise out of social life. We like to be rewarded for what our bodies and minds can do. Unfortunately, many people never get the chance to learn to do what is valued by those who can dispense rewards.

We can see that social experience conditions our bodies to react to the world in certain ways. Suppose you looked up from the page right now and saw a wizened old man with bulging eyes and flecks of spittle on his chin coming at you with a knife in one hand and a rattlesnake in the other. What would you do? You might shriek, freeze, run, cower, or throw this book at him. In any case, you would surely have a bodily reaction—your heart would pound, your chest would tighten—and this reaction would be a result of how your body has been conditioned to respond to scenes you interpret as threatening.

This odd example serves to illustrate the point that our bodies, not only our minds, react to the world in ways that result from how we have been conditioned to react. Recognizing that these responses are conditioned is important because it reminds us that we do not control all our reactions to the world. What is important to see is that some ways of responding to the world are more valued, more useful than others, and more likely to lead to inequality.

Imagine that you are invited to give a public talk about sociological mindfulness. The talk should be about an hour long and is set for a week from today. Your family, friends, and teachers will be there, along with most of the leaders of the community in which you live. You can expect an audience of about 1,500 people, not counting reporters and photographers. When you speak, you will be representing not only yourself but all the people and groups to which you belong. If you do well, you will receive more honors and probably several job offers.

The prospect of giving such a talk would make many people extremely anxious. They would worry about looking unpoised, about saying the wrong thing, about embarrassing themselves and others. A person who reacted this way might think, "I am so nervous I can't think straight. I can't prepare adequately in just a week! I know I am going to blow it. My heart pounds when I imagine getting up in front of all those people. I can't do this!" This sort of reaction might make it hard to do a good job, thus leading to the bad performance that is so feared.

Another person chosen to give the same talk might say, "Thank you for this honor. A week will be plenty of time to prepare. I'll get to work right away and do my best." Then, brimming with self-confidence, this person brushes up on sociological mindfulness and studies the speeches of great orators throughout history. S/he then writes a first draft, revises it, gets comments from others, revises it again, practices giving the talk, revises some more, and then, finally, on the big day, does a great job, makes everyone proud, and launches a brilliant career.

Why might two people react so differently to the prospect of giving a public talk? It is not much help to say, "Some people are more comfortable speaking in public than others." That is an observation, not an explanation.

Being sociologically mindful we would ask, What *experiences* led one person to be so confident and the other to be so anxious and afraid? How did one person *learn* to have faith in his or her abilities and the other person not? We would try to understand how it happened that these people learned to feel so differently about their abilities and about the challenge of using them.

We should also be mindful that ways of responding to the world, the ways that are conditioned into us, are patterned. Some types of people are more likely to be conditioned to respond to problems with calm faith in their own abilities and worth. If you are white, male, and upper middle class, you will probably have more experiences that nurture your talents, affirm your sense of worth as a person, and give you confidence that you can do whatever you set your mind to than if you are a black woman growing up in poverty.

Obviously this is not true in every case. Some white men from rich families can be plagued by self-doubt. And there are many women of color, from all kinds of backgrounds, whose families and communities instill in them tremendous abilities and pride. Yet on the whole, on average, the pattern holds, as it must, in a society that is run by and privileges whites, males, and those with wealth. In general, those who are born with more visible resources have better chances of acquiring the inner resources that lead to further advantages.

Reconditioning Ourselves

Upon hearing this argument about inner resources, a student said, "But isn't this a lot like in nature? You know, those who survive and succeed are the fittest—the ones who are, for whatever reason, best adapted to the environment." I said yes, the situation could be seen that way, but there are two differences.

One difference is that in nature, creatures are what they are by virtue of genetic endowment; they do not become what they are by going to school, learning skills, and acquiring the habits and dispositions that allow them to survive. In the social world, however, we must devote conscious effort to all the tasks needed to turn children into fully functioning, capable adults. If we don't do this, human beings can be damaged or stunted.

The second way things are different with humans, I said, is that our environment is not simply given to us by nature but is socially constructed. The survival-of-the-fittest analogy is thus wrong, because the social world *can* be changed to make it safe and nurturing for all kinds of people. We do not have to sacrifice human beings as if they were little fish deserving to be eaten by bigger fish. That kind of predatory arrangement does not make for a very humane world.

Reconditioning ourselves is always a possibility. If a lack of self-confidence is the problem, we can practice setting achievable goals and then work to achieve them, thus boosting our self-confidence. We can also learn new skills, habits, and ideas at any time. This becomes more difficult, of course, as we get older and settle into comfortable ruts. It might also be that others whose ruts run parallel to ours will resist our efforts to change.

Yet with support from others, remarkable change remains possible. If our relationships with others make us what we are, then we can potentially remake ourselves by relating differently to others or by forming relationships with different others. As long as there exists the possibility of doing this, of making these kinds of changes, we need not resign ourselves to accepting everything that has been instilled in us by a particular form of social life. We can always pursue growth and change in directions of our own choosing.

Being sociologically mindful, we can see how certain highly visible facts of social life—such as huge inequalities in wealth, status, and power—can lead to inequalities in the distribution of invisible resources. The old adage "To them that have shall be given" is a poetic way of making the same point, which is that advantages tend to accumulate. If we are mindful of the bad results that arise from this tendency, we can decide to reorganize ourselves to make things turn out differently, with greater justice for all.

False Parallels

One time I was talking about how women are hurt by occupational segregation, which is the practice of steering women into jobs that pay less than "men's jobs." A man in the class said, "Men are hurt by occupational segregation, too." When I asked how, he explained that he wanted to become an elementary school teacher but that, as a man, he had been discouraged from doing so. He argued that just as women are oppressed if they are directed away from high-paying "men's jobs" (e.g., engineer, surgeon), he was oppressed because his wish to be an elementary school teacher was not being honored.

His statement evoked a great deal of sympathy. Most people in the class seemed to agree that there was something unfair about his being discouraged from being an elementary school teacher, a job that is usually held by women. His example implied that occupational segregation was equally bad for women and men. He was suggesting that women did not have it any worse than men, because men experienced parallel problems.

I asked the young man who was discouraging him. "My dad and my uncles," he said. I asked if he was being discouraged by anyone in the university or in the public school system. "No, if anything they want more men to go into elementary education," he said. I asked why, if the future for men in elementary education looked so bright, his dad and uncles were discouraging him. "They say it's a woman's job, and that I could do better," he said. At that point the parallel broke down.

This young man's experience was *not* like what women experience when they seek jobs typically held by men. In seeking to become an elementary school teacher, this young man wasn't being told, "You are not good enough for this kind of job." He was being told, "This job is not good enough for you." But even this message did not come from anyone with any power to keep him out. It was his dad and uncles who said he was setting his sights too low. A young woman who wanted to become an engineer or a surgeon would probably not get that sort of message.

Despite all this, I urged the young man to stick to his goals if he wanted to teach children. Then he said, "It's not so much that I want to teach children. I figured I'd teach for a few years and then go into administration. A lot of school systems are eager to hire men as elementary school principals, and from there you can go on to be a superintendent." I was disappointed to hear him say this. The young man who claimed to be oppressed had in fact calculated that his gender would *aid* his career. There was no parallel here to women's experiences of exclusion from the most rewarding jobs.

Taking History and Context into Account

Another false parallel often comes up when talking about racism. If I talk about white racism, someone will invariably say, "Yeah, but blacks can be racist, too." I ask how that can be, and someone will explain, "You see it all the time. Like in the cafeteria. Blacks sit by themselves and exclude white students. They also make disparaging remarks about whites, just like some whites do about blacks. That's racism." Actually, while this behavior might reflect prejudice, it is not racism. Being sociologically mindful, we can see why accusing blacks of racism—for keeping to themselves or for satirizing whites—is a false parallel.

Part of being sociologically mindful is taking history and context into account. If we do that, we can see two things. One is that it was not Africans but Europeans who invented the racial categories "black" and "white" to justify colonization and slavery. If any group is racist, it is the group that invents and imposes such categories. It makes no sense to call the victims racist.

We can also see that in the United States blacks have never had the power to oppress or exploit whites, nor have whites had to suffer daily indignities at the hands of a black majority. When it comes to oppression, exploitation, and disrespect, the situation has been, and remains, entirely the other way around. Blacks have suffered, not benefited, from the idea of "race" and the social arrangements built on this idea.

So if blacks, who are still a relatively powerless minority in the United States, disparage whites and try to maintain solidarity among themselves, this is not racism but *resistance* to racism. To say that blacks who are unfriendly to whites or who tell jokes about whites are "just as racist" as whites who do the same things to blacks is a false parallel. It is false because it ignores the historical responsibility for racism; it ignores the huge differences in power between blacks and whites; and it ignores the different consequences that arise, depending on who is disparaging whom.

Anyone can exhibit prejudice if they embrace stereotypes about members of another group. And so if some blacks see all whites as untrustworthy bigots, we can call this "being prejudiced." Understandably, many white people resent this stereotype. But since blacks as a group do not have the power to discriminate against whites, any prejudice harbored by blacks is of little consequence. Without power it is simply impossible to "do racism." Being sociologically mindful, we can see that doing racism requires not only prejudice but also the *power to discriminate* in ways that hurt others.

Often I can make this point about power and discrimination by asking how many students believe that to get their first big job they will have to please a black employer. So far no one has raised a hand when I've asked that question. I then ask how many students believe that their career success will depend on the judgments of black employers. Again, no hands.

The difference in power between racial groups in the United States also suggests why it is a false parallel to say that when blacks exclude whites from their gatherings, this is the same as whites excluding blacks. If whites hold most positions of power and tend to give such positions to others who are like them—others who are in their network—then people who are excluded from these networks will suffer; they will be locked out and kept powerless. Blacks, in contrast, have relatively little power and wealth, so if they say, "We prefer not to associate with people who look down on us," that is not cause for much suffering among whites.

Recall the student who mentioned blacks sitting by themselves in the cafeteria. It is curious that this example comes up so often. It's a good example of a false parallel that is made just to avoid seeing what is really going on.

I once asked a white student who cited the pattern of separate seating to explain why it bothered him. "Are you bothered because you want to sit at a table with your black friends and suddenly, when they're together, they don't want you to join them?" I asked. He said no, that wasn't it; he said that the black students he was thinking of weren't even his friends. So I asked, "If they aren't your friends, why do you want to sit with them?"

While he was thinking, a black woman raised her hand and said, "People sit with their friends if there's room. It's just that white students are more likely to have white friends and black students more likely to have black friends." She was trying to make peace. Then another black woman said, "It isn't that white students want to sit with us. It's that whites are so used to being able to go wherever they want and sit wherever they want, they resent it if there's even one place where they don't feel free to go." All of the black students and about half of the whites nodded their heads in agreement. It seemed that she had hit the nail on the head.

False Gender Parallels

In discussing the problem of sexual violence, I try to make the point that part of the problem (one of the enabling conditions) is men's practice of sexually objectifying women. This refers to men talking about and treating women as targets of sexual conquest rather than as human beings. When I make this point, often someone will say, "Yes, but women also sexually objectify men. Women talk about men as 'hunks,' and remember there was that television commercial where the secretaries ogled the male construction worker."

To equate women's sexual objectification of men with men's sexual objectification of women is false for two reasons. One is that men do it more often, because showing sexual interest in women—showing that you are attracted to their bodies as sexual objects—is part of signifying (heterosexual) manhood in U.S. culture. The more important reason is that the consequences of objectification are different in the two cases, because men have greater power to harm women physically and economically.

A woman who is treated as a sexual object is not being respected as a complete human being. It is this lesser respect for a woman's personhood that underlies rape and other forms of sexual coercion. It also underlies discrimination in the workplace (it is hard to appreciate the intellect and skill of a person who is perceived as a set of body parts). Again, it is men who, because of their physical strength and institutional power, can cause harm to women—harm that grows out of treating others as objects. Women generally do not have the power to harm men, so the sexual objectification in which women engage is rarely a threat to any man's body, status, or career.

Being sociologically mindful does not lead to the conclusion that it's wrong for men to objectify women but okay if women do it to men. To objectify others is wrong because it is likely to produce harm, if only by reinforcing the habit of ignoring the humanity of other people. We must be mindful, however, of how the consequences of objectification can be very different, depending on who is objectifying whom, under what conditions. When there is a serious imbalance in power, and especially the power to cause harm, we must take this imbalance into account and not let a false parallel keep us from seeing which acts of objectification are more dangerous and damaging.

Patterns in True Parallels

One time I was talking about death rates from stress-related diseases, such as heart attacks, strokes, and liver failure. I pointed out that the rates were higher for black men and for working-class men than for white men and middle-class men. In response, a student said, "But there are a lot of executives who have stress-related health problems, too." I said that while this was true, the data on death rates contained a more important lesson: inequality in U.S. society is one reason that some men, those on the lower end of the economic ladder, die sooner than others.

Instead of grasping this lesson, the student tried to conjure a parallel, as if to say, "Sure, workers have their health troubles, but then so do executives." While this is not literally false, to put matters this way distorts reality. If executives are stressed, it is often because they are trying to hold on to power; when workers are stressed, it is often because they lack power. Invoking a parallel between workers and executives also implies that both groups suffer equally—a notion that is clearly false, as shown by the differences in death rates.

Being sociologically mindful does not mean ignoring all parallels. In fact, it is good to look for them, since true parallels can reveal important things about how the social world works. Perhaps, for example, there is a commonality in the troubles experienced by working-class *men* and executive *men*. Both groups of men might be striving, in parallel ways, for control over their lives. This would be worth looking into. Still, we should not presume that a parallel, even if it is a true parallel, is necessarily an equivalence.

Being sociologically mindful does not mean ignoring the troubles of people in privileged groups, nor does it mean overlooking the misbehavior of people in oppressed groups. Being mindful means paying attention to context, to history, and to power, so that we can see when differences are inequalities and when false parallels make inequalities seem to disappear.

Self-Justification and a Test for Justice

We could say that people make false parallels, refuse to see inequalities, or try to portray inequalities as mere differences because they are not being sociologically mindful. But what is behind the resistance to being mindful in these matters? Perhaps it is a desire to justify one's place in the world. People who enjoy privileges because of their race, gender, income, or sexuality usually seek to justify the arrangements that provide these privileges.

It is hard to change people's thinking when their view of the social world also supports a favorable view of themselves. Someone who has status, wealth, and power is likely to embrace a view of society as a place of fair and open competition, since this view implies that they have done well through their own merits. A critical view of society might threaten this view of themselves. Nor is it very useful to say, "Think harder, stop deluding yourself, and face up to reality." Most privileged people will respond by thinking harder about how to justify holding on to the version of reality they prefer.

It is possible, however, to get people to consider a different way of seeing, if a way can be found to preempt their need to self-justify. How can this be done? One way I have tried to do this is with an exercise (inspired by the thinking of philosopher John Rawls) that might be called a "test for justice." It is a collective thought experiment that comes with these instructions:

> A new society is in the works. The principles of distributive justice on which this new society will operate remain to be formulated. Your job is to formulate them. You have been chosen to do this precisely because you don't know anything else about this new society. More important, you don't know what your place in this new society is going to be. Thus you are perfectly situated to come up with principles that will produce a fair distribution of wealth, since you can't know how to tilt the game to your advantage. Your task, then, is to do the following:
>
> 1. Formulate the rule or rules by which it will be determined who gets how much wealth in this new society.
> 2. Formulate the rule or rules by which it will be determined what each person must contribute to this new society.
> 3. Show how the rules you formulate will maximize justice and equality. (Obviously, you need to define what you mean by "justice" and "equality.") Be sure to consider how your rules will produce fair results even in unusual cases.

This is a difficult exercise for most people. For one thing, it is hard to imagine not knowing who we would be in a new society, since we are so used to being who we are. For another thing, we are unused to anyone asking us how to distribute wealth in a just way. Yet the basic idea behind the exercise is simple: *if you don't know what your position will be in this new society, you have no privileges to justify and every reason to devise rules that will ensure justice for everyone.*

Here are some of the rules that my students and others have proposed for determining who gets how much wealth: (i) everybody gets a share of wealth that is in proportion to what they contribute to society; (ii) everybody gets exactly the same equal share of society's collective wealth; and (iii) everybody gets whatever amount of wealth they need to live a decent life, plus some extra if they have special hardships.

Some of these rules don't work so well when we get to the third part of the exercise, because what at first glance seems fair—such as distributing wealth based on contributions to society—can produce unfair results in many cases, such as when people are disabled and can't do as much work as others. Even the strict equality rule—everybody gets an equal share of the wealth—runs into trouble because some people (e.g., those raising several children) have greater needs than others (e.g., those who are single, with no dependents). To give everyone an equal share would thus produce an unjust result because some people would get more than they need, while others would get less than they need.

It is interesting to see the problems that arise when trying to formulate a rule for determining what each person must contribute to the new society. You might wonder why such a rule is necessary. For one thing, every society depends on people doing what is necessary to keep the society going. Someone has to grow and sell food, build houses, clean up, care for children, and do thousands of other unglamorous tasks. No society could last if everyone decided to sit back and live off the fruits of other people's labors.

Another reason for formulating a rule about contributions is to ensure fairness in the new society. No one should have to do more than their share of the necessary labor, and no one (who is able to work) should get away with a free ride. So what kind of rule can we devise to ensure that fairness prevails? Here is one possibility: we will calculate how much time it takes to do all the work necessary to keep society going and then divide up this work equally among all who are able to work. Perhaps it will turn out that we need twenty hours a week from everyone to keep society running. If so, then the rule becomes "everyone must put in their twenty hours a week."

A rule like this is just a starting point; we would still have to figure out who gets to do what kind of work. Many people might say, "I'll do my twenty hours a week as a brain surgeon, because that seems most interesting." Probably too few people would say, "I'll put in my twenty hours as a garbage collector, because I like stench and filth." We would thus have to come up with a rule to deal with inequalities in different types of work, to make sure that pleasant work and unpleasant work were fairly distributed. Perhaps we would need a rule like this: everyone must do a share of the dirty work; no one gets to do fun and interesting work all the time; and no one gets stuck doing dirty work all the time.

There are many possible rules, all of which solve some problems of justice while creating others. But that is inevitable; we always have to keep thinking about how to make sure that our abstract rules, principles, and guidelines lead to good results in concrete circumstances. That is in large part what human intelligence is for. Being sociologically mindful means bringing this intelligence to bear on problems in the social world.

The goal of the test-for-justice exercise is not to arrive at a single vision of what a just society would look like. The goal is to encourage thinking and conversation about justice and about how well our current society produces just or unjust results. This exercise seems to make it easier for people to see problems in existing society because they do not get so caught up in justifying arrangements that benefit them. Instead they think about the kinds of arrangements that would produce better results for everyone.

I have also noticed that one idea never comes up during this exercise. No one has ever said, "To maximize justice and equality, all we need to do is use the same rules that govern U.S. society right now." No one says this, I think, because once the incentive for self-justification is gone, they are free to be more sociologically mindful than usual.

Dialogue

Inconvenience and Oppression

The section on false parallels has elicited more false parallels. For example, several times I have heard something like this: "What if a white person has a black person for a boss, and that black person treats whites unfairly? Isn't that racism?" A variation on this theme is the female boss who treats men badly. Of course this sort of thing can happen; white males have no monopoly on the abuse of power. We should be mindful, however, that discriminatory acts by members of subordinate groups are relatively rare and do not constitute systematic oppression.

To explain this, I should say what I mean by "oppression." This is not just political rhetoric. It can be a useful analytic term if we take a moment to define it.

To say that people are oppressed is to say that certain things are done to them. Namely, when people are oppressed they are *devalued* (i.e., defined as worth less than people in other groups), *discriminated against* (i.e., given fewer chances to develop, display, and be rewarded for their abilities), and *exploited* (i.e., not fairly rewarded for their ideas, time, and labor). Oppression thus presupposes inequality between groups, because no one can be devalued, discriminated against, or exploited except by someone more powerful. To say that a group is *systematically* oppressed is to say that its members face obstacles every which way they turn.

The philosopher Marilyn Frye uses the metaphor of a birdcage to describe systematic oppression. Think of a bird in a wire cage. If the cage has only one wire, it isn't much of a cage; the bird can just fly around the wire and be free. But imagine a cage with many wires close together, surrounding the bird on all sides. Now, no matter which way the bird turns, a wire blocks its way. That is what systematic oppression is like.

There is a difference, then, between systematic oppression and situational inconvenience. The former is like being in the complete cage; the latter is like facing a single wire that can easily be avoided. Here is a longer example (based on a true story) that I have used in class to spark discussion of these matters.

A young white man, a pre-med student at a large university in North Carolina, was returning to school after spending summer vacation with his family in Connecticut. Near Washington, D.C., he got off the freeway to get a bite to eat. After a few blocks, he found a restaurant and went inside. He was the only white person there, on either side of the counter. He waited in line to place his order, but then, when it seemed to be his turn, the young woman behind the counter ignored him and took someone else's order. When he thought it was his turn again, the young woman ignored him again. Finally, on the third try, she took his order. He got his food and left, returning to his life as a college student.

I tell this story in class and then ask a simple question: is the young white man oppressed? Most students, if they have been given a sociological definition of oppression, say no. They recognize that the hungry young man has male privilege, white privilege, and is on his way to considerable class privilege. So it makes no sense to say that he is oppressed. Yet a few students always insist that he *is* oppressed, *in the restaurant.*

Actually, it seems to me more sensible to say that the young man is situationally inconvenienced. He is not denied service, insulted, or threatened. At worst, he is unfairly made to wait an extra minute before ordering his burger. But then, once he has his food, he is on his way back to a life of opportunity, privilege, and comfort. To use the birdcage metaphor again, we might say that he has had to face, for just a moment, one slim wire that is of no serious consequence.

When I use this story in class, I ask two other questions to prompt discussion. I ask, first, What if the young man had decided to complain about how he was treated? To whom is it likely that he would end up speaking? The manager of a fast-food restaurant in a black neighborhood of Washington, D.C., might well have been black, too. But since the restaurant was part of a national chain, chances are, if the young man went up the corporate ladder, he would end up speaking to another white male.

I point out, then, that the young white man's experience, if he made a complaint, would likely be different from that of a black person who did the same thing. While the young white man could count on eventually speaking to someone like himself, and thus getting a sympathetic hearing, a black person who pursued a complaint would probably end up dealing with less similar and less sympathetic people. A black person might thus face the wire of situational disrespect and then face another wire—not being listened to or taken seriously—if s/he decided to press a complaint.

The other question I ask about the burger story is this: does racism have anything to do with what happened in the restaurant? In response, I can always count on someone to say, "Yes, the young woman behind the counter was being racist." Fortunately, I can also count on someone else to offer a more mindful analysis.

It is fair to say, however, that the young woman behaves in a discriminatory way. She makes the young white man wait while she serves black customers. If that seems rude or unfair, well, it's hard to disagree, given our culture's rules about serving customers in restaurants. But why might she behave this way? What might her behavior possibly have to do with racism?

There is no way to know for sure what she was thinking. But it seems plausible to suppose a few things: her minimum-wage job probably did not fill her with joy; she might have felt that her job opportunities were limited by anti-black discrimination; she might have resented the privileges taken for granted by whites; and, over the course of her life, she might have been disrespected many times by white people. In other words, it is not unreasonable to suppose that, as a black woman in a society fraught with racism and sexism, she would have a few things to be angry about.

And now across the counter appears a young white guy—a college student, she guesses—pretending not to be nervous in a restaurant full of her people. Maybe she thinks that this is a good experience for him. Maybe she thinks that he is learning a lesson about what it feels like to be in the minority. Maybe she thinks it's also a chance for a tiny bit of payback. Make him wait a minute to place his order.

It's not as if she thinks this particular white guy deserves to be punished. He might be perfectly nice. But then she has been treated all her life, by white people, first as a member of a category and only secondarily, if at all, as an individual. So here, in this one rare instance, she can give a representative member of the dominant group a small taste of what black folks like her experience every day. Maybe that's what she was thinking.

So if her behavior has anything to do with racism, it is a reaction to living as a black woman in a society dominated by white males. On making this point, I also say, speaking to white students, that if they would prefer to live in a society where such situations do not arise—where white people do not occasionally have to face even mild expressions of anger from black people—then they ought to work against racism. Which is to say that we should go after the root of the problem and not fool ourselves into thinking that all will be well if everyone just smiles and says, "Have a nice day."

Once again, in the restaurant example, we see that to really understand what is going on in a face-to-face encounter we must take larger circumstances into account. Being sociologically mindful, we might ask, To what groups do the people in this encounter belong? How have these groups related to each other historically? Has one group used its power to oppress the other? Does one group still have far more power than the other? The answers to these questions will surely shape our interpretation of what happens when people from different groups come together.

By taking history and the larger context into account, we can avoid making false parallels, which are, as I say in the chapter, obstacles to understanding. At the very least, we should not confuse inconvenience (which can indeed be unpleasant) with oppression (which is pervasive and life threatening). In terms of the birdcage metaphor, being sociologically mindful means examining not only individual wires, but also how the wires are created and how they are connected.

A Note on Common Wealth

The first time I heard the word *infrastructure*, I thought, "What an ugly piece of jargon!" It was a word I never wanted to use. But then I realized that it meant something like what I had previously learned to think of as "the commons," which originally referred to a plot of land on which everyone in a medieval town could graze their livestock or grow food. And so I came to see *infrastructure*, though still an ungainly word, as referring to something of value: the shared resources that sustain a community.

These days, it's rare that any place in the United States has a real commons where people can graze their cows or plant a garden. But most communities do have a lot of infrastructure or, to use the term I prefer, *common wealth*, that exists in other forms. This common wealth consists of all the buildings, machinery, places, organizations, and other resources that people in a community create to help them get things done together and generally enrich their lives.

Parks, playgrounds, and libraries are examples of a community's common wealth. So are public schools, roads, bridges, and public transportation systems. So are public hospitals, fire departments, police departments, health departments, courts, and local governments. I would also include water and sewage treatment plants, airports, and other public utilities. Whenever people in a community pool their money and efforts to create something from which everyone can benefit, they are adding to their common wealth.

Part of what makes a community's common wealth so valuable is that everyone has equal access to it, or is supposed to. If this principle is followed, then people can help themselves by drawing on resources that might not otherwise be available to them. A body of common wealth to which everyone has equal access also gives everyone a stake in the community—that is, it gives them incentive to be responsible, contributing members. A community can begin to break down, however, if some people acquire so much power that they can unfairly exploit the common wealth for private gain. This is why mindful communities create policies not only to ensure equal access to the common wealth, but also to ensure that it remains common.

Paths for Reflection

1. Perhaps you are in school in hopes that it will help you to avoid getting stuck in a lousy job—the kind that pays badly, offers little challenge, gets you no respect, and leaves you vulnerable to the whims of nasty bosses. It's understandable that you would want to avoid this fate; an awful job can make a person's life miserable. But of course many millions of people will, through no fault of their own, end up in awful jobs their entire lives, while others will, because of class, race, and gender privileges, end up in good jobs. Who benefits and who pays when a society works this way? How might we reorganize things so that people are not permanently stuck in jobs that make it impossible to live a good life?

2. I have heard it said that economic equality is a bad idea "because that means everyone would be the same." This objection to equality has always struck me as strange, since it is obvious that people who have the same amount of money are often very different in other ways. There is, in other words, a lot of diversity *within* economic classes. If you consider what enables people to develop their potentials, how might reducing economic inequality—if only by eliminating poverty—actually increase the amount of interesting diversity in society? Suppose, too, that we democratically

decided to adopt the following policy: *no one will have more wealth than they need until everyone has at least as much as they need.* Putting this policy into practice would reduce economic inequality. How might it help to reduce non-economic inequalities as well?

3. Upon learning about the extent and harmfulness of inequality in our society, some people will say, "Yes, it is sad." I have often wondered about this expression. It is not the same as saying, "These facts about inequality make me feel sad," or "I am saddened to see how people are hurt by inequality," either of which makes it clear that the speaker or writer is claiming to have an emotional response. To say of inequality "it is sad" uses the language of feeling but implies detachment. How do you interpret and explain the use of this expression? What do you suppose are the consequences if people look at inequality and injustice and feel sad (or merely say they do) rather than angry or outraged?

Related Readings

Albert, Michael, & Hahnel, Robin. (1999). *Looking Forward: Participatory Economics for the Twenty-first Century.* Boston: South End Press.

Bonilla-Silva, Eduardo. (2013). *Racism without Racists: Color-Blind Racism and the Persistence of Racial Inequality in the United States* (4th ed.). Lanham, MD: Rowman & Littlefield.

Frye, Marilyn. (1981). "Oppression." Pp. 1–16 in *The Politics of Reality.* Freedom, CA: Crossing Press.

Johnson, Allan. (2006). *Privilege, Power, and Difference* (2nd ed.). New York: McGraw–Hill.

McIntosh, Peggy. (1997). "White Privilege and Male Privilege: A Personal Account of Coming to See Correspondences through Work in Women's Studies." Pp. 76–87 in Margaret Anderson & Patricia Hill Collins, Eds., *Race, Class, and Gender: An Anthology.* Belmont, CA: Wadsworth.

Rawls, John. (1971). *A Theory of Justice.* Cambridge, MA: Harvard University Press.

Schwalbe, Michael. (2014). *Rigging the Game: How Inequality Is Reproduced in Everyday Life* (2nd ed.). New York: Oxford University Press.

Walljasper, Jay. (2010). *All That We Share.* New York: The New Press.

Wellman, David. (1993). *Portraits of White Racism* (2nd ed.). New York: Cambridge University Press.

Williams, Christine. (1992). "The Glass Escalator: Hidden Advantages for Men in the 'Female' Professions." *Social Problems* 39:253–267.

Wright, Erik Olin. (2015). *Understanding Class.* London: Verso.

CHAPTER 12

....

Seeing the Social in the Natural

Once while driving on a country road I saw an old dump truck in a field. Rusted metal showed through bare spots in the truck's yellow paint. There was a spider-web crack in the middle of the windshield. I was struck by how the ruined truck stood out against a backdrop of green trees and grass, so I stopped to take a photograph. The owner of the field came by as I was getting out of my car. After we had talked for a while, he began to complain about the zoning laws that kept him from building a subdivision. "Look at this," he said, gesturing at the field and trees. "The land's not doing anyone any good. It's just sticks and mice."

It was clear that the land had different meanings for him than it did for me. I saw it as something to pass through and enjoy looking at. He saw it as a resource from which to make money, and letting it remain woodlots and empty fields seemed like a waste, perhaps even a threat to his livelihood.

One lesson contained in this incident is that nature is not the same thing for everyone. Nature is one thing for a farmer trying to raise crops, another thing for a developer who wants to build houses, another thing for a wildlife advocate, another thing for an energy company investor seeking to extract resources and make a profit, another thing for a landscape photographer, and so on. Nature in its physical form—soil and minerals, hills and streams, plants and animals—exists no matter what we think about it. But what matters to us about nature depends on our purposes.

Here is another nature story. One time a guest was standing on our deck looking into our backyard. He said, "You've sure got a lot of nature here." He was referring to the bamboo thicket and other trees that blocked the view of our neighbor's house and to the layer of English ivy that covered the ground and climbed the trees. It was green and lush. But was it nature?

The bamboo had been planted by a previous homeowner, as had the azaleas and shrubs near the deck. I had planted the holly trees that filled in between the oaks, maples, dogwoods, and longleaf pines. Even these larger trees were not, as foresters say, "original growth." They were trees that grew after the land had been cleared in the 1700s and 1800s. The English ivy was also an import. European immigrants brought it to North America in the 1800s as an ornamental plant. So even though our backyard is green and lush, it is hardly natural.

This story suggests another lesson about what we see when we see nature. In this case, a scene that appeared natural—because it was full of trees and plants and was not tended like a garden—had been profoundly shaped by human intervention. Being sociologically mindful about nature, we will keep this possibility in mind—the possibility that what might seem natural, in the sense of being *wild*, is not that at all, but rather is the product of human activity. We might even think of nature as a kind of text that can be read, if we know how, as a record of human interaction with the environment.

When I was driving through the countryside enjoying the scenery and looking for something to photograph, the situation was much the same as in the case of my backyard. Even though I thought of the trees and green fields as "nature," it was a humanly shaped nature. The fields and woodlots looked as they did because of hundreds of years of intervention by people who tried to make a living from the land by logging and farming. What seemed natural about the scene was no less a reflection of human presence than the old truck.

It is ironic, too, that my experience of nature while touring the countryside depended on much else that was unnatural: roads, cars, cameras, maps. If not for these human inventions, I would not have had access to, or the same interest in, the scene I stopped to photograph. So not only was the (seemingly natural) scene a reflection of centuries of human presence, so was my presence as a witness. Even my attraction to the scene—the visual and emotional appeal it held for me—arose from an acquired cultural notion that nature is purer, nobler than what is humanly made.

Here is one more story. About ten years ago we put a new roof on our house. When the roofer removed two layers of old shingles, he discovered that some of the underlying wood sheets were rotten and needed to be replaced. "That's not unusual," he explained. "You have to remember that nature is always trying to reclaim your house." Anyone who has ever seen an abandoned, decaying house knows the truth of this statement. Much of nature may be affected, even shaped, by human action, but this does not mean that we fully control it. In the end, nature can reclaim anything we build.

The way I have written these accounts—of stopping to photograph the old truck; of our woodsy backyard; of putting on a new roof—might seem to imply that nature is a distinct entity that affects us even as we affect it. This is a common-sense way of thinking about how we are connected to nature, and it is not unreasonable to think this way. But there is another message in these accounts: we are not as separable from nature as we often imagine. The key to being sociologically mindful about this is learning to see what is social about the natural and what is natural about the social.

Unnatural Disasters

A fire, flood, storm, volcanic eruption, avalanche, or earthquake that doesn't affect people is just an occurrence, not a disaster. It is only when such events cause major harm to people that we speak of disasters. This way of looking at things suggests that whenever we are tempted to speak of *natural* disasters, we should think of how the harm they cause depends on social behavior.

Earthquakes, for example, cause harm mainly by making buildings collapse, crushing those inside them. This is why the deadliest earthquakes occur in places where buildings are made of stone or other heavy, inflexible materials. In modern industrial societies, it is possible to make buildings able to resist earthquakes, thus minimizing the loss of life. So if we are thinking about the damage caused by earthquakes, we must take into account how people build the structures in which they live and work.

Building practices also matter in cases of fires, floods, and storms. Some materials burn more easily than others, and if structures made from combustible materials are close together, the risk of a disastrous fire is high. Some kinds of buildings can withstand hurricane-force winds; others can be flattened by strong gusts. Buildings can also be located in places where floods are more or less likely. Those on high ground are much less vulnerable than those built on flood plains. Perhaps this all seems obvious. Yet the language of natural disasters encourages us to forget how human choices affect how much harm occurs to whom. Being sociologically mindful, we will try to see what is unnatural about so-called natural disasters.

When it comes to disasters such as floods or fires, the problem is not just that people take risks by building on flood plains or with highly combustible materials. It might be that no other building materials or locations are feasible, given local resources, technologies, and land formations. But it might also be that some people—perhaps the poor and powerless—are forced to build in risky places, using cheap and dangerous materials. If this is the case, then we can say that vulnerability to natural disaster is not natural at all. It is a consequence of inequality.

The case of Hurricane Katrina and the damage it caused to the city of New Orleans in August 2005 is a good example of an unnatural natural disaster. The storm itself was natural, but its unequal effects were not. Those who got hurt the most were most vulnerable because of the political environment in which they lived.

Because New Orleans is built below sea level, it requires an elaborate system of levees, drainage canals, and pumps to protect against flooding. It might be said that Katrina was such a powerful storm that it simply overwhelmed the city's protective system. But in fact it was known for years that the poorest parts of the city—the Ninth Ward, in particular, where many low-income people of color lived—were especially vulnerable because the levees were badly designed and not well maintained. Many people were thus not surprised when the levees broke and the poor parts of the city were devastated.

It was not just that many people (1,836) lost their lives and property to the flooding. In the aftermath of the storm, the poorest people—again, most of them African American—continued to suffer disproportionately. Tens of thousands of displaced people were herded into the Superdome (a sports stadium) and forced to get by with inadequate water, plumbing, and other supplies. People who tried to escape the flooding on foot were sometimes turned back by armed whites in less-affected areas. Lack of wealth also made it harder for poor people to support themselves during the storm-related disruption of their lives, as well as harder to rebuild their lives later. The inequality of the damage caused by the storm paralleled other social and economic inequalities.

Another example of an unnatural natural disaster is the tsunami that hit northeastern Japan in March 2011. The tsunami—a giant wave triggered by an undersea earthquake—caused terrible damage. More than a million buildings were destroyed and 18,000 people were killed in the coastal areas of the Fukushima, Miyagi, and Iwate prefectures. Again, the destructive effects of a natural event depended on local building practices and people's choices of where to live. An added element in this case was the destruction of a nuclear power plant in Fukushima.

Nuclear engineers underestimated the tsunami threat. The 33-foot sea wall built to protect the plant was overwhelmed by a wave that was 50 to 60 feet high. Other safety features—backup power sources, steel containment vessels—also failed. Three nuclear cores thus melted down and released radioactivity into the groundwater, the air, and the sea. This led to a massive evacuation: 159,128 people were moved out of a 310 square mile "exclusion zone" around the facility. Today (2016), it is still not clear how, if it all, the people who were evicted will be compensated for their losses. As in the case of Katrina, those with the fewest resources have faced the greatest hardships in rebuilding.

As was also the case with Katrina, the risks of disaster were not entirely unknown. Some scientists and environmentalists have long argued that nuclear power plants are extremely risky because of their vulnerability to human error (e.g., Three Mile Island, Chernobyl), earthquakes, tsunamis, and terrorist attacks. They are also enormously expensive to build, create radioactive waste that is dangerous for thousands of years, and must be dismantled, at high cost, after about forty or fifty years. But power companies and governments have often built nuclear power plants anyway—ignoring the wishes of ordinary citizens—for the sake of generating not just electricity but profits. What this means is that use of a risky and expensive way to generate power is itself a reflection of inequalities in political power.

Japanese health officials have said that no deaths were caused by exposure to radiation from the ruined Fukushima facility. Other health scientists argue that even if short-term exposure did not cause any immediate deaths, rates of radiation-related death and disease will rise in the years ahead. They also note that more than 1,500 people died from stresses related to forced evacuation from the exclusion zone. It thus seems fair to say that the tsunami, the destruction of the power plants, and the release of radiation were catastrophic events, with consequences that continue to unfold.

The Fukushima case also shows that human judgments about safety can be skewed by inequality. Those with the most status and power—corporate executives, government officials, and nuclear engineers—underestimated nature and overestimated themselves. Perhaps they didn't grasp the limits of their knowledge, or perhaps they cared too little about the people whose lives they put in danger. Perhaps it was both. In any case, the scope of the disaster cannot be understood without being mindful of inequality in political power and the tendency of the powerful to pursue their interests with excessive confidence in the correctness of their actions.

Both cases, Katrina and Fukushima, are examples of how natural events can combine with social arrangements to yield disasters. Both are also examples of how vulnerabilities, exposure to risk of harm, and actual harm are related to inequalities in wealth, status, and power. Being sociologically mindful about "natural" disasters, we thus see that their consequences—especially the unequal distribution of harmful consequences—are often socially determined. At the least, we should always try to see, whenever an event is labeled a natural disaster, how it is linked to human social behavior.

Unintended Environmental Consequences

Sometimes the connections between social arrangements and the damage done by natural events are easy to see, as in the cases of Katrina and Fukushima. Other times the connections are less obvious. For example, in the town where I live there are several small creeks that run through commercial and residential areas. For centuries these creeks, which at times are nearly dry, could easily handle the runoff from heavy rains. Now, floods happen every year.

The problem is not just that more houses and businesses have been built in flood-prone areas. In one sense, this is true. But it is also true, and perhaps more important to recognize, that the areas at risk have expanded. Is this because it rains more today than it used to? No. It's because most rain used to be absorbed by the ground where it fell. Now it lands on hard surfaces—roads, parking lots, rooftops—and runs into creeks that can't drain off all that water fast enough. And so areas that used to flood only rarely now do so regularly.

In this case, there is a connection between the growth of the town and a flooding problem that is getting worse. But there is even more to it. The kind of growth also matters.

Rain is not just bouncing off the rooftops of houses. It is bouncing off apartment complexes, malls, and shopping centers surrounded by acres of parking lots—and off wider roads built to handle the related auto traffic. This kind of growth occurs because it is the most profitable kind, aggressively sought by builders, businesses, investors, and real estate developers. Because these people are often wealthy and powerful (at least by local standards), politicians cater to their desires. And because politicians fear being voted out if they raise taxes, the revenue needed to deal with the flooding problem—by building a better drainage system—is not available.

By comparison to major disasters, our local flooding is a minor problem. Yet it shows the importance of seeing connections between the natural and the social. The flooding problem *seems* natural—it rains hard, then it floods—but it is more complex, involving not only rain and creeks but also dollars and votes. Being sociologically mindful, we will try to see, as this example shows, how natural processes are linked to social ones.

The flooding example illustrates one more principle: seemingly natural problems can arise as unintended consequences of social action. Not even the greediest real estate developer aims to create floods that damage people's homes. In fact, the intentions might be good: trying to give people more places to live or more places to shop. Still, the consequences can be bad. Sometimes this happens because of limited knowledge about how human action will affect the environment. Sometimes it happens because of an inability or refusal to be mindful of connections between the social and the natural.

In thinking about these matters, it is useful to distinguish between two kinds of unintended consequences. Some are unintended but foreseen. For example, corporate executives might decide to release pollutants into the air, knowing that doing so will cause higher rates of death and disease in downwind communities. The executives do not intend to harm anyone; they intend only to increase profits by not spending money on pollution control equipment. This kind of consequence is called an "externality," meaning that a cost of doing business is imposed on others—it is *externalized*—rather than being paid for by the corporation itself.

Other kinds of consequences are not foreseen and result from the combined actions of many people. These consequences can be called *structural costs* because they arise from how a society and its economy operate, with nearly everyone being implicated in some way. These costs arise, in other words, because of how society is organized—or "structured"—on a large scale.

The United States, for example, is an industrial society that requires vast quantities of fossil fuels—oil, coal, and natural gas—for its existence. It is also a capitalist society in which a tiny portion of the population controls most economic resources and dominates government. These are not superficial features of U.S. society but fundamental ones that affect every aspect of social life. Although there are variations, most modern capitalist societies operate similarly. One unintended consequence of these arrangements, a consequence that will have enormous costs, is global warming.

Global warming has occurred in large part because burning fossil fuels creates carbon dioxide, a "greenhouse gas" that traps heat inside the earth's atmosphere. As a result of this warming, sea levels are rising, storms are becoming more severe, and crop-destroying droughts are becoming more common in some parts of the world. These climate changes are expected to produce major social disruptions, as millions of people flee coastal cities in the 21st century, cope with the wreckage caused by great storms, and try to find more hospitable places to live. All this migration is likely to entail considerable conflict.

When the age of industrialism powered by fossil fuels began in the mid-1800s, no one could foresee global climate change as a consequence. Nor were most people in industrial societies, up through the 20th century, aware that their consumption of fossil fuels could affect the climate in a harmful way. It was only around the turn of the 21st century that the problem of global warming gained much public attention. What's more, this is not a problem caused by a handful of short-sighted capitalists. Everyone who participates in a modern industrial economy is implicated; we all depend on fossil fuels to heat and light our homes, drive our cars, ride mass transit, grow food, and obtain the consumer goods we use in everyday life.

Global warming and the problems it is going to create can thus be seen as structural costs in that they arise out of how industrial capitalist societies are organized. If we are mindful of this connection between the natural and the social, we realize that dealing with these costs will require changes in how we live. Not only will we have to adapt to more extreme weather and massive population shifts, we will also have to learn to generate and use power differently. And if capitalists and politicians refuse to respond adequately to the climate change problem, we will have to learn to govern ourselves differently. Far more democracy might be necessary to avoid facing costs that will be impossible to bear.

What I have been pointing to is the need to consider how problems we might think of as arising from nature can be the unintended results of human behavior. In some cases, it might be easy to trace a problem, such as exposure to a specific toxic pollutant, to the action of a single corporation. But even when there is one obvious culprit, other people (e.g., government officials) and other kinds of action (e.g., law making, law enforcement) are always implicated. Being sociologically mindful, we would try to see all the relationships and behaviors that go into creating a seemingly unintended environmental problem.

In other cases, such as global warming, the relationships and behaviors are even more complex. In these cases we need to be sociologically mindful of how problems arise out of the way a society is organized and how ordinary people conduct their everyday lives. Problems on this scale are not only harder to analyze—because they require more knowledge of how natural and social processes operate and are affected by each other— but also harder to face. We can more easily accept the need to correct the behavior of a single polluter than we can accept the need to change a form of economy, government, or way of using energy. Yet we might recognize, if we are mindful of connections between the social and natural, that current ways of life are not sustainable.

Being sociologically mindful of unintended environmental consequences requires recognizing two seemingly contradictory things at once: national boundaries don't matter; and nations matter greatly. On the one hand, national boundaries don't matter, in that the earth's ecosystem takes no note of them. Lines on a map do not affect how air or ocean currents flow, or the formation and movement of storms, or the temperature of the planet. Consequences do not stop at national borders; what happens in one place, one country, can have global reach. Thus to understand our relationship to planetary nature, we must temporarily suspend belief in nations as discrete entities.

On the other hand, nations matter because national governments make laws regulating corporate and individual behavior that affects the environment. It is also within nations that people are most likely to act together to challenge harmful laws and economic behaviors. So, national boundaries don't matter—the carbon dioxide generated in the United States and other industrialized nations affects the warming of the whole planet—yet they do matter, because nations are sovereign entities that make laws regulating what goes on within them. This is why environmentalists often advise people to "think globally and act locally." Of course, acting locally, which is the best most of us can do, can have global consequences, for better or worse.

I have been referring to relationships between the natural and the social as if the social is over here and the natural is over there, and we can glance back and forth between them to see how they're connected. This way of looking at things is useful for some purposes. As I've said, we can look at social behaviors—building practices, food production, energy extraction and consumption, and so on—and ask how they affect the environment. Analyzing our "impacts" on the environment in these ways can help us see unintended consequences and perhaps make changes before we cause damage and create high costs for ourselves.

Yet the talk of impacts tends to perpetuate the dangerous idea that we are separate from nature, that we merely *affect* it. But if we are mindful of our origins in nature, our inescapable dependence on nature, and the effects we have on the rest of the natural world, it is hard to sustain belief in this dualism or, as it is sometimes called, "human exceptionalism." The truth is that we are never apart from nature but always a part of nature. This becomes even clearer when we turn from looking at the nature that surrounds us to the nature that constitutes us, which is to say, looking at our bodies.

The Body as a Social Product

As a boy, I threw baseballs thousands of times. And so even today, if I throw a baseball with my right arm, I can put my whole body into it, throw smoothly and fast, and usually hit what I am aiming at. If someone watched me do this, they might think that I naturally throw like a boy or a man. But if they watched me throw with my left arm, they would get a different impression. Quite possibly they would think that I throw like a girl.

In truth, boys and girls do not throw baseballs (or snowballs, or anything else) differently because they are boys or girls. If people throw differently—with a smooth, powerful, whole-body motion, or with a jerky, weak, arm-only motion—it is a result of differences in training and practice. Because of the sports boys and girls are taught to play in U.S. culture, boys usually get more of this kind of training and practice than do girls. So, "throwing like a girl" is just a sexist way of saying "throwing like someone who has not done much throwing."

Someone who does not understand the importance of learning how to throw with whole-body motion, or the importance of throwing thousands of times (perhaps more) to perfect this kind of motion, could mistakenly think that what is called throwing like a girl is a consequence of nature. Boys' bodies, a person might think, are just naturally better suited to throwing than girls' bodies. In this case, a result of social life—boys being taught how to throw and devoting many hours to practice—is misinterpreted as a result of nature.

I use the example of throwing not to say that there aren't differences between male and female bodies, but that often we fail to see how all human bodies are shaped by social life. Just as we sometimes fail to see how the nature around us is shaped by human behavior, we sometimes fail to see how the nature inside us—the interior environment—is shaped by how we organize society, the cultural beliefs we embrace, and how we interact with others. Before I say more about this, I want to return briefly to the idea of the body as a *natural* object and unpack what this means.

Human bodies are, first of all, products of evolution. Analysis of our DNA shows that we are related to all other creatures on earth—most closely to other great apes, then to other mammals, then to other vertebrates, and so on back to protozoa. The size, shape, sensory abilities, and neurological capacities of the human body are results of our species' evolutionary history. We look as we do, and can do what we do, because of natural selection, sexual selection, genetic drift, and genetic mutation. Scientists might argue over the relative importance of these processes, but there is no disagreement that nature has made us what we are, biologically.

In some ways, we are like all other organisms. We are born, we grow, we age, we decline, and we die. Our biological nature also sets limits and endows us with certain capacities: we require nutrients of the kind our bodies can use; we can tolerate a limited range of temperatures; we must breathe the mix of nitrogen, oxygen, and argon we call "air"; we are susceptible to injury and disease; we can perceive only a limited amount of the information available in the world around us; we can move in some ways and not others—we can crawl, walk, swim, or run, but no matter how hard we try, we can't fly. We are, in short, a kind of animal, evolved to occupy a particular ecological niche.

For most people, it is not hard to see how we are natural creatures. Just thinking about human bodies as products of evolution reminds us of this. What is often harder to see is how our seemingly natural bodies are also products of social life. Again, what tends to remain unexamined, or less deeply examined, is the social in the natural.

The earlier example of throwing a baseball shows how our bodies are conditioned—developed in some ways and not others—as a result of culture. This kind of conditioning goes beyond throwing. If some people are encouraged to run and jump and climb and lift and hit and explore and engage vigorously with the world, while others are discouraged, or even prevented, from doing these things, different capacities will be developed. Those in the former group will tend to develop more strength, agility, and confidence in their bodies than those in the latter group.

230 THE SOCIOLOGICALLY EXAMINED LIFE

What the above example alludes to is a pattern of gender socialization still common in U.S. culture. It is not always the case, of course, but usually it is boys who are encouraged to play in ways that more fully develop their bodily capacities and instill a sense of physical competence. These differences, as with "throwing like a girl" (or "swaggering like a dude"), are then often misperceived as being the results of nature rather than of how nature—in this case, the human body—is shaped by culture.

Here is an example that isn't about physical performance. Perhaps you have been at a party, talking to a person or a few people around you, and then suddenly—through the hum and buzz of noise in the room—you hear your name (or perhaps you hear "sociological mindfulness") spoken by someone at a distance. You weren't trying to listen to conversations across the room; all you could hear was a background murmur of voices. Yet somehow, out of the chaos of sound, you caught a word or phrase that had special meaning for you.

This "cocktail party effect" (as social psychologists call it) occurs because your brain and mind are conditioned to pay attention to sounds selectively. Being selective is necessary because it would be overwhelming to try to perceive and interpret every sound coming from the world around you. But when a sound wave contains a bit of information relevant to your interests or concerns, your mind instantly interprets it and "lets it through to consciousness," so to speak. This happens automatically, as a result of prior conditioning—much like picking up a baseball and throwing it with a smooth, whole-body motion. It's a seemingly natural ability, yet one that originates in social experience.

Brain scientists often get these matters backward. A common mistake is to study the brains of adult women and men, note some difference—for example, that women's brains respond differently to images of violence or to requests to perform emotional tasks—and then claim that these physical differences explain differences in women's and men's behavior in everyday life. This unsociological view ignores at least two things: behavior is more powerfully shaped by context and interaction than by individual traits; and the brain, like other parts of the body, is shaped by experience. Alleged differences in brains are thus more likely to be the consequences than the causes of social behavior and experience.

Whenever we look at differences in bodily function between people in major social categories—categories that are associated with disparities in resources, power, and stress—we should suspect that differences in function result from social experiences. The temptation, if we are not sociologically mindful, is to think that physical differences cause social differences.

But this is almost never the case, especially if we are looking at categories of people who are subjected to deprivation, abuse, exploitation, or discrimination. What we are usually seeing, when we see bodies growing or functioning differently, are the biological consequences of inequality.

The world of sports offers many easy-to-see examples of how the body is shaped by social experience. Achieving a high level of fitness for a sport is obviously a result of choices people make about how to develop their bodies—choices that stem from the experience of being drawn into a *community* of athletes and a *culture* of competitive sports. When we see athletes devote years of their lives to training their bodies to do extraordinary things, there is no doubt that we are seeing how the body can be conditioned by a social process. But the social shaping of the body is also a generic process—it happens to everyone, not just athletes or people subjected to high levels of chronic stress.

Consider what seems most natural about each of us: height. We tend to think of a person's height as determined by genes. This is not quite true. Height depends not only on genes but also on nutrition. It is similar to what happens with plants. Seeds that are genetically identical offspring from the same parent plant will grow to different heights depending on the sunlight, water, and soil nutrients they are given. Likewise, children who are nutritionally deprived will not grow as tall as they would under better conditions. This is why we have seen the average height of people in some parts of the world increase as nutrition has improved.

Weight is another aspect of the body that is affected by social life. For example, in the past thirty-five years adult obesity rates in the United States have doubled. Today, more than a third of U.S. adults are obese, and more than two-thirds are overweight or obese. About a third of children and teenagers are now overweight or obese. According to the National Center for Health Statistics, the average American is nearly twenty-five pounds heavier today than in 1960.

Health scientists argue about what has caused this rise in obesity. The causes they point to include children and adults engaging in less physical play and less physical work; people spending more time sitting in front of television and computer screens; more reliance on cheap, high-calorie fast food; and more consumption of high-calorie sugars (especially fructose from corn syrup) that corporations use to make processed foods taste better. The relative importance of these causes remains to be determined, but they are all in the realm of the social. American bodies have changed because of changes in culture and economics, not genetics.

Obesity is not the only bodily consequence of these social changes. Increasing obesity has in turn boosted rates of diabetes, high blood pressure, heart disease, joint deterioration, and mobility problems. If we are not aware of how these diseases are linked to obesity and of how obesity is linked to culture and economics, we might think that obesity is occurring naturally. If we can see the social in the natural, we will not make this mistake. We will also see that to overcome these health problems it is necessary to change the social conditions that create them.

Many types of harm to our bodies can be traced to social behavior. Cancers and other diseases can be caused by toxins that corporations release into the environment, as well as by other substances—tobacco smoke, alcohol—people choose to put into their bodies. Heart attacks and strokes can be caused by chronically stressful work. Even seemingly natural diseases can be traced to social behaviors. Cholera, for example, is largely a consequence of poor water treatment and sanitation practices. The actual spread of disease is also a result of how we interact with others (e.g., hand shaking, gathering in small spaces, sharing food, having unprotected sex) in everyday life.

Injuries, too, usually arise from social life: reckless behavior undertaken to impress others; the negligent or reckless behavior of others; an employer's refusal to invest in proper safety equipment; the making and selling of defective or dangerous consumer products. In all such instances, human choices and behaviors end up affecting our bodies. It is of course possible to be hit by lightning or a falling tree, but only rarely are we victims of unaided nature. Usually it is our own behavior, or the behavior of powerful others, that is the source of what ails us.

The upshot is that human bodies are products of what we *know* (how to stay healthy, prevent disease, repair injury, and cure illness); what we *make* (foods, drugs, machines, toxins); and what we *do* (eat, work, exercise, gather, reproduce). In fancier terms, we can say that symbolic culture, material culture, and social organization make our bodies what they are. To be aware of how these aspects of social life shape our bodies is another way of being sociologically mindful of the social in the natural.

Trying to see the social in the natural does not mean ignoring the natural. As noted earlier, the human body is a product of evolution. In that sense, it is as natural as anything can be.

So how do we take the body's naturalness into account while being mindful of its social construction? By recognizing two things: first, how we are affected by social life is a result of what nature has made us: if evolution had given us different bodies (including different brains), social life might affect us differently; second, the size, shape, fitness, health, needs, and abilities of our bodies result from how nature and social life interact. What we are as creatures is not a result of nature *or* nurture, the natural *or* the social, but of both at once. Being mindful of this helps us see that human bodies are as much products of society as of nature and that it takes mindful effort to discern precisely how.

Social Realities and Natural Illusions

When it is said that race is a fiction—a set of false notions about how groups of people are genetically different in ways that bestow greater or lesser intelligence, morality, creativity, or ambition—some people will respond by insisting that race is real because they can see it. But what they see is not race. What they see are differences in skin tone, hair texture, and facial features. These outer differences are then imagined to reflect differences in the character of people in so-called racial groups. These imagined inner differences are in turn used to explain and justify the dominance of some groups over others—the idea being that it is only natural and right for groups with superior qualities to rule those with inferior qualities. *That* is what race is.

Yet even if race is a fiction, it is a fiction that persists in part because there are real, genetically based, bodily differences between some groups of people. Skin tone, hair texture, and facial features are all genetically heritable traits. The problem, however, is that the association of these traits with social groups is often misunderstood to be purely a consequence of nature. In fact, social behavior has everything to do with why these bodily differences exist and persist. The concept of a gene pool is useful for understanding this.

Genes are biological instructions or recipes for how to make and assemble proteins into a living organism. Human chromosomes carry the genes (tiny strings of DNA) that encode the instructions for assembling proteins into the various parts of a human body. All the instructions for all the possible ways of making an organism that we would recognize as human exist in the gene pool of our species. This includes the gene variations that give people different kinds of hair, skin tone, facial features, eye colors, and so on.

But here is a complication: because of geography and culture, smaller gene pools can form within the larger pool. Technically, these smaller pools do not consist of different genes but of gene variations or "alleles." It is worth remembering that all humans, as members of the same species, have the same genes. What makes us different from each other are gene variations.

If people in a place mate with each other—and not with outsiders—then any gene variations they share will spread throughout the local population (presuming that the variation doesn't keep people from reproducing). If the variation that comes to be widely shared is for a visible bodily feature, such as skin tone or hair texture, then people in the local population will develop a shared aspect of appearance that distinguishes them from people elsewhere. Even if every member of the population doesn't have the feature, it might be so common as to be seen, by insiders and outsiders alike, as a mark of membership in the population.

Geography can matter in another way if climatic differences, over a long period of time, lead to visible adaptations. The best example is skin tone. Melanin, which is what makes skin darker, is protective against skin cancer in sunny, equatorial climates. Skin that contains less melanin is better at converting the limited sunshine available in cloudy northern regions into vitamin D, a vitamin necessary for survival. This adaptation, a result of early humans moving out of Africa and into less sunny parts of the world, has created visible bodily differences. Skin tone is thus natural, genetic, and inherited, yet skin tone differences among groups exist and persist because of social behavior: where people chose to live and with whom to mate.

Culture matters because it is another basis for mate selection. Most of the time, cultural insiders are seen as more desirable mates than outsiders. Culture also tends to emerge out of geographic proximity—people who live and work together in a place tend to develop shared values, attitudes, beliefs, tastes, and customs. Geography and culture thus often combine to strengthen boundaries between populations in which certain gene variations are more or less frequent. A possible result is the emergence of cultural differences that correspond to gene pool variations.

Cultural boundaries that correspond to gene pool variations can also be upheld by inequalities in power. When a powerful group targets a group of people who "look different" for exploitation, this usually entails the creation of rules about who can mate with whom. Members of the dominant, higher-status group might be forbidden from mating with members of the subordinate, lower-status group. Although such rules are often violated, to the extent that they are followed, group differences in the frequency of gene variations will be preserved, along with any visible differences they might produce. Here again we see social behavior leading to what might otherwise be thought of as the outcome of a purely natural process.

The process I have been describing is one in which the natural, social, and political are intertwined. It is this process, unfolding over many generations, that gives rise to distinct communities that correspond to heritable differences in appearance. The illusion this can create is that differences in appearance reflect underlying biological differences that *cause* cultural differences. But what is really going on is that local gene variations (or, more correctly, the frequencies of gene variations in local populations) are being perpetuated by geography, culture, and politics. Variations in group appearance—variations that are commonly misunderstood as "race"—are thus further instances of the social in the natural.

Seeing the Natural in the Social

Because it is usually harder for people in U.S. culture to see the social in the natural, that is the matter I have tackled here. By being more mindful of the social in the natural, we can better understand the environment and how we are connected to it. With this understanding, we are less likely to be misled by claims that social arrangements are "natural" and must therefore be accepted without question. To fully understand how we are connected to nature it is of course also important to turn things around and consider the natural in the social.

One thing we might see, in looking for the natural in the social, is that the *built environment*, or what is also called "material culture," is a reflection of our biological nature. We build the kinds of shelters we do because of the limited range of temperatures our bodies can tolerate. We grow the kinds of foods we do because of what our bodies need to consume. We build the kind of vehicles we do because of what our bodies can and cannot do when it comes to getting from one place to another.

We build the kinds of scientific instruments we do because of our limited abilities to see what is going on with the matter and energy around us. We build the kinds of tools and machines we do because of the limited force and precision with which we can wield our bodies. In fact, everything we build is in some way tied to our biological nature—either as a matter of enhancing our bodily powers, protecting our bodies, or meeting our physical survival needs. To recognize this is to recognize the natural in the social.

The natural capacities of our bodies are also tied to social control. Because of how we experience the taste and texture of food, even a hungry person probably would not find a skunk tail sandwich to be as strong an incentive for good behavior as a piece of fresh apple pie. And if it was necessary to use force to make a person obey, a feather duster would be a less effective tool than a cattle prod. These might seem like silly examples, but they illustrate the same principle that is used to leverage our behavior in real life. We can be compelled to do things, or not to do things, because of what our bodies lead us to experience as pleasurable or painful.

Our bodies, we might say, are information-gathering and information-generating devices for our brains and minds. We see light, hear sounds, detect odors. We feel the pull of gravity, the pressure of the wind, the texture and temperature of objects. What we can sense—in every way the body makes possible—is stimulus for the brain and information for the mind. All that information helps us construct mental images of the outer world and of ourselves.

It also matters that our bodies are not rooted in place but can move around to gather information from multiple vantage points. Movement itself, because of the sensations that accompany it, generates information that is channeled to our brains. In these ways the natural capacities of the body help to shape the growth of our minds—how we come to habitually perceive, interpret, and respond to the world around us. If our sensory and perceptual abilities were different, we would likely develop quite different minds. We might know, as the philosopher Thomas Nagel famously considered, what it's like to be a bat.

The natural is also evident in the social in that all human societies must devise ways of handling reproduction, child rearing, aging, and death. Were we not the creatures we are—vulnerable at birth, vigorous in youth, strong in adulthood, weak when old, *mortal*—we would not have the social arrangements we have. Many familiar social institutions—families, schools, hospitals, workplaces—might not exist at all if not for what our bodies require of us, enable us to do, and keep us from doing. In this sense, every social arrangement and every cultural practice in some way reflects the part of nature that is us.

Even though I have said more in this chapter about the social in the natural than about the natural in the social, it should be clear that being sociologically mindful means seeing both. It means recognizing that what we sometimes take to be natural is shaped by human intervention and that what we sometimes take to be social is shaped by nature. Precisely how and to what extent this shaping occurs, precisely how the natural and the social are intertwined, must be discovered in any given case. But what we are likely to find, in the end, is that we are not looking at two distinct realities, the natural and the social, but two sides of one.

Dialogue

The Limits of Technology

Modern humans are good at inventing tools and machines to solve problems. We are so good at this that many people have a near religious faith in technology, believing that no matter what problem we face, some new invention will come along, like a benevolent god, to solve it. This tendency is evident in the case of global warming. Many people believe that the solution to the problem will be technological—a matter of creative engineering more than anything else.

The problem is of course in part technological, since it stems from how we extract and use energy to keep our industrial societies going. If we did not build engines, electrical power plants, and furnaces that burn fossil fuels as they do, we would not be putting billions of tons of carbon dioxide into the atmosphere every year, causing the planet to get warmer. Given that the problem is linked to our current technologies, it makes sense to think that the problem could be mitigated by changes in these technologies.

One set of technological fixes involves turning from fossil fuels to alternative energy sources: wind, sun, tides, rivers, volcanic heat. To the extent that we can derive energy from these sources, we will burn less fossil fuel, generate less carbon dioxide, and avoid further warming the planet. Developing technologies that allow us to extract, store, and distribute energy from these sources is thus seen by many people as an essential part of the solution to the problem of global warming.

Another set of proposed fixes goes by the name "geoengineering." This term refers to trying to change nature in a way that reduces planetary warming. Some proposals include scattering sulfate particles in the stratosphere to reflect sunlight away from the earth; taking carbon dioxide out of the air and burying it in the ground or under the sea; stirring the surface of the sea into froth to reflect sunlight and keep the water cooler; and scattering iron powder on the ocean to promote the growth of plankton, which absorbs carbon dioxide.

Controversy surrounds all of these proposals. Advocates of alternative energy sources point out that we already know how to tap most of these sources. Critics say that all of these sources, together, cannot replace the 82 percent of the world's primary energy that now comes from fossil fuels. Others argue that nuclear power is the solution. But critics of nuclear power point out that at present it provides only about 5 percent of the world's primary energy and that we would need to build one new nuclear power plant every week for fifty years just to replace one-third of the energy we now derive from fossil fuels—presuming a willingness to accept the other risks associated with nuclear power.

Geoengineering is even more controversial. Critics of this approach say that the proposed schemes, even if possible in theory, would be impossible to implement on a scale large enough to make a difference and would be prohibitively expensive. The greatest concern, however, is that tinkering with the planet's climate system could produce unforeseen, catastrophic consequences. Proponents of geoengineering respond by saying that global warming is itself a result of human "tinkering" and that solving the problem will require taking risks, perhaps big ones.

These responses to global warming are mainly technological. They all depend on cleverer use of tools and machines, ones that now exist or that we might someday invent. If there is a solution to the problem of global warming, it will no doubt require action along these lines—the scientific and technological. But if we think of solutions only in scientific and technological terms, we miss what is most important: the beliefs, practices, and social arrangements that affect our prospects for finding any kind of solution.

People must first believe that there is a problem. If lawmakers deny that global warming is a problem, then serious legislative action is unlikely. If people in general do not believe global warming is a problem, then they will not pressure lawmakers to take action. *Climate scientists* realize that there is a problem, but if people do not believe what climate scientists say—perhaps because of intentional efforts to sow doubt about the findings of climate research (see the following Note on Ignorance)—then, once more, a serious response will be impeded. These and other beliefs determine whether a solution will even be pursued.

Everyday practices matter, too. For example, in the United States it is not uncommon to see a single person driving a 5,000-pound SUV to and from the grocery store or to and from work. Given how our towns and cities are designed, given where homes and stores and workplaces are located, and given the lack of public transportation, many people feel they have no choice but to use fossil-fuel vehicles in this way. It is partly a matter of convenience and partly a matter of necessity. In any case, it is the kind of ordinary, entrenched practice—one that most people are understandably reluctant to give up—that adds to the global warming problem.

But suppose that most people came to believe that global warming is a serious problem. Suppose, too, that most people wanted to take corrective action in their personal lives (e.g., by driving less or by heating their homes with solar power) and wanted political leaders to take action on a larger scale. Would this get us moving toward a solution? Perhaps not, as we can see if we are mindful of how political and economic arrangements bear on the problem.

I don't mean anything mysterious by "arrangements." I just mean the ways that power is distributed and exercised in politics and the economy. Democracy, for example, is a kind of arrangement in which the power to make laws is distributed equally among the people subject to those laws. Plutocracy is a different kind of arrangement. In this case, most or all law-making power is in the hands of the rich, usually along with the power to interpret and enforce laws.

Capitalism is a kind of arrangement in which control of society's major economic resources is legally concentrated in the hands of a relative few. Because capitalism tends to cause wealth to concentrate in fewer and fewer hands and because wealth can be used to influence people who make, interpret, and enforce laws, capitalism tends to undermine democracy and foster plutocracy. Consider, then, how these political and economic arrangements—the concentration of wealth and political power in the hands of a small percentage of the population— could affect the chances of dealing effectively with a problem like global warming.

Under these conditions, if the small percentage of the population that dominates government and the economy benefits tremendously from keeping things as they are—that is, from *not* changing the ways fossil fuels are extracted, bought and sold for profit, and used wastefully—then a serious response to global warming is unlikely. Government action that might change society's ways of using energy—a shift away from burning fossil fuels—will be thwarted because it poses too much of a threat to capitalist wealth and power. This is not a hypothetical example. It is in fact how things have unfolded so far in the United States when it comes to mustering an adequate response to global warming.

Matters are further complicated by other social arrangements: the existence of nations whose economic and political elites compete with each other for power and wealth. Global warming is not a problem that can be solved by any one nation alone. It will require cooperation. But how will this cooperation be achieved? And what if people of all nations want to achieve the same level of material wealth found in Western Europe and North America? This will not be possible without exacerbating global warming. It might not even be possible at all, given that this level of global development would require the resources of three earths.

So how will these potential conflicts be handled? Figuring out what to do will require compassion, understanding, and breaking down the usual boundaries that are erected between people, as well as commitments to justice and democracy. No tools and machines, no technology, can do this kind of work for us.

I realize that this discussion of the limits of technology is not encouraging and can make the situation seem hopeless. No solution is possible, however, if we don't acknowledge that the problem of global warming is far more than a technological problem. If we are mindful that the problem is also cultural, political, and economic, we will be less likely to sit back and wait for a breakthrough that will save us. We will perhaps be more likely to see how social arrangements block the path to a solution and then try to change those arrangements.

A Note on Ignorance

The American humorist Will Rogers (1879–1935) once said that everybody is ignorant, only on different subjects. He was right, of course. A person can know a lot about mathematics or physics, yet know little about history or sociology. In such cases, ignorance is a result of people being interested in different things or of just not having the time to learn about everything. On the other hand, ignorance can also be intentionally cultivated.

We usually think of people as cultivating knowledge and trying to overcome ignorance. This is what people who want to understand the world try to do. Scientists, intellectuals, students, and many other people seek new ideas and information to help them figure out what's going on in society or in nature. Perhaps this is done for the sake of inventing new technologies, formulating good public policies, or just the joy of learning. Given the benefits of knowledge, who would want to cultivate ignorance?

It's possible that some people avoid learning things that might cause discomfort. After all, new ideas and information can be unsettling. It's also possible that people in powerful groups have blind spots that arise from being dominant—for example, an inability to grasp the perspectives and experiences of people in less powerful groups. If people strive to hold onto the power and privilege that induce blind spots, this could be called a form of cultivating ignorance. In this case, however, ignorance is not a goal; it's a by-product of inequality.

Another possibility is that power can be used to keep people ignorant and vulnerable. A classic example is the tobacco industry. As far back as the 1950s, tobacco industry executives knew that smoking caused lung disease and that nicotine was addictive. This was knowledge that they wanted to keep from others—government officials who might impose regulations and people who might decide to quit smoking, or not start.

Even after 1964, when the U.S. surgeon general's report documented that smoking caused emphysema and lung cancer, the tobacco industry publicly denied that there was a proven link between smoking and disease. Into the 1990s they denied that nicotine was addictive. Worse still, tobacco company executives conspired and used their wealth to create doubt in many people's minds that smoking was harmful. They did all this, aware that they were lying about the hazards of smoking and the addictiveness of nicotine, as a way to stall regulation and keep people buying their products. One result has been that millions more people have died from tobacco-related disease than might have died if the tobacco companies had not worked so hard to deny the truth.

Fossil fuel companies have acted similarly in regard to climate change. By the late 1970s, energy industry scientists were finding evidence of global warming caused by the burning of fossil fuels. Industry executives knew this. But instead of admitting the problem and offering to help find solutions, they funded think tanks and public relations campaigns to foster doubt about whether global warming was occurring and whether humans had anything to do with it. As with the tobacco industry, the goal was to stall government regulation that could cut into profits. As a result of this cultivated ignorance, serious steps to counter global warming have not yet been taken.

In both of these cases, ignorance was the result of special efforts by capitalist corporations to promote it, to keep people from acquiring knowledge. Even though I have written about these cases in the past tense, the problems created by these campaigns to foster public ignorance are not behind us. Doubt about the harmfulness of smoking still helps to impede effective regulation and to get teenagers addicted to cigarettes. Doubt about global warming is still slowing action to deal with it. The costs of ignorance in these matters continue to mount.

According to an old saying, knowledge is power. This is true, in that knowledge enables us to exert control over things in the world and to make informed choices that best serve our interests. The opposite is true as well: ignorance is weakness. These twin principles make it possible to gain power not only by seeking knowledge but also by fostering ignorance and unwarranted doubt. Being sociologically mindful, we will be alert to the possibility that ignorance is not the innocent result of people being interested in different things, but the result of calculated efforts by some people to exploit others.

Paths for Reflection

1. A busy downtown street in a megacity might seem like the very opposite of nature. Most objects in the scene, other than people, are made of concrete, steel, asphalt, glass, or other artificial materials. But even here nature is not absent or without consequence. If you were in such a seemingly nonnatural place, what might you see that reflects the presence and power of nature? If you find it hard to put yourself (imaginarily or physically) in an intense urban scene, just use whatever is handy and familiar to you—be it the center of a small town, a campus brickyard, or a parking lot. How is nature present there? How has it been shaped by human intervention? What might happen, over time, if this intervention ceased?

2. In the foregoing chapter I said that we are all implicated in the problem of global warming. By "we" I meant everyone who adds to the problem—especially those of us in developed countries who consume most of the world's fossil fuels—and everyone who stands to be affected by the problem—which includes pretty much all of humanity. But to say that we are all *implicated* is not to say that we are all equally responsible or have equal power to solve the problem. So who bears the heaviest burden of responsibility? Who has the most power to do something about global warming? If those who have the most power refuse to act, what should be done?

3. It is not possible for a human to know what it is like to be a bat, Thomas Nagel argues, because "what it is like to be a bat" consists of the subjective experience of a bat, and this is a kind of experience to which humans—being different kinds of creatures—have no access. So while we can *imagine* what it would be like to fly, eat bugs, and echolocate, we are always doing this imagining from the standpoint of a human, which is not the same standpoint as a creature that is a bat and nothing but a bat. But since we similarly cannot get inside the skin of another person, does this mean we can never know what it's like to be another person? Or is there something about being human that allows us to "get inside" another person's experience? What makes it harder or easier to do this?

Related Readings

Berry, Wendell. (2015). *Our Only World*. Berkeley, CA: Counterpoint.
Birke, Lynda. (1999). *Feminism and the Biological Body*. New Brunswick, NJ: Rutgers University Press.

Fine, Cordelia. (2011). *Delusions of Gender: How Our Minds, Society, and Neurosexism Create Difference*. New York: Norton.

Gould, Kenneth, A., & Lewis, Tammy L., Eds. (2015). *Twenty Lessons in Environmental Sociology* (2nd ed.). New York: Oxford University Press.

Jones, Jacqueline. (2013). *A Dreadful Deceit: The Myth of Race from the Colonial Era to Obama's America*. New York: Basic Books.

Jordan-Young, Rebecca. (2011). *Brain Storm: The Flaws in the Science of Sex Differences*. Cambridge, MA: Harvard University Press.

Magdoff, Fred, & Foster, John Bellamy. (2011). *What Every Environmentalist Needs to Know about Capitalism*. New York: Monthly Review Press.

Oreskes, Naomi, & Conway, Erik. (2010). *Merchants of Doubt*. New York: Bloomsbury.

Proctor, Robert N. (2011). *Golden Holocaust: Origins of the Cigarette Catastrophe and the Case for Abolition*. Berkeley, CA: University of California Press.

Turner, Bryan S. (2008). *The Body and Society* (3rd ed.). Thousand Oaks, CA: Sage.

....

CHAPTER 13

Unpacking Process

Being sociologically mindful is not a contest, though it seems clear that some people are better at it than others. Suppose we were asked to explain this difference in ability. We could invoke the notion of "talent" and say that some people just have more talent for being sociologically mindful than others, perhaps because they were lucky enough to get the mindfulness gene. I hope by now that such an explanation seems silly. A better approach would be to look at the processes through which people develop the ability to think sociologically.

Yet talent is a powerful notion in U.S. culture. Outstanding performance—in sports, art, academia, business, and other fields of activity—is said to flow from talent, and winners are said to win because they have more talent than others. But if we are sociologically mindful about process, we will see that this explanation is flawed.

Consider how it is that a person is deemed to have talent: by performing excellently. Excellent performance is thus taken as evidence of talent, which is taken to be the cause of excellent performance. This is circular reasoning. If you asked why an object is hot and someone said, "Because it possesses a quality called 'heat,' which is evident in the fact that the object is hot," you would recognize that this is no explanation. Likewise with talent as an explanation for excellence. Unless there is a way to verify its existence *prior to* and *independent of* excellent performance, it can't be the explanation. There must be something else going on.

To show what else is going on, I will use swimmers as an example (at least for now) because, as it turns out, we know a lot about what leads to excellent performance among swimmers, thanks to the work of sociologist Daniel Chambliss. A swimmer and swimming coach himself, Chambliss spent years studying swimmers, from the country club level to the Olympic level. He wanted to understand how it happened that some swimmers greatly improved, rose through the ranks of the sport, and became champions.

What he found is that excellence does not come just from swimming more miles or "trying harder" to go fast. The best competitive swimmers do swim more miles than others. And relative to recreational swimmers, they do try harder. But this isn't enough.

What matters, Chambliss found, is that the best swimmers strive to do all the little things right—starts, strokes, kicks, breathing, turns—and to weave these elements of technique into a seamless whole. They try to do these things right *all the time* and use lots and lots of practice to make it a matter of habit to do so. Excellence is thus a result not so much of quantitative changes (more miles) but of qualitative changes in technique, discipline, and attitude.

Social worlds are also important. As swimmers move up in the sport, they interact with different people: more knowledgeable coaches, as well as other swimmers who are also striving to improve. At each higher level of the sport, more people are determined to become as good as they can be. Training and competition thus get more intense, and this fosters further improvement. So achieving excellence isn't simply a matter of swimmers figuring things out for themselves and trying hard to get better. It's a matter of spending more time around others who know what it takes to be a champion and are themselves dedicated to doing these things on a regular basis.

Chambliss concludes that excellence comes from doing ordinary things that don't require extraordinary abilities. In principle, anyone can learn the elements of good technique; anyone can strive to weave these elements into a seamless whole; anyone can commit to practicing a lot and making it a habit to do all the little things right all the time. One must get into the social worlds where correct knowledge is shared and the right practices are reinforced, but this doesn't require extraordinary ability, either; it requires resources and luck. Attributing excellence to "talent" makes it hard to see all this.

Chambliss knows that bodies matter. He doesn't claim that anyone can be an Olympic medalist if they just practice enough. Success in a sport always depends in part on having the right kind of body for doing what the sport demands, and bodily potentials are set by genetics. But if we assume a rough equality of potential among participants in a sport, then what matters are the things people do to develop their potential. What matters, in other words, are all the things that Chambliss points to. It also often happens that people with great potential are surpassed by people with less potential because the latter more fully develop the potential they possess.

Unless you're a competitive swimmer or a fan of competitive swimming, you probably feel that I've said enough about excellence in swimming. I agree. Here, then, is the point that really matters: unpacking process is an important part of being sociologically mindful. Chambliss's study is a nice example of how to do this. He takes something that many people have a hard time explaining—consistent superior performance in a sport—and examines the process that produces it.

To think of it a little differently, imagine a black box with a spout on one side, and out of this spout comes excellence (I know this image seems strange, but please bear with me). Now imagine asking how the box produces excellence and being told only that the box contains "talent." This would not be a satisfying answer. After all, the box is opaque, which means you can't see through its walls to know if what you've been told is correct. If you were truly curious about how excellence is made, you'd want to open the box and see what's going on inside. Being sociologically mindful means opening the box.

When Chambliss opened the box he found mundane things— identifiable and ordinary things, perhaps combined in complex ways and not easy to do, but not magical, either. He thus gained insight that dispelled the unhelpful mystery created by the notion of talent. But if excellent performance among swimmers is just a case of a more general phenomenon, it should be possible to open other boxes and see similar things going on. Suppose that the box we want to open is the one that produces excellent academic performance in college.

A belief in talent would lead us to say that some people do better in college—do better academic work and get higher grades—because they're smarter than others. No doubt it's true that some people are better *prepared* than others when they start college, and so they already have skills and habits that enable them to do well right off the bat and make progress quickly. But these skills and habits aren't mysterious, nor are they matters of talent. They are the result of doing ordinary things that anyone could do.

At the risk of shattering the illusion of smartness, I'll tell you what these things are: doing assigned readings carefully and on time; going to class and paying attention to what's being said; asking questions in class and taking notes; starting assignments early to allow enough time to do them well; revising and editing papers rather than turning in drafts written at the last minute; talking to professors outside of class; getting feedback on your work and using that feedback to improve; doing extra reading related to your courses; and hanging out with other good students. None of these things demands special ability. Anyone can do them. So the secret is this: if you do all of these little things consistently and make them matters of habit, you can do excellent academic work and get labeled "smart."

On the other hand, being sociologically mindful we can see why doing these things is harder for some people than for others. Students who must work or take care of family members may have limited time to study. Differences in class, race, or gender can make it feel awkward to talk to professors or hang out with students who do well. Weak skills in reading and writing, as a result of poor prior education, can make it hard to get the most out of reading and writing assignments in college, even if one takes those assignments seriously. So, yes, achieving excellence in college is more complicated than is implied by a list of correct actions.

An added complication is that excellence in academic work is not measured by a stopwatch. While it is almost always possible to be certain who swims the fastest, there is room for judgment when it comes to saying who is the best scientist or scholar or student or professor. The same performance might be judged differently, depending on the values of those doing the judging. This tends to be true in most areas of life outside of sports. There are few places where excellence can be measured with the precision and impartiality of a stopwatch.

But even with these complications taken into account, there is still a process that can be studied and understood. We don't have to accept the notion that excellence and mediocrity arise from mysterious forces. If we are sociologically mindful, we recognize, first, that *everything* in social life, from individual performances to major historical events, is the result of a process. The second thing we recognize is that, if it is important enough to do so, we can investigate the process. With the right tools, we can open the box and see what's going on.

Opening a Bigger Box

The largest capitalist corporations each have hundreds of thousands of employees. Corporations that are merely big can have thousands or tens of thousands of employees. You can think of an individual corporation as shaped like a pyramid, with a few very powerful, extremely well-paid executives at the top, a smaller number of middle managers and staff who earn less and have less power, and then a mass of low-paid, mostly power-less workers at the bottom. The details will vary depending on what kind of corporation it is, what it produces, and what kind of people it employs. But a concentration of wealth and power at the top is a feature of all capitalist corporations.

Suppose we notice that in nearly all large capitalist corporations few of the top executives are women or people of color. We might thus suspect that the white males who occupy the top positions are sexist and racist and behave in discriminatory ways to keep out women and people of color. This would be a plausible hypothesis. How could we find out if it is correct? Perhaps we could look at a single corporation and treat it as a black box with a spout that produces white male executives. We could then try to open the box and see what produces this result.

One way to proceed would be to approach all the white male executives and ask, *Could you please explain how racism and sexism affect your choices of whom to hire and promote into the ranks of top executives in your company?* This would have the virtue of directness, but it would be a poor research strategy. One reason is that most people become defensive and do not respond honestly if a question presumes that they are doing something wrong. Another reason is that people are often unaware of how they participate in processes that reproduce inequality, especially if these processes extend over long periods of time. So direct questioning is not always the best approach when trying to find out what people are doing and why they do it.

Suppose, however, that we tried, in some way that would not provoke defensiveness, to get white male executives to admit to being racist, sexist, and discriminatory. Suppose, too, that no matter how cleverly we probed, the answers never revealed any prejudice or discriminatory intent. Perhaps what we hear, over and again, is something like this: "When we promote people to executive positions, we consider talent, experience, trustworthi-ness, willingness to be a team player, and how comfortable we feel with the person. Race, gender, nationality, religion, and so on have nothing to do with it." What now? Is our hypothesis about discrimination kaput?

We might suspect that the white male executives are excellent liars and that our interviewing skills are not good enough to get at the truth. Another possibility, however, is that the executives are telling the truth, *as they see it.* This is in fact quite likely, although it doesn't mean our original hypothesis is wrong. If we are sociologically mindful, we recognize that discrimination can happen without conscious awareness or intent. To see this, we need to do more than ask questions of people who might have an interest in not seeing what's going on.

So now we are going to open the box—look inside the organization—and try to see how it happens that white males are the ones who become top executives. To develop the example, it's important to specify a starting condition. Let us imagine, then, that the first thing we see is that all the top executives are white males, but that there are many women and people of color at the middle and lower levels of the organization. Let us also imagine that many of these people aspire to move up and become top executives someday. Yet, even over time, they never get that far; they bump into some kind of invisible barrier and go no higher.

What should we look for if we open the box and try to figure out what's happening? One thing to look for is mentoring. We know (from many studies) that having a good mentor is crucial for career success. A mentor is a more experienced, more knowledgeable person who shows you the ropes, teaches you the tricks of the trade, clues you in about how things really work, and helps you avoid mistakes. A person who lacks a mentor might never learn these things or take a long time to learn them, making many mistakes along the way. A person who finds a good mentor, or is found by a good mentor, gets much valuable help in advancing his or her career.

So one thing we might see when we open the box is inequality in mentoring. Perhaps this is because the people who have been around the longest and are best equipped to be good mentors are mostly white males, and they "naturally" tend to connect with the younger white males who remind them of themselves. It's not that they dislike women or people of color and want to see them fail. It's just that they feel more at ease with people who look like them, talk like them, and have similar tastes in food, clothing, music, sports, politics, hobbies, and so on. The result is that some of the younger employees—white males—get more help in advancing their careers than others—women and people of color—even though no one intends for this to happen.

Another thing we might look for is sponsoring. This happens when a person higher up in an organization takes an interest in a younger person's career and steers advantages and opportunities toward the younger person. An example would be recommending the younger person for a spot on an important project team, so that s/he makes connections and gets valuable experience. Or it could be "putting in a good word" for the younger person when promotion decisions are being made. In any case, sponsoring, like mentoring, is a form of extra help that can be unequally distributed.

Here again, inequality is not necessarily the result of ill will. More likely, sponsors, who are already successful in the organization, see younger people who remind them of themselves and want those younger people to succeed. Perhaps, back in the day, the sponsors had sponsors, and now they want to help a younger person get ahead, just as they once were helped. But if the people powerful enough to be sponsors are all white males, and if they sponsor people who remind them of themselves when they were young, then again it is white males who will get a career boost.

One more thing we might see happening is network formation. This means people making connections with others who are willing and able to share information and offer support. Getting coached by a good mentor is crucial, as noted earlier. But forming networks with peers (people at the same level in the organization) also matters. A person without a good peer network in an organization is less likely to know what's going on, less likely to get help in solving problems, and less likely to feel and appear dedicated to the organization. To be in such a situation is to be at a disadvantage when it comes to getting ahead.

As with mentoring and sponsoring, network formation can be a result of social closeness; that is, people tend to connect with others with whom they feel comfortable because of similarities in background, interests, and tastes. This is why it is often hard for women and people of color who are in the numerical minority—"tokens," as it is sometimes said—to form strong and extensive networks with helpful others in big organizations. There are fewer similar others with whom to connect, and perhaps fewer of the *different* others (members of the majority group) make an effort to connect. The result, without anyone intending it, can be disadvantages— poorer networks through which to obtain information and support—for women and people of color.

Network inequalities can arise unintentionally, but sometimes they are a result of a conscious strategy. When ambitious peers think about the people with whom they would like to connect, they are typically drawn to those who seem likely to rise to the top. Who are these rising stars likely to be? People who look like those already at the top. In the case of our hypothetical big corporation, these people would be white males. If most people follow this strategy of making connections, it means that those who don't look like the organization's past and current leaders are likely to be excluded from networks of ambitious peers. This is another way that disadvantage can be created for women and people of color.

Suppose these are the things we've seen upon opening the box. Now we need to watch what happens over time. If white males get good mentors who teach them practical skills and socialize them into the culture of the organization; if they get more chances to gain experience and meet key people; and if they are included in helpful peer networks, then, after a while, they will be better prepared for high-level positions. Eventually, they will acquire the qualities that make them look like the best candidates to be the organization's new leaders. This is why top executives might be telling the truth when they say that their promotion decisions are not prejudicial. It's not so much that their decisions are biased, it's that a long, complex discriminatory process has been operating *in the organization as a whole* to make their decisions seem reasonable.

In this hypothetical case, we could have been misled by the sincere denials of white male executives who always replaced themselves with other white males. We could have thought that bias and discrimination had nothing to do with who rises to the top of the organization. But by looking at how processes play out over time, we could see how unconscious biases and subtle discriminatory actions affected women and people of color. Real life can be even more complicated than this hypothetical example suggests, which makes it all the more important to open the box and pay close attention to process.

Seeing Processes as Generic

Earlier I said that excellence in academic work is achieved in much the same way that it is achieved in swimming. It's not a result of innate talent or brilliance, but a result of doing all the little things right—things that anyone could do—and making it a matter of habit, through much practice, to do them right all the time. Another way to put it is to say that the process of achieving excellence is *generic*, meaning that it occurs similarly in many places. Part of being sociologically mindful is seeing how processes that occur in one place might be occurring in other places in similar, if not identical, ways.

In the example of the big corporation, I pointed to several generic processes: mentoring, sponsoring, and network formation. These processes occur in many places. Wherever older, more experienced and knowledgeable people make special efforts to nurture the abilities of younger people, there is mentoring going on. This often happens in big organizations. But it can happen in small ones as well and outside of organizations entirely. What matters is that there is a distinct kind of one-on-one teaching going on. If we wanted to know more about how this process works, we could study mentoring in many different settings.

Sponsoring, too, is generic. Perhaps it occurs most often in formal organizations, such as big corporations or government bureaucracies, where a person "higher up" can use his or her power to aid the rise of a person at a lower level. But again we could say that wherever a more powerful or higher-status person intervenes to aid the advancement of a younger person in some kind of hierarchy, there is sponsoring going on. We might thus expect to find sponsoring in smaller, less formal organizations and groups, such as churches, clubs, and gangs.

Network formation likewise occurs whenever people meet each other and begin to exchange information, support, or other resources. How these relationships get started, how they're kept up, and how they're used will vary depending on circumstances. Still, in modern social life, this process of network formation goes on all the time and implicates everyone who knows at least one other person. Which is to say, it implicates us all. If we wanted to, we could look in any direction and see some part of the process of network formation going on.

In the big corporation example, something more specific is going on. The example described not just a process of network formation but also more specific processes of inclusion and exclusion. Inclusion means being greeted, invited to participate, spoken to, encouraged to stay in touch. Exclusion means receiving no such warm outreach and perhaps even being rebuffed when trying to connect with others who are already connected to each other. These, too, are processes that occur in many places. And, as in the corporation example, they are often part of a larger process of reproducing inequality.

If we think of these processes as generic, we can avoid being misled by particulars. In the big corporation example, I said that white males at the top were replacing themselves with new white males, to the detriment of women and people of color who also sought to get ahead. I said "white males" because this reflects current reality in the United States (about 90% of chief executive officers at Fortune 500 corporations are white males). But if we are mindful of generic processes, we can see that what's going on does not arise from a fault peculiar to white males. Similar processes would occur if any group dominated the top positions in an organization in which different kinds of people competed for those positions.

Being mindful of processes as generic does not mean seeing the exact same thing occurring wherever we look. Mentoring might be similar but somewhat different inside and outside of big organizations; it might be similar but somewhat different depending on the ages of the people involved; it might be similar but somewhat different depending on the kinds of knowledge and skills being transmitted. In each case, we would see mentoring going on, but in each case it might be a little different. Being sociologically mindful would help us recognize that there *is* a similar process going on. After that, if we wanted, we could examine specific cases to try to understand why mentoring occurs a bit differently under different conditions.

Consider again the example of the big corporation. Perhaps this corporation, when it operates normally, puts enormous wealth and power into the hands of a few top managers and shareholders. Perhaps it also produces harmful products, or violates tax laws, or causes environmental damage. If we noticed similar things going on in other capitalist corporations, we might wonder if there is something about the nature of capitalist corporations that tends to make these kinds of things happen. We might wonder, in other words, if there is a generic process occurring in capitalist corporations that tends to produce harmful results. If we found this to be true, we might also wonder how much benefit will come from replacing the white males at the top with other kinds of people who will enact the same processes and produce the same results.

Processes and Conditions

Everyone is born into a set of social conditions. Examples of "conditions" are a society's type of economy, its level of technology, its type of government, and the degree of conflict among groups. To be born into an industrial capitalist society with an electoral democracy and peaceful cooperation among various groups is to be born into one set of conditions. To be born into an agricultural society that is run by warlords who battle each other for power is to be born into very different conditions.

We can also think about conditions on a smaller scale. For example, to be born into a low-income, single-parent family in a deteriorating inner-city neighborhood in the United States is to be born into one set of conditions. To be born into an upper-middle-class, two-parent family in a safe, affluent suburb in the United States is to be born into a different set of conditions. So even when *societal* conditions are the same—that is, the same kind of economy, government, level of technology, and so on—the *nearby* conditions of people's lives can vary greatly.

Being sociologically mindful about social conditions means recognizing several things: no one chooses the conditions into which they are born; these conditions create harder or easier lives for people; and these conditions affect how people think, feel, and learn to behave. These are important points to remember. But here, in the context of thinking about processes, I want to make a different point: what we usually think of as conditions are really processes.

Take capitalism, for example. We usually think of capitalism as a type of economy in which a tiny percentage of the population (less than 2% in the United States) controls the major means of production and uses this control to dominate working people, government, and most societal institutions (e.g., education, health care). Capitalism is thus often thought of as a stable set of political and economic arrangements. We should be wary, however, of thinking of these arrangements as immutable conditions.

What capitalism—or any form of economy—really consists of is people doing things together in patterned, orderly ways, on a regular basis. This is the sense in which it is a process. If workers and managers, buyers and sellers, bankers and borrowers, brokers and investors, and many other types of people did not interact every day and do things together according to the rules of capitalism (see "Rules as Constructed Causes" in Chapter 8), then capitalism would not exist. Because capitalism has been going on for several centuries, we usually think of it as a stable condition—that is, as a fixed feature of the landscape—rather than as a process.

Sometimes it is perfectly fine to think of capitalism as a condition. As I said earlier, the form of economy that exists in a society is one kind of social condition into which we are born. It is also a condition that we have no choice but to deal with, and precisely how we do so matters a lot for how our lives unfold. Recognizing these facts is part of being sociologically mindful. But if we forget that conditions are also processes, we might also forget that what we call "conditions" are subject to change.

Being sociologically mindful, we recognize that all parts of the social world are processes. Even the large and seemingly solid parts of the social world—corporations, economies, governments, nations—consist of nothing more than people doing things together in patterned, orderly ways, on a regular basis. What's more, this orderliness persists only because people act on shared understandings of who they are and how they ought to do things together. One implication is that if people develop new understandings of who they are and how they should do things together, then the processes that make up the social world can change.

Recognizing that what we usually call conditions are actually processes helps us appreciate the possibility of change. If we see current conditions as processes rather than as fixed features of the universe, then we are less likely to conclude that change is impossible. If we understand the social world as made up of processes, we recognize that change is not only possible—if we can develop new ideas about how we should do things together—but is going on all the time, though often in ways too small to see. Whenever we do things together a little differently, we are tweaking the process and nudging change along. The only thing that is truly impossible is stopping change.

Here is another example of something that we usually think of as fixed but is really a process: gender. Of course the maleness or femaleness of our bodies is fixed by biology and evolution; it is true that humans as a species usually come in the types we call "male" and "female," distinguished by differences in reproductive anatomy. But body parts are not gender. Gender consists of beliefs and practices—beliefs about how males and females are different kinds of people and should therefore think, feel, and behave differently; and practices through which these beliefs are upheld and made to seem correct.

This way of looking at gender might seem at odds with common sense, which tells us that a male adult is a man and a female adult is a woman, end of story. But the common-sense view confuses biological sex with gender. From a sociological perspective, the former is about anatomy and the latter is about ideas and customary behavior. As soon as we start thinking about how the creatures we call "male," "female," "boys," "girls," "women," and "men" *should* think, feel, behave, and identify themselves, we are in the realm of gender—a realm that humans enter from the moment of birth, sometimes sooner.

My point is that once we begin to see gender as depending on ideas and on conformity to rules of behavior, it becomes possible to see that gender is not at all a fixed thing. As it is sometimes said, gender is not so much something we *have* as it is something we *do*. And so, like anything humans do that depends on ideas, the actual doing changes as ideas change. We can see this if we look across cultures and over time; when people hold different ideas about what it means to be a man or a woman, gender changes. In principle, if we had no such ideas, gender might not exist at all, just like race would not exist if we had no notion of racial categories.

Remember, too, that ideas don't persist on their own; it takes other forms of doing to uphold them. Ideas about gender must thus be taught and frequently reaffirmed, much like the ideas that unite religious communities. Without schools of theology, sacred texts, teaching of doctrine to children, rituals, and regular services, religions tend to dissolve. It is much the same with gender. To keep gender from dissolving requires that people engage in all kinds of gender-supporting practices. If we don't recognize ourselves as practicing a religion of gender, so to speak, it is mainly because the practices involved are usually so taken for granted as to be invisible.

As deeply attached as many people are to seeing gender as a natural part of the human condition, most people are not too threatened by seeing ideas about gender as varying somewhat across cultures and over time. Nor is it terribly threatening to accept that ideas about gender change through some kind of social process. After all, even people who are in college today (2016) can see that some ideas about gender—for example, the acceptability of gay marriage—have changed within their lifetimes. A more challenging idea, one that many people have a hard time accepting, is that our identities as women or men (or however we might define ourselves) are also upheld by processes of doing.

The kind of doing I am referring to is sometimes called self-presentation. This means speaking, dressing, gesturing, moving, and generally acting in ways that express who and what we are. When others observe and interpret this expressive behavior, they imagine that we possess a certain kind of inner character; they see us, in other words, as being a particular kind of person. Assuming that they do not see us as pretending for some reason, others then treat us as the kind of person they take us to be. This is why self-presentations are so consequential. No matter what might be going on in our heads or hearts, people still treat us based on how they interpret whatever expressive behavior they perceive.

This view of self-presentation implies that when others recognize us as women or men and treat us as such, they do so because of our expressive behavior. Others listen to what we say and how we say it, they observe how we dress, gesture, move, and otherwise act and, on the basis of this information, perceive us as women or men. We do the same thing when we interact with others, observing and interpreting their expressive behavior. Most of us present ourselves to others so that our gender identities are "legible," which is to say, easily *readable* by others. We expect to be able to do this interpretive work quickly and with little effort. When we cannot—when a person's gender identity is not immediately legible—it can be unsettling.

What does all this have to do with process? Two things. First, even something as seemingly obvious, unambiguous, and settled as our gender identities is based on a process of conveying and interpreting information. For gender identities to exist as part of human social life, we have to do these things, and do them all the time. We have to keep up the doing—we have to maintain the process—to keep on seeing ourselves as, and believing ourselves to be, women and men. If this process were to stop for some reason, our seemingly obvious, unambiguous, and settled gender identities would melt away.

The second connection to process has to do with the invisibility of many processes in social life. Gender is an excellent example. Expressing our gender identities—presenting ourselves to others as women and men; then being recognized, affirmed, and treated as such—is so habitual as to occur beneath conscious awareness most of the time. We take part in an elaborate process of conveying and interpreting information about ourselves and each other, yet we rarely see it. We thus experience gender as a solid part of the natural world, something that is "just there," without realizing that gender exists only because we constantly recreate it in everyday life.

One way to keep in mind the importance of process, whenever looking at social conditions, is to ask, *How were these conditions created?* and *What must people do together, on a regular basis, to maintain them?* If we seek answers to these questions, we are likely to find that what seems solid is actually fluid. As historians say, everything has a history that continues to unfold. Sociological mindfulness offers a similar insight: the social conditions that seem to be solid and natural are created and constituted by people doing things together in patterned, orderly ways, on a regular basis. The things that make up the social world are not "things" in the usual sense but are ever-evolving processes of collective doing.

Multiple Processes at Once

When I said that some processes are "generic" (in that they happen in similar ways in many places), you might have wondered if there are other types as well. There are. People who study processes can describe many kinds. Mechanical, chemical, and electrical engineers can even design and build many kinds of processes. But that's more than we need to worry about. To understand the social world sociologically, there are three types of processes—in addition to generic processes—that are important to be able to see.

The first type is an escalating process. Here is an example. Imagine a child born into a family with two highly educated parents who earn good salaries and who live in a safe, comfortable, book-filled home. Imagine that the child is well cared for, happy, and well behaved and develops the abilities to read and write before going to school. It is likely, then, that when this child goes to school, s/he will be seen by teachers as an ideal student. Such a child is likely to get a lot of friendly, supportive, and encouraging attention from teachers.

The child in this case will grow in self-confidence and ability as a result of nurturing from teachers. These gains can in turn make the child more willing to tackle hard problems and learn new things, further bolstering self-confidence and ability. Success in school can translate into motivation and ability to learn more outside of school—from lessons, summer camps, workshops, reading, and travel. When this child graduates from college, s/he will possess superior knowledge and skills that will pay off well in the job market and, indeed, for a lifetime.

What I have just described is a process in which advantages compound, like interest on a savings account. Because advantages at one stage in the process can produce advantages at a later stage, and advantages at this stage can produce even more advantages at a still later stage, and so on, we can say that the process is escalating. More at one time leads to more at a later time. This can also be called a "positive feedback" process because the results of one stage feed back into the process in a way that keeps driving it forward.

It is not always easy to observe escalating processes, even when we suspect that they exist. In the case of the child described above, it might seem as if success in school (and throughout years of schooling) is a result of innate ability. This is because much of what is happening occurs without conscious intent and becomes invisible unless we pay close attention in a sociologically mindful way. Looking closely, we might see that success in school, and later in the job market, is a result of advantages that have been compounding since early childhood. This is an important kind of process to examine when trying to understand how inequality is reproduced in U.S. society.

Another kind of process that occurs often in the social world is called a dialectical process. I know that this sounds esoteric, but the basic idea is not difficult. "Dialectical," in this context, means approximately this: *driven by a conflict between opposites*. So a dialectical process is one that produces change through a conflict between opposing forces.

Dialectical processes often play out in politics. Imagine, for example, a society in which people are denied basic rights and freedoms. Such repression is likely to provoke anger, resistance, and struggles to obtain rights and freedoms. The elites who benefit from repression might first try to crack down on dissent but then realize that if they don't make concessions, the conflict will tear society apart. So a few rights and freedoms are granted. And then, as time goes by, people win more rights and freedoms. But then elites realize that they are losing control completely, so they try to crack down again, and this works for a while—until people begin trying more aggressively to restore and expand their freedoms.

In this example, historical change is driven by conflict between opposites. On the one hand, elites desire control (for the sake of continuing to enrich themselves) and try to limit the rights and freedoms of others. Non-elites, on the other hand, want to resist being controlled and exploited, so they fight for rights and freedoms. Change occurs as these groups clash. This kind of process has a back-and-forth quality to it. For a time, one side gains the upper hand, but this simultaneously produces pressures for change—pressures that mount until the other side begins to resist and push the pendulum back in the opposite direction.

A swinging pendulum, however, is not quite the right image, because a pendulum returns to where it began. With people, things are more complicated. When tensions mount and groups clash, a new situation is created. Sometimes it is said that in a dialectical process the conflict between opposing forces produces a "synthesis," a condition different from the one that existed before the period of conflict reached a peak. This kind of process is not exactly like a pendulum swinging back and forth or the tide going out and coming in. Rather, every cycle of tension and conflict changes the social world in some way; even when the conflict is resolved, things are never the same again.

Dialectical processes can also occur on smaller scales. For example, groups can oppose each other within organizations. Imagine a government or a large corporation in which groups of people (or "factions") compete for control and resources. If such groups have opposing visions or opposing agendas and they struggle against each other to see whose vision or agenda will prevail, then a dialectical process can unfold. One group might gain power for a time, causing resentment and tensions to mount. The other group might then eventually turn to disruption, sabotage, or withholding of cooperation as a way to force negotiation of change. Out of this process comes a new set of arrangements, a slightly different organization.

Part of being sociologically mindful is being alert for conflicts that are built into routine ways of doing things together. For example, an economy organized in a way that allows a small group of elites to control the economic resources on which everyone else depends is likely to generate conflict, because most people dislike being vulnerable to exploitation and domination by others. Another part of being sociologically mindful is being alert to how these kinds of social arrangements, ones that pit groups of people against each other, generate dialectical processes.

Yet conflict does not always entail an obvious clash of opposites. We might see more modest, less fundamental forms of conflict. What we should try to see, in any case, is how change proceeding in one direction can simultaneously produce pressures for change in the opposite direction. This can help us appreciate that change in the social world does not always unfold in a linear, one-step-after-another way. Instead, change can be messy, moving in more than one direction, even opposite directions, at once, and thus be surprising.

The third kind of process that is important to see is called an iterative process. An iterative process is one that repeats over and again in the same way, using output from one time as input for the next. Suppose, for example, that I am trying to write a chapter about how to be sociologically mindful of various kinds of processes in human social life. I will begin with some notes and a rough idea of what I want to say. Then I will try to turn these notes and ideas into sentences and the sentences into paragraphs. If I do this day after day, the paragraphs will add up and begin to fill pages. Eventually this process will result in a draft of the chapter.

But this first draft is unlikely to be very good. Some sentences will be clunky or unclear. Some paragraphs will not hang together well. Some examples will be too complicated; others will be too simple. The threads of some arguments will be hard to follow. Important ideas will be left out and irrelevant ideas will sneak in like weeds. If there are all these problems, what should I do?

I would not start over from scratch. Rather, I would begin revising the draft, which becomes the initial input for the next step—the next *iteration*—of the process. I would go back through the draft and try to fix the problems. I would try to say things better, clarify the examples, make the threads of argument easier to follow, get rid of irrelevant ideas, and add important ideas that were left out the first time. Eventually, I would have a better second draft. Then I would repeat the process, doing it as many times as necessary to create a draft that I was satisfied with.

But the process would not end there. I would give the draft to others to read. They might say that I have not done as good a job as I had thought. Using their reactions, I would revise again. More iterations! Finally, at some point, I would have to give up and say, "This is the best I can do. I hope it works." That version is the one you have in your hands.

Iterative processes occur in many places in social life. Any time human beings build something, evaluate the results, and use those results as the starting point for doing better the next time, an iterative process is occurring. Science, for example, proceeds in this way. Scientists make proposals (called hypotheses) about how things work, then gather evidence to see if those proposals are correct, then modify the proposals so that they better fit the evidence, eventually developing the best proposals into theories. Each iteration of this process is supposed to get rid of false ideas and refine ones that appear to be true. It is as if science as a whole is a draft that we continually work on revising.

Material culture develops in much the same way. Early humans made tools out of rocks, huts out of thatch and mud, clothes out of animal skins, and weapons out of tree branches—and then tried to improve on what they had made. Each piece of material culture, once brought into being, became the starting point for the next try. When the next try produced something better, that result became the starting point for seeking further improvements. It is this upwardly ratcheting iterative process that has given us, millennia later, our modern world of smartphones, spacecraft, computers, particle accelerators, drones, and nuclear weapons. For better or worse, it will give us even more powerful tools in the future.

When it comes to non-material human inventions, it's harder to agree on what amounts to an improvement. Not everyone would agree, for example, that democracy is better than monarchy. Be that as it may, we can see iterative processes occurring when people create ways of doing things together—ways of governing society, ways of educating the young, ways of delivering health care—and then evaluate those practices and arrangements, seeking and adopting ways of making things work better. In these cases, however, it's hard to count on a continual ratcheting in the direction of "better," given that what powerful elites think of as better is often what others think of as worse.

Being sociologically mindful, we cultivate the habit of asking, *What is going on here?* I don't mean that we learn to blurt out demands that people explain themselves to us. I mean that we develop the habit of trying to understand how the social world works, rather than taking it for granted. If the social world is, as I said earlier, a process, then the answer to the question *What is going on here?* will almost certainly point to some kind of process. We are thus likely to find, when we ask what is going on, a generic process, an iterative process, a dialectical process, or an escalating process. We might even find all of these occurring at once.

The Sociologically Examined Life is in fact part of multiple processes. It is part of a dialectical process in that I wrote it to oppose the drab portrayal of sociology that is found in many textbooks. It is part of an escalating process in that the supportive encounters I had with teachers when I was young helped me become a better learner, and learn more, as I grew older. It is the result of an iterative writing process. The generic processes of gatekeeping, mentoring, and network formation also affected my entry into academic life and my trajectory through it. And now, with each new reader, this book plays a part in more lives. The process is still unfolding.

Dialogue

Achieving Analytic Distance

Some students who read Daniel Chambliss's study of what makes for excellence in swimming remain unconvinced. They insist that talent is real and that it is what really matters. Part of this resistance may stem from not understanding the difference between what can be learned through careful, systematic, long-term research (which is what Chambliss did) and what seems to be true based on casual observation. As I said in this chapter, many processes that occur in social life are hard to see unless one pays close attention in a rigorous way. So it is not surprising that some people are troubled by studies that expose processes that challenge common-sense notions about how the world works.

Sometimes, after students have read Chambliss's article about the mundanity of excellence and we have discussed it in class, I ask, "Are there emotional reasons why someone might be attached to the notion of 'talent' as an explanation for success?" At first, this question is puzzling. What does emotion have to do with it? But eventually someone says, approximately, "If you think success comes from natural talent, then you don't have to feel bad about yourself if you fail." This answer contains a useful insight. Believing in talent is a way to avoid blaming oneself for not doing the things that could produce excellence. After all, if you don't have natural talent, it's not your fault for being mediocre.

In U.S. culture we are taught that success or failure depends largely on individual qualities. This means that most people are inclined to blame themselves when trying to understand why they haven't done better. The tendency to focus on individual qualities also means that looking for a way to let oneself off the hook—by embracing the notion of talent—makes a lot of sense. If you weren't lucky enough to get the genes for whatever kind of talent you think matters, well, that's not your fault, so you shouldn't feel too bad about it. On the other hand, if you have achieved some kind of success, then you can attribute it to your own outstanding character and feel good about yourself.

So there are at least two reasons why the notion of talent is hard to dislodge. First, we're taught to explain people's behavior and its outcomes—especially success or failure—by pointing to individual qualities rather than to social processes. Second, we want to feel good about ourselves, no matter what we do or where we end up in life, and we have learned to use the idea of talent to produce this feeling. If we can't overcome these obstacles to thinking mindfully about processes, we will fail to see important things about how the social world works.

A further benefit of thinking about process is that it makes the social world more amenable to analysis. Instead of seeing the social world as "just there," as a fixed set of conditions, we can see it as a complex set of goings-on: people interacting in orderly ways that can be studied and explained. Looking at the social world in this way allows us to achieve analytic distance. Instead of asking, What's wrong and who is to blame?, we ask, How do these things work? and What process is unfolding? Asking questions about process can help us see that the social world is not only more complicated than we thought, but also more understandable.

Achieving analytic distance by focusing on process can also help us gain perspective on ourselves. We can do this by looking at a process occurring around us and asking, How are we implicated in this process? How did we become implicated? How do our choices and actions keep this process going? Is there any way we could choose to act differently, if we wanted to change the process? These are simple but powerful questions. They give us a way to look at ourselves that neither imposes blame nor takes us off the hook. If we can come up with good answers to these questions, we can arrive at better understandings of who we are, how we participate in the world, and how we might change the world.

Asking questions about social processes and how we are implicated in them does not require sociological genius; anyone can learn to ask these kinds of questions. Coming up with good answers sometimes requires advanced investigatory skills, but these skills are also learnable; they do not arise from talent but from opportunity, effort, and practice. Beyond this, being sociologically mindful of process requires only curiosity and a desire to know. The component techniques are mundane. The results can be extraordinary.

A Note on Life-Stage and Generational Differences

We move through life in stages. When we are young, we are occupied with growing, playing, and learning; when we are a little older, we strive for independence and adult status; in mid-life our energies often go into achieving and accumulating; and then, in later life, we must face decline and death. Of course, life is not as scripted as this sequence implies. We can continue to play and learn and create throughout life, and sometimes death comes early. Still, it can be useful to think about life as a process that unfolds in stages.

One thing that such a perspective helps us understand is why people of different ages have different concerns. For example, young people—from teen years through college—who are striving for autonomy from parents and adult authorities tend to care a great deal about peer judgments of what is cool and about being popular with some subgroup of like-minded friends. These concerns can be overwhelming for a time, causing much drama and anguish, and then fade in importance just a few years later.

During the early-adult and mid-life stages what often becomes most important are those things that aid or impede career success and the accumulation of wealth. This is not to say that people stop caring about fitting in with friends or become selfish, money-grubbing careerists, but that the need to make a living—and perhaps also to support a family—tends to make people care more about whatever helps or hinders this process. At this life stage, drama and anguish tend to revolve around jobs, the workplace, debts, bills, and getting ahead economically.

Adult and mid-life stages are also often dominated by concerns for relationships with partners, spouses, children, and aging parents. For many people at mid-life, these relationships provide a sense of purpose and stability. Important identities—grateful child, responsible parent, good partner or spouse—are staked on these relationships. Concerns for these relationships and for economic security are often linked; being a responsible parent might be seen by many people as dependent on having a job and a steady income. This is why job and family concerns often crowd out other concerns (e.g., political ones) during adult and mid-life stages.

Later in life, many people find their concerns shifting to matters of health and how best to use their remaining years. They might think about their legacy, about what they will leave behind, about what they have accomplished or failed to accomplish. Here again it is not that concerns with economic security or family relationships disappear after a certain age. Surely, these can remain important. It is just that as the body begins to wear out and the end of life is in sight, new concerns arise that perhaps were not present, or barely considered, earlier.

The pattern of life-stage concerns I have described is general; it does not fit everyone. What people care about or worry about, and how much, depends on their circumstances. A young person with a serious illness might worry about dying. A mid-life adult with a secure fortune might care little about a job. But these are departures from the general pattern, which tends to hold true for most people in modern industrial societies. The point, in any case, is to recognize that many generational differences— in goals, problems, worries, values, outlooks, and so on—are a result of how human lives tend to unfold in stages.

A life-stage perspective can help us understand generational differences in other ways. My grandparents, for example, were young adults during the Great Depression of the 1930s. This experience of economic hardship instilled in them a strong concern for thrift. Throughout the rest of their lives they abhorred any wasteful or imprudent use of money. Many other members of their generation developed similar attitudes because the Great Depression caused widespread fear of becoming jobless and destitute.

Not every generation experiences a Great Depression or a world war. But every generation experiences some set of economic conditions and political events that create a generational outlook. Many people who witnessed or joined in the democratic movements of the 1960s and 1970s—the civil rights, women's rights, consumer rights, environmental, and anti-war movements—learned at least two things: political and economic elites often lie to protect their interests and preserve their power; and when people organize and act collectively, elite power can be successfully challenged. This is why many people of this generation embrace a critical view of elites and still think it is worth fighting for social change.

Yes, I am generalizing again. Not every member of every generation experiences conditions and events in the same way. If people are positioned differently—because of social class, race, ethnicity, gender, sexuality, subculture, or geography—they will see and experience different things and learn different lessons. People of the same generation can also observe the same conditions and events but interpret them differently and thus be affected differently. Even so, members of the same generation often have common touchstones—matters about which most people of that generation are aware—that create a kind of unity, if not unanimity.

Culture matters, too. Consider how changes in music and fashion can occur within generations (teens might see the music and fashion tastes of college students as out of date). Changes in technology can also be profound within decades. When I was in college, there were no personal computers, tablets were made of paper, and only the rich had portable phones, which were the size of shoeboxes. The Internet did not exist. No one had ever heard of "social media." There was no hip-hop music, and the only people who had tattoos were prisoners, sailors, and circus performers. College students today experience a different cultural and technological environment than I did at the same age.

Being mindful of these differences in life-stage concerns and in exposure to economic, political, cultural, and technological conditions, we can understand why it is sometimes hard for young people and older people to talk to each other. It is as if they live in different social worlds, at least in some ways. One way to bridge these gaps is to marvel at the differences and then try to connect over what we have in common.

What we have in common is struggling to figure out how to care for those we love, how to support ourselves with dignity, how to deal with people who treat us unfairly, how to decide what is moral, how to develop our potentials and accept our limitations, how to cope with loss and grief, how to keep anger and sadness from overwhelming us, and how to come to terms with mortality. These are the problems we face in being human at any time. Being mindful that we are not on this journey alone can help us see, in turn, that the wisdom we need to make the journey can be found in voices at each life stage and in every generation, if we know how to listen.

Paths for Reflection

1. Most students who write papers for college courses write them at the last minute, turning in what are really first drafts, not polished texts. This way of working—the writing process most students use—sacrifices the quality that can come from using the iterative process of writing, getting feedback, revising, getting feedback, revising again, editing, and polishing. Many students might even be aware that an iterative writing process would yield far better results, yet they still submit inferior work written just before a deadline. How would you explain this pattern of behavior? What might this behavior have to do with the way schooling is organized, the way courses are taught, and how the purpose of higher education is often defined?

2. One time, when I said in class that everything in social life is a process, a student raised her hand and said, "What about love at first sight? That's not a process. It just happens." I thought about it for a moment, then said that even this is a process. In this case, the process begins long before the moment of attraction. The people involved must have had prior experiences that shaped their ideas of who and what is attractive; they had to learn what kinds of feelings constitute or can be defined as "love"; they had to take paths that allowed them to meet each other at just the right moment;

they had to successfully communicate with each other; and then they had to arrive at a shared definition of the feelings generated by this interaction as love. Upon reflection, "love at first sight" is indeed a complicated process. Think of some other seemingly instant happening in social life (e.g., the entertainer who becomes an "overnight success"), look at it closely, and try to analyze it as the result of a process.

3. The 6th century BCE Greek philosopher Heraclitus is often quoted (somewhat inaccurately) as saying that you can't step into the same river twice. Most people take this to mean (again, in a way not quite true to Heraclitus's original point) that life is always in flux—that things are always changing, and that when we come back to them, they are not what they were before. The image of a river captures this idea nicely; most of us understand rivers as flowing, dynamic, and capable of changing shape over time. But what about a book? Except for microscopic decay, a book doesn't change physically over time. If you read a book today, put it away for a year, and then read it again, it's the same book. Or is it? If books don't change as physical objects, what process might explain why we can never open the same book twice?

Related Readings

Abbott, Andrew. (2016). *Processual Sociology*. Chicago: University of Chicago Press.

Becker, Howard S. (2014). *What about Murder? What about Mozart? Reasoning from Cases*. Chicago: University of Chicago Press.

Blumer, Herbert. (1969). *Symbolic Interactionism*. New York: Prentice Hall.

Chambliss, Daniel. (1989). "The Mundanity of Excellence: An Ethnographic Report on Stratification and Olympic Swimmers." *Sociological Theory* 7(1): 70–86.

Dweck, Carol. (2007). *Mindset*. New York: Ballantine.

Ericsson, Anders, & Pool, Robert. (2016). *Peak: Secrets from the New Science of Expertise*. New York: Houghton Mifflin Harcourt.

Lareau, Annette. (2011). *Unequal Childhoods: Class, Race, and Family Life* (2nd ed.). Berkeley: University of California Press.

Schwalbe, Michael, Godwin, Sandra, Holden, Daphne, Schrock, Douglas, Thompson, Shealy, & Wolkomir, Michelle. (2000). "Generic Processes in the Reproduction of Inequality: An Interactionist Analysis." *Social Forces* 79(2): 419–452.

CHAPTER 14

....

Studying and Changing
the Social World

I f I said that the central processor in my computer is not a silicon chip but a positronic wafer that operates at 10^3 gigahertz by sending modulated gravimetric pulses through a high-density tachyon field at twice the speed of light, you might not know whether to believe me. Perhaps this sounds plausible. After all, do you really know what goes on inside a computer? Maybe I'm just bragging about my fancy computer by spouting jargon that is unfamiliar to you.

If you know anything about physics, however, you know that my computer story is silly. The reference to things traveling "at twice the speed of light" gives away the joke. Even if you didn't know that the speed of light is unexceedable, but you knew a little about computers and kept up with the news, you could still guess that the story is outrageous, since it is implausible that "positronic wafers," "gravimetric pulses," "high-density tachyon fields," and a processor operating at "10^3 gigahertz" somehow ended up in a home computer without being widely reported.

This example shows how we can know things through deduction. You had to know only one fact—that nothing can go faster than the speed of light—to deduce that my story about the positronic wafer is nonsense. Or you might have known that powerful computing technologies do not first appear in home computers. In any case, the point is that by knowing one thing, or just a few things, and then reasoning carefully, we can arrive at conclusions that help us sort sense from nonsense.

Here is another example. Without looking up any statistics, can you say whether there are more poor black people or poor white people in the United States? A common mistake, because blacks are often represented as being poor, is to say that there are more poor black people than poor white people. But blacks make up only about 12 percent of the U.S. population. And even though the rate of poverty is higher among blacks (about 26%) than among whites (about 10%), the much larger size of the white population means that there are twice as many whites as blacks living in poverty. Again, a few facts and a bit of logic make this easy to figure out.

So logical deduction is one way to know things or to find out the implications of what we know. Much of what we know comes straight from others. It is passed on to us by parents, teachers, friends, and so on. We can also know things from personal experience or observation, from systematic research, and from mystical revelation. It is possible, too, that some knowledge is instinctive, as, for example, when an infant "knows" that it should suck on whatever is put in its mouth.

It is interesting to think about where our knowledge comes from. What usually concerns us more, however, is how to be sure that our knowledge is valid and reliable. Each source of knowledge has limitations in these respects. Part of being sociologically mindful is being aware of these limitations.

Logical deduction, for instance, is a fine way to elaborate our knowledge—except that if our *premises* are wrong, then our conclusions will also be wrong; we will simply reason our way to further ignorance. One strength of logical deduction, however, is that others can check up on our assumptions and our reasoning and thus correct us if we go astray.

Relying on what others tell us is necessary and is often a good way to learn. But how do we know that what others tell us is right? Surely you have had the experience of being told—by a parent, teacher, or mentor—something that later turned out to be wrong. Then there is the problem of deciding between different versions of the truth that come to us from sources that seem equally credible. How do we decide who is right?

Personal experience and observation are good sources of knowledge, except that it is easy to misjudge and overgeneralize from these sources. For example, your own observations might tell you that the sun revolves around the earth, or that all Lithuanians are slobs because both of the Lithuanians you've met in your life were a bit slobby, or that there is no ruling class in the United States because you've never seen it gathered in one place, or that crime is rising because you were just robbed. The problem in each case is not that you don't know what you've seen, but that what you've seen isn't enough to support the conclusion you reached.

As for mystical revelation, it is perhaps a way to gain spiritual knowledge for one's self, but it is not a good way to learn about the social world, since there is no way for others to check up on or to refute another person's mystical revelations. If you claimed to know—because the notion just popped into your head—that this book is a tool of the devil, how could I disagree? I suppose I could say that I had a mystical revelation myself and, on this basis, I know that this book is a gift from Hermes—and you should believe me because, after all, it is my book. But this would be a very strange and irresolvable argument to get into.

Advantages of Systematic Research

Careful research is perhaps the best way to create valid and reliable knowledge about the state of the social world and how it works. It is the best way for several reasons. First, by using standard, widely accepted means of finding things out, we can control personal biases. If we can do this, we are less likely to mistake what we would like to be true for what is really true.

Suppose, for example, I believe that democratic work organizations are better than authoritarian ones and would therefore like to believe that they are also more efficient. My bias would be to look only for evidence that supports my belief. But if I use a standard method of assessing efficiency and use it carefully and fairly to compare democratic and authoritarian work organizations, I will have to accept whatever I find. My bias would thus be canceled out or at least controlled.

Second, research can get us beyond personal experience and casual observation, because to re-*search* is to look beyond what is obvious to us from where we stand. It is to look for ideas and information that might challenge the common sense that gets us through daily life. It means considering the quality and correctness of knowledge created by others, even if we find their knowledge irritating. All this can be difficult, because our usual habit is to settle comfortably into believing that what we already know is right.

A third reason for doing research is that it lets us check up on each other. If we use methods that others agree are proper, they can look at our results and say, "Hmmm, yes, you did it right; these results must be correct." Or they can say, "Ah, you went astray here at this point, so your conclusions are not trustworthy." We can make the same judgments when others offer us knowledge they have created. In this way, by working together, we can do better at dispelling illusions and, in the long run, creating knowledge that is valid and reliable.

Perhaps you noticed that I had only good things to say about knowledge that comes from research. Does this mean that one should accept as true whatever is published in a scientific or scholarly journal? No. Knowledge from any source should be critically interrogated. Careful research is just a way to avoid problems that are common when knowledge is created in other ways. And if research is not done properly, it can yield as much foolishness as any other method.

The larger point here is that we should be mindful, to the extent we can, of where our own knowledge comes from. We can be mindful in this way by asking ourselves how we know what we claim to know. Is some piece of knowledge a result of logical deduction? (If so, have we reasoned correctly? How do we know that our premises are correct?) Is some piece of knowledge a hand-me-down from others? (If so, where did *their* knowledge come from? How can we be sure it is correct?) Is some piece of knowledge a result of personal experience or observation? (If so, are we claiming to know more than our personal experience can warrant? Is it possible that we have observed only what we want to believe is true or that our observations have been limited in some crucial way?)

The point of asking ourselves these questions is not to arrive at a paralyzing state of doubt about what we know, but to more wisely decide how much trust to put in what we know. If we can do this, we can open ourselves to new knowledge without fear of surrendering our minds to yet another fishy belief system. Being sociologically mindful, we can get a better view of what is coming at us by way of new knowledge and where it is coming from. We can also see what is worth catching.

The Kinds of Questions We Can Ask

All attempts to create knowledge are responses to questions, and knowledge must be created in a way that suits the question. For example, if you asked, "How much does this book weigh?" the proper way to get an answer is to weigh it. How many words does it contain? Count them. Will it fly like a boomerang? Give it a throw and observe the result. These are *empirical* questions, which means that they are answerable by measuring, counting, or looking to see what happens.

But suppose you asked, "Is the cover of this book beautiful?" What then? You could ask ten artists for their opinions. What if seven said it was ugly, two were ambivalent, and one thought it was beautiful? In this case no measuring stick will settle the matter, because you have asked an *aesthetic* question—a question about what is subjectively pleasing to the senses—and aesthetic questions are not answerable with data. We can try to say why something strikes us as ugly or beautiful, tasteful or crass, but no evidence or logic will prove us right and others wrong.

Here is another kind of question: was it worthwhile for me to write this book, considering what else I might have done with my time? Again, this is not an empirical question, since there is no way to get an answer by measuring, counting, or observing. It is a *moral* question, since it calls for a judgment about what is right to do. I could say why it seemed to me a good thing to write this book, but my reasons would be based on moral precepts and on my sense of how the future is likely to unfold. There is no data I can show, no standard analysis, to prove that my answer is right. All I can do is to offer reasonable arguments.

There are also questions of *interpretation*, the simplest of which is, What does this thing mean? Such questions often arise when we confront works of art. We might look at a painting or read a novel and wonder what the writer or artist wanted us to understand. But any fact, object, gesture, phrase, or behavior—anything that has meaning—can raise a question of interpretation.

Sometimes we can get an answer by asking for clarification. Perhaps the writer or artist can tell us what s/he meant (although writers and artists can't always fully explain what their work means). Or perhaps there is expert opinion available to help us make sense of things. Other times there might be so much ambiguity that no clear interpretation can be nailed down. All anyone can do then is to give reasons to support the plausibility of a particular interpretation.

You can perhaps see now that research is better suited to answering some questions than others. It is a good way to answer empirical questions. It can also be useful for answering interpretive questions, because we can sometimes dig up evidence that supports the plausibility of an interpretation. And although it is wise to search for ideas and information to help guide our moral and aesthetic judgments, research will not tell us which judgments are correct.

It is good to be mindful of the kind of question we are facing. Sometimes we get into fruitless debates because we are not clear about this. There is no point, for example, in trading opinions about the correct answer to a simple empirical question. Are crime rates rising? Go to the library or get on the Web and look up the best answer you can find. If it is the answer to an empirical question that is in dispute, we should stop disputing and go get the answer.

Interpreting the Answers to Empirical Questions

Sometimes the answer to an empirical question can create a great deal of interpretive trouble. For example, to ask, What are the rates of poverty among blacks and whites living in the United States? is to ask an empirical question. We can look up the answers because someone else (the U.S. Census Bureau) has already done the counting and the arithmetic. As I noted earlier, the poverty rate among blacks is about 26 percent and among whites it is about 10 percent (these figures fluctuate somewhat and can also vary depending on how poverty is defined). But what do these figures mean? How can we interpret them?

I once presented these figures during a discussion of racial inequality. The class suddenly got quiet. No one wanted to comment on the meaning of the percentages. When I pressed for some reaction, a white student said, "I think no one is talking because the figures are embarrassing." Did he mean that the figures were embarrassing because they pointed out a failure to overcome racial inequality? I wasn't sure, so I asked him to be more explicit. "The figures are embarrassing," he said with some hesitation, "to black students." I was baffled by this.

After further conversation, it became clear that the student who spoke about the figures being "embarrassing to black students" saw the figures as evidence of black inferiority. His presumption was that the poverty rate of a group was an indicator of the capability of people in that group. I saw the figures as evidence of racism and discrimination. In this case, the facts about poverty rates were clear, but they did not speak for themselves. The same facts lent themselves to nearly opposite interpretations.

To support my interpretation, I might have said that, in the United States, millions of people, black and white, are poor because they can't find jobs that pay a decent wage, or they can't find jobs at all. Sometimes the jobs available in an area don't match people's skills. Or else the jobs disappear when employers move factories to foreign countries where they can pay workers less. And so people can end up poor, or very nearly poor, even though they are able and willing to work.

I might have added that the higher poverty rate among blacks is a result of factories being closed in inner cities in the North, where a lot of the black population is concentrated. It's a result of schools that do not serve black children well. It's a result of discrimination in hiring and network advantages enjoyed by whites. In some cases, part of the problem is a lack of marketable skills, but that's because access to education and train-ing is limited, not because people's natural abilities are limited.

I might have said all this—and probably did—but was it enough to establish my interpretation as correct? Although I am sure that my state-ment helped some people see why the white student's interpretation was wrong, others who preferred to hold on to that interpretation could point out, correctly, that I had not really *proven*—by anything I'd said or any evidence I'd shown—that blacks were not inferior to whites. All I had done was to suggest that "black inferiority" was not a plausible explanation, if other things were taken into account, if those other things were true, and if no significant counterevidence was being overlooked.

My interpretation was not, however, a matter of opinion. My interpre-tation was based on previously answered empirical questions. Have jobs disappeared in areas heavily populated by blacks? Do employers discrimi-nate against blacks? Do whites enjoy network advantages when it comes to getting jobs? Do schools serve black kids as well as they serve white kids? Is there a lack of access to education and job training? With knowledge of the answers to these empirical questions, we can determine which inter-pretation of the poverty-rate figures is most likely to be correct.

Resolving Disagreement

Why argue about this stuff? You might think, "People are going to believe what they want to believe, and you can't convince them otherwise." Unfor-tunately, that is true about some people. They will not be persuaded to give up beliefs and interpretations that make them feel good about themselves. Even so, conversation can often get us to surprising places if we don't give up too soon. One thing that helps is to figure out what kind of question is bogging us down.

If the answer to an empirical question is at issue, we can say, "Neither of us knows the answer right now, but we can find one." Then we can decide whether to go on without an answer or go look one up. What we do will depend on what we are trying to understand and how important the matter is to us. Even if we don't break off a conversation and dash to the library or start Googling, perhaps we will make a mental note to look something up later. That, too, is progress, since it will allow us to bring more information to a future conversation.

It is much the same when we disagree about answers to interpretive questions. What we must do, if we wish to figure out where the disagree-ment lies, is to try to explain the assumptions on which our interpretations are based. This is a matter of being mindful about the ideas on which we draw to say what something means. If we can explain to others "where we are coming from," we are more likely to arrive at an understanding of why our interpretations differ and how the difference might be settled.

Disagreements about aesthetic and moral questions are not easy to resolve. Some may even be impossible to resolve. Perhaps the best we can do then is to explain, as fully as possible, the grounds for preferring one answer over another. This might not lead to agreement, but it will lead to better understanding. And if we can commit to keeping the conversation going, this will preclude the use of violence as a way to end a disagreement. Unfortunately, many human beings, being less than mindful or heartful, have had great difficulty committing to this practice.

Mindful Skepticism

Once, during a discussion of the benefits of education, a black woman said she was outraged to learn that, on average, a high school diploma was likely to yield higher earnings (by mid-life) for a white man than a college degree was likely to yield for a black woman. When she said this, another student, a white male said, "I don't believe it. How can you possibly know that?" Before she could answer, I said, "She probably read the article that was assigned for today. If you look on page 34 in the text, you'll see a table that shows what she's referring to." He paged through his book and found the table. After studying it for a few moments, he harumphed and said, "Well, anybody can make up numbers."

As a teacher, I was irritated by this response, because it meant this: no matter what information I am presented with, if it does not suit my prior beliefs, if it does not make me comfortable, I will discount it, so I can continue to believe what I want to believe. An attitude like this leaves little room for education to make a dent. I wondered why this student would bother to study anything at all, or read any books at all, if he was so intent on being unchanged.

And yet I could not say that his attitude was entirely foolish. Numbers are often cooked up to mislead us, and numbers can be wrong because of honest mistakes, so it is reasonable to be skeptical of numbers, whatever the source. Is there any way to tell which numbers are right? Yes, it can be done; it just requires training. Since most people do not have such training, however, it is understandable that they might say, "I can't tell what's right or wrong, so I'm going to treat all statistics as hogwash."

This is clearly not a mindful response to the situation. It is like saying, "I can't read, so I am going to treat all books as hogwash." It would be better to learn to read and to learn also what is necessary to distinguish the hog from the wash. This is hard but not impossible. What helps is being mindfully, rather than indiscriminately, skeptical of new information.

One of the difficulties in learning about the social world is that we must rely on information created and filtered by others. We can't check out everything for ourselves, even if we know how. This being the case, we must pay attention to how information (in the form of words or numbers) is created, by whom, for what purposes. We must ask, Who stands to benefit if this information is accepted as true? Being mindful in these ways puts us on alert against fraud, yet it does not cut us off from learning.

We should also seek alternative views, since this can help us see the limits of our own knowledge. A bit of conventional knowledge—that Columbus discovered America, for instance—seems simple and true until an alternative is suggested: Columbus launched a brutal invasion of an already populated continent. This is not just a different way to describe the same events, but a different way of seeing what those events were. If we try out this alternative view, we can look at what passes for conventional knowledge and see that it is, at the very least, contestable.

What is conventional and what is alternative depends, of course, on where you stand. A view that you consider alternative might seem conventional to someone else. Recognizing this relativity of perspectives is part of being sociologically mindful. But there is more to it. Being sociologically mindful, we can also see that these alternative perspectives create the possibility of understanding the world more fully, because they give us more angles from which to view it.

Perhaps by looking for and seriously considering alternative views—and there are always multiple alternatives—we will eventually get closer to a better version of the truth. This is something to aim for. In the meantime, it is wise to consider alternative views, because doing so can help us see how competing versions of the truth are created. In this way we can learn more about how others see the world, how we have come to see the world, and what more we might see if we are willing to suffer a bit of uncertainty.

Partial Truth and Inevitable Uncertainty

The student who said "anyone can make up numbers" did not want to suffer uncertainty. Perhaps he was afraid that if he let go of what he already believed, he would end up lost, not knowing what to believe. He did not know how to be mindfully skeptical.

Part of what we fear is losing what we think is the truth. If we are sociologically mindful, however, we know that we never possess the absolute, complete truth. What we have is a head full of humanly created images, representations, and accounts that seem to pretty well make sense of the world as we know it. Why not stand ready, as we see and experience more of the world, to invent or borrow new ways of making sense?

If we can admit that there is more to the world than we have yet seen or experienced—and more than we could see and experience in a lifetime— perhaps we can also say to ourselves, "In anticipation of learning more about the world, as I surely will do, I will treat my current beliefs as provisional and explore alternative ways of making sense of things, because one of these ways might come in handy someday."

To adopt this stance toward knowledge does not mean flitting from one belief to another. It is like the deliberate movement of wading upstream in a river. To move ahead you must take gentle steps, making sure of your footing before you shift your weight forward. You must stay flexible and lean into the current. If you rush or lose concentration, you will end up all wet. So you pay attention, moving mindfully when it makes sense to move.

Being sociologically mindful, we know that we never get to the whole truth about the social world. All the truths that we invent or borrow—all the images, representations, and accounts we come upon—are partial views of a whole that is unknowable because it is always changing in ways that run ahead of our ability to understand. We thus need not fear that new ideas and information will wrest the truth from us. They might, however, give us a larger, more complex, and unruly truth to contend with, and that can be unsettling.

For some people it is scary to think of never being sure of having it right. Imagining that one has it right, now and forever, is comforting. The problem, however, is that other people see things differently, and when conflicts arise, others will neither happily conform to the version of truth that comforts us nor lay down their knowledge to embrace ours. And so, if we want to understand and get along with others, we must be willing to seriously consider their perspectives and to tolerate the uncertainty that comes with this openness.

Perpetual Inquiry and Conversation

I have been recommending a mindful skepticism toward all knowledge— that which we already possess and that which strikes us as new and strange. In this way we can avoid the dead ends of nihilism ("There is no truth. Anyone can make up numbers. You might as well believe what you want.") and fanaticism ("There is only one truth and my people know it! All other beliefs are false or insane!"). These are dead ends because they make conversation pointless and offer no hope of resolving conflict.

A mindful skepticism toward knowledge keeps us inquiring, observing, and trying to make better sense of things; it keeps us trying to create more accurate, complete, and useful representations; it keeps us open to new information; and it keeps us connected to others as we try to do all this. Conversation is both a means to this end and an end in itself—at least it is if we believe that it is better to try to understand others than to ignore or to hurt them. Be mindfully skeptical, then, of all knowledge, including that which I have offered in this book. After fair consideration, take and use what is helpful for making sense and for keeping the conversation going.

Changing One's Self and the World

If you could live forever, would life get boring? Some people might say, "Yes, because it would be the same old thing, day after day, forever." But here is another possibility: life would get more *interesting* because, as one learned more about the world, one would see more complexities, more mysteries, more problems to be solved, and more things to be done. Why might some people see life as holding such great promise? I think it is because they are full of curiosity, care, and hope.

If there is no curiosity about the nature of things and how they work, then the world will seem like a drab backdrop against which life is endured until it is over. If there is no care about anything outside one's self or beyond one's time, then it will seem pointless to worry about things that don't matter for getting through the day. Without hope, it will seem pointless to invest much effort in analyzing the social world. So it seems that we need curiosity, care, and hope to spark a desire to pay attention to the social world, to try to understand it as it is, and to use this awareness to pursue change.

Sometimes the conditions of people's lives do not inspire much curiosity, care, or hope. There might be so much day-to-day hardship and sameness, and so few prospects for change, that people limit their attention to each day's tasks and fleeting amusements. Other people might be so comfortable that they too lose interest in critically examining the world beyond their cocoon of privilege. Under these conditions, people are not likely to develop much sociological mindfulness. Then again, perhaps the process can be turned around. Perhaps a lesson in mindfulness can spark curiosity, care, and hope.

Being mindful that the world is a complex and mysterious place, and that penetrating these mysteries is satisfying, ought to arouse our curiosity. Being mindful of how our actions affect others' experiences of joy and suffering ought to encourage feelings of care. And being mindful of how human action creates the world ought to give us hope that we can make the world a better place. Obviously these are expressions of my own wishes, yet I have tried to do more than put them forth as wishes.

I have tried to show how much there is to be curious about: the connections, patterns, contingencies, interdependencies, and processes that constitute the social world; the ways that people try to solve problems together and end up creating cultural habits; the ways that some people create social arrangements to benefit themselves at the expense of others; the ways that people create the images, accounts, and representations that make up our knowledge of social reality; and how the natural and the social affect each other. We could study these matters forever and always be learning something new.

I have also shown that sociological mindfulness gives us reasons for caring. The more we pay attention to and understand connections, interdependencies, and contingencies, the better we can see how *our* ways of thinking and acting affect *others'* chances for good lives. We can see, too, that what others think and do affects us as well. Being sociologically mindful helps us to see how this is true in a way that goes beyond what is obvious in everyday life as we interact with others who are close to us.

And just as we care about the others who are close to us, we can, if we are sociologically mindful, come to care about the distant others whose lives are intertwined with ours. At the least, we can thus see new reasons for caring about the social arrangements that bind us to others, for better or worse.

Perhaps you are thinking, "What about hope? It seems that 'being sociologically mindful' just makes us aware of how messed up the social world is. How is *that* supposed to inspire hope?" Actually, mere awareness of problems—inequalities, exploitation, the suffering of others—is not supposed to inspire hope. It is supposed to inspire concern, perhaps outrage, and a desire to change things. Unfortunately, when awareness of problems is combined with feelings of powerlessness, the result is often despair.

Being sociologically mindful, however, we know that the social world is, for all its seeming solidity, a social construction. All the ideas, habits, arrangements, and so on that make up the social world are human creations. We know, too, that the social world keeps going as it does because of the beliefs people share and because of how they keep doing things together on an everyday basis. If we are mindful of all this, we can see that the problems that exist now need not exist forever; they are all within our power to overcome.

Of course it will not be easy, because many powerful people benefit from the arrangements that cause problems for so many others. There is also the problem of changing the arrangements that are devised to keep things from changing. Yet the *possibility* of change always exists, if only people can organize to make it happen, and that is a good reason for hope.

Mindfulness can get us out of the rut of despair by reminding us that we cannot change a society overnight by ourselves. It is silly to say, "I failed to bring about a revolution this week, even though I tried very hard. That proves it's hopeless. I guess I'll give up and just march along with everyone else." Yet many people fall into this kind of trap. The way out is through awareness that change requires working with others to challenge existing arrangements and to create new ones. We cannot do it alone.

There is no point in despairing because we cannot single-handedly change the world. Of course we can't. We can, however, try to find or organize others who recognize a need for change and are willing to work for it. It is amazing how being in community with others can help alleviate the despair that arises from failed dreams of heroism.

Here, then, is a practical suggestion. Instead of lamenting your inability to change the world by yourself, think of the one issue or problem that most bothers you. Be as specific as you can. Perhaps it is excessive military spending, or environmental destruction, or low wages for the service workers in your school. Whatever the issue or problem might be, chances are that some people are already working on it. Find those people (ask around) and get involved with what they are doing. Add your energy and intelligence to theirs, and you will be doing your part to move the social world in a positive direction.

Sociological mindfulness also reminds us that we *can* change a small part of the social world single-handedly. If we treat others with more respect and compassion, if we refuse to participate in recreating inequalities even in little ways, if we raise questions about official representations of reality, if we refuse to work in destructive industries, then we are making change. We do not have to join a group or organize a protest to make these kinds of changes. We can make them on our own, by deciding to live differently.

Perhaps our modest efforts will resonate with others and inspire them to live differently. Or perhaps no one will notice, or they will notice but think we are strange. And so you might think, "If no one is going to notice that I am a superior moral being, then what is the point? Why bother to be different and risk ridicule?" That is one way to look at it. Being sociologically mindful, however, suggests a different thought: I cannot be sure that *anything* I do will change things for the better, yet I can be sure that if I do not at least *try*, then I will fail to do what I think is right and will be contributing to keeping things the same; therefore I will opt to do what is right, whether much or little comes of it.

In the end, sociological mindfulness must be about more than studying how the social world works. It must also do more than inspire curiosity, care, and hope—although these we cannot do without. If it is to be worth practicing, sociological mindfulness must help us change ourselves and our ways of doing things together, so that we can live more peacefully and productively with others, without exploitation, disrespect, and inequality. Sociological mindfulness is a way to see where we are and what needs to be done. It is a path to heartful membership in a conversation that ought to have no end.

Dialogue

Knowledge and Action

Several teachers have suggested that I split this chapter into one on research and one on social change. As you can see, I have not done this. One reason is that I would rather devote *TSEL* to the problem of how to think about information, since there are already plenty of books that teach about how to gather it. The main reason, however, for keeping this chapter intact is that I do not think it is wise to separate knowledge from action.

In real life, we create knowledge through action. Observing what happens when we act is a powerful way to discover patterns in how the world works. Then, by thinking a little harder, we can derive general principles to account for the patterns we see. We can go further and weave these principles into conceptual schemes. When scientists do this, we say they are "building theory." When people do the same thing in everyday life, we say that they are acquiring common sense.

We also test our knowledge through action. If common sense consists of theories we have about how the world works, then every action guided by those theories is like an experiment. If we can at least roughly predict the results of our actions, then our knowledge passes a kind of utility test. We can say, in other words, that our knowledge provides a useful guide to action, in which case we will continue to embrace it. But if our knowledge does not help us to act effectively, then we must revise it.

One purpose of *TSEL* is to equip readers to create for themselves more and better knowledge of the social world. Such knowledge can result from perceiving the world with a higher degree of sociological mindfulness. And perhaps, if I have done a good job here, you have acquired an ability to see things you did not see before. If so, this ability will, by itself, lead to the creation of new knowledge. But for the payoff to be greatest, a new way of seeing must be linked to action.

There are two ways to think about this. One is to say that new ideas are best grasped by trying to put them into practice. This is why teaching often includes exercises through which students practice the skills they seek to master. Whether in art, craft, or scholarship, an apprentice learns by doing, under the guidance of an experienced teacher. The same principle applies to sociological mindfulness. It is best learned by doing; that is, by using the ideas offered here to make sense of the social world (or some part of it) through writing or talk. A good teacher can aid the process considerably.

Another way to think about the link between knowledge and action is suggested by something I tell students in my course on social inequality. I say, "A good way to learn how inequality is perpetuated is to watch what happens when you try to abolish it." What I mean is that, under normal conditions, it can be hard to see how certain social arrangements are upheld. But then, if we try to change those arrangements, we can learn very quickly who is willing to do what to protect them. Such an attempt to change the world could make for a good test of our ideas about how the world works.

If our everyday worlds pose no fresh challenges, and we fail to seek them, then our knowledge may cease to grow. If we live safely and comfortably in a rut, we learn a lot about how to trudge along one path. By being sociologically mindful, however, we can gain perspective on both the path and our manner of trudging. But to learn more, to see the limits of our old knowledge and to create new knowledge, we may need to try new paths. How can we map new territory if we don't take the risk of exploring it?

This metaphor of knowledge as a map is useful for explaining what it means to create new representations of the world and how we must go about doing it. But the metaphor is not perfect, because the social world is not quite like the surface of the earth. Here is the difference: the surface of the earth waits for us to explore it and doesn't change when we draw a map of it. The social world, however, is what it is because of how people act based on their understandings of it. Which means that the social world itself can change as new understandings lead to new behaviors.

And so, unlike the surface of the earth, the social world is changed by our efforts to understand it. We do not simply extend our knowledge through action. We extend the social world by acting differently based on the knowledge our prior action creates.

There is another reason that I have been reluctant to separate what I say about research and knowledge from what I say about social change. In a nutshell, it is this: in a world so full of violence and suffering caused by inequality, it seems to me that the most morally compelling reason to learn about the social world is to try to change it. Being sociologically mindful is a means to that end.

It is good to remember, finally, that one person's ignorance is another person's advantage. In other words, what you don't know can be used against you by powerful others. Lack of information and a failure to think critically also limit our ability to act in morally responsible ways. So, if you desire nothing more than to live a responsible life, then I would say that you are obligated to learn as much as you can about the social world to which you belong and which you help to reproduce through your actions. Being sociologically mindful is a way to see more clearly what's going on. Deciding what to do about it is up to you.

A Note on Teaching Others

One of the hardest questions I was ever asked by a student who had read *The Sociologically Examined Life* is this: how can I get others to be sociologically mindful? I suggested that he give them *TSEL*, or part of it, to read and then have a conversation about it. The student accepted that answer, but I realized later that it wasn't adequate, because the answer didn't acknowledge how complicated and challenging it can be to try to teach things that others might not be eager to learn.

If I were asked that question again, I might respond, "It depends on *who* you want to be sociologically mindful about *what*, and *why* you think they aren't." It makes a difference if the other person is a same-age friend, a new acquaintance, an intimate partner, or an adult family member. People listen to us differently depending on the relationship we have with them. An approach that works with a friend might not work with a parent.

What the issue is and what that issue means to the person we are trying to teach also make a difference. If someone has a strong interest in *not* thinking critically about some part of the social world—perhaps because to do so would threaten a cherished self-conception—then it might be hard to find an approach that works. Then I recommend patience and a continued effort to better understand the other person. All good teachers know that, whatever the message, it has to be delivered in a way that others can hear.

In general, I advise gentle tugs rather than pushes. Saying, "Another way to look at the matter is like this . . ." or "It might also make sense to look at it like so . . ." can be effective. Usually, the less pushed around people feel, the more willing they are to listen.

I also suggest starting with questions rather than arguments. By taking this approach you might find that a person is reasoning perfectly well but is beginning with dubious assumptions (perhaps based on incorrect or incomplete information). Bringing these assumptions into the open allows them to be examined. Perhaps then a conversation about these assumptions will lead to new understandings. Again, if you want to teach someone something new, it's important to know where they're starting from, because that's where a teacher must start too.

Paths for Reflection

1. If you are lucky, school has partly satisfied your hunger for knowledge and, at the same time, increased that hunger. If you have not been so lucky, don't worry, because the problem can be overcome. All you need to do, as a first step, is to recognize this: *you are responsible for your own education.* In other words, you must go after the knowledge you are hungry for and not wait for teachers to feed you. To get started, make a list of things that you would like to know about. Since you can't do everything at once, pick one of these things and come up with three steps you can take to learn about it (e.g., read a book, talk to an expert, take a class). How might you *use* your teachers to help you pursue your own education? What other resources, human or material, can you draw on to learn what you want to learn?

2. Some people say that the problems of inequality and injustice in our society are unsolvable, because those with wealth and power will resist all efforts to change the conditions from which they benefit. This is an oddly pessimistic view, in light of the successful struggles for social justice that have occurred in the past century. Why do you suppose some middle-class people might find comfort in this pessimistic view? Consider the struggles led by Susan B. Anthony, Martin Luther King Jr., Mohandas Gandhi, and Nelson Mandela. They all challenged social arrangements that were backed by enormous wealth and power—and won, despite the odds against them. How did they do it? What resources and strategies

were used to overcome those who had far greater economic, political, and military power?

3. As I have taught it in this book, sociological mindfulness is largely an intellectual practice—a way of seeing and making sense of the social world. Perhaps I have given the impression that one can be sociologically mindful and yet live in a detached way, looking and analyzing but not acting on what one sees and figures out. Although I suppose this is possible, I would like to think that understanding the social world differently will lead people to live differently. How do you think this might be true in your case? If you are the kind of person who cares about the problems of injustice and inequality that sociological mindfulness brings to light, how might you act in a way that is consistent with these values and with your new understandings?

Related Readings

Engler, Mark, & Engler, Paul. (2016). *This Is an Uprising.* New York: Nation Books.

Fay, Brian. (1975). *Social Theory and Political Practice.* London: Allen & Unwin.

Godfrey-Smith, Peter. (2001). *Theory and Reality: An Introduction to the Philosophy of Science.* Chicago: University of Chicago Press.

Kivel, Paul. (2011). *Uprooting Racism: How White People Can Work for Racial Justice* (3rd ed.). Gabriola Island, BC: New Society Press.

Korgen, Kathleen O., White, Jonathan, M., & White, Shelly K. (2014). *Sociologists in Action: Sociology, Social Change, and Social Justice.* Thousand Oaks, CA: Sage.

McLeod, Melvin, ed. (2006). *Mindful Politics.* Boston: Wisdom.

O'Hear, Anthony. (1989). *An Introduction to the Philosophy of Science.* New York: Oxford University Press.

Stout, Linda. (2011). *Collective Visioning.* San Francisco: Berrett–Koehler.

Zinn, Howard. (1993). *Failure to Quit: Reflections of an Optimistic Historian.* Monroe, ME: Common Courage Press.

INDEX

....